Strategy for Tourism

John Tribe

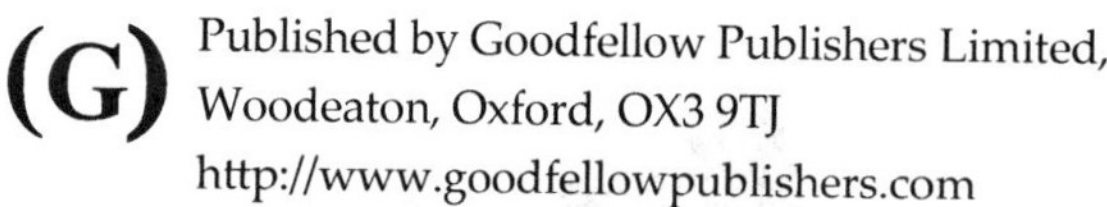
Published by Goodfellow Publishers Limited,
Woodeaton, Oxford, OX3 9TJ
http://www.goodfellowpublishers.com

British Library Cataloguing in Publication Data: a catalogue record for this title is available from the British Library.

Library of Congress Catalog Card Number: on file.

ISBN: 978-1-906884-07-9

Design and typesetting by P.K. McBride

Printed by Lightning Source, www.lightningsource.com

Contents

About the author

Professor John Tribe is Head of Tourism at the University of Surrey, UK. His undergraduate, postgraduate and doctoral studies were all under-taken at the University of London. He is a Fellow of the Higher Education Academy, Fellow of the International Academy for the Study of Tourism and Academician of the Academy of the Social Sciences.

His research concentrates on sustainability, epistemology and education and he has authored books on strategy, philosophy, economics, education and environmental management in tourism. Funded research projects have included sustainable tourism and forests in the European Union, curriculum development in Moldova, quality in tourism education and the use of visual images in tourism. He is past Chair of the UK Association for Tourism in Higher Education (ATHE) and was the specialist advisor for tourism for the UK 2008 Research Assessment Exercise. He is co-chair of the United Nations World Tourism Organisation Education and Science Council and editor of *Annals of Tourism Research* and *The Journal of Hospitality, Leisure Sport and Tourism Education* (JOHLSTE).

Part I
Strategic Purpose

This section provides an insight into the purpose of tourism strategy.

Chapter 1 provides an introduction to the subject and presents a framework for examining the whole strategy process based around four of its key component parts:

- Strategic purpose
- Strategic analysis
- Strategic choice
- Strategic implementation.

These four areas in turn provide the headings for the four parts of this book.

Chapter 2 examines in detail the concept of strategic mission. It analyses the aims and purposes of tourism entities and introduces the idea of stakeholders.

The relationship between culture and strategy is investigated in Chapter 3

These initial chapters provide the essential toolkit to engage in the first part of this strategic process.

1 Introduction to Strategy

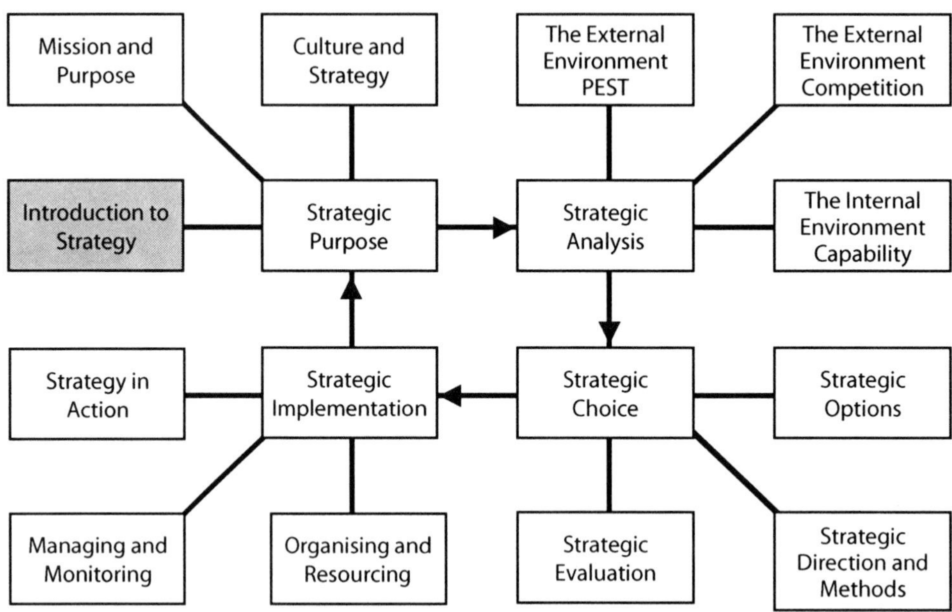

Figure 1.1

Learning outcomes

After studying this chapter and related materials you should be able to understand:

- The meaning of strategy
- The process of strategy
- The importance of strategy
- The contexts and uses of strategy in tourism
- Competing approaches to strategy

and critically evaluate, explain and apply the above concepts.

Introduction

Figure 1.1 shows both the structure of this book and of this chapter. The main body of this chapter starts with the case study of the strategy which was developed for tourism in New Zealand. It uses this case study to answer some of the basic questions about strategy. Starting with its definition, strategy is defined as 'the planning of a desirable future and the design and testing of suitable ways of bringing it about'. Next the process of strategy is examined. Here the steps that need to be taken to design and implement a successful strategy – mission, strategic analysis, strategic choice and strategic implementation – are set out. The chapter then discusses why it is important to have a strategy as a guiding and overarching plan of action since this will help an organisation to achieve its aims and avoid mission-drift. It is then noted that the use of strategy is not confined to business organisations and the other contexts for strategy, including governments, destinations, and not-for-profit entities, are also examined. Finally a brief review is offered of different approaches to strategy where it is revealed to be a contested practice subject to uncertainty, complexity and fallibility.

Case Study 1: The Tourism Strategy for New Zealand

Tourism is a significant sector for the economy of New Zealand. At the time of writing, it contributes approximately 10% to New Zealand's gross domestic product. It also provides employment for about one in every ten New Zealanders. Additionally it is an important export sector accounting for some 20% of New Zealand's overall export earnings. So it is important that a strategic approach is taken to developing the country's tourism product.

100% Pure New Zealand. Picture courtesy of Tourism New Zealand

On 7 November 2007 New Zealand's Tourism Strategy 2015 (NZTS 2015) (Tourism New Zealand, 2007) was launched by the Prime Minister, Rt. Hon Helen Clark. Looking back, Prime Minister Clark noted that 'in the first year of our government in 2000, we brought together stakeholders from across the tourism industry and central and local government to develop the first New Zealand Tourism Strategy ... that first strategy was launched in 2001'.

The need for an updated strategy is underlined by the important changes that have occurred since 2001 in the domestic and global environments for New Zealand tourism. The 2015 strategy notes three key changes in the global environment as:

- Concerns about the impact of travel on climate change
- Greater use of IT by consumers – particularly the Internet and online bookings
- Higher fuel prices.

At the domestic level, the tourism industry is seen to face particular challenges in:

- Recruitment of skilled staff
- Developing a more environmentally sustainable product
- Provision of tourism infrastructure.

The New Zealand Tourism Strategy 2015 is guided by its vision statement:

> "In 2015, tourism is valued as the leading contributor to a sustainable New Zealand economy".

It is also underpinned by two key values of *arekaitiakitanga* (guardianship) and *manaaki-tanga* (hospitality) which are found in Maori culture. But a vision needs unpacking into more specific outcomes and for NZTS 2015 these are:

- 'New Zealand delivers a world-class visitor experience
- New Zealand's tourism sector is prosperous and attracts ongoing investment
- The tourism sector takes a leading role in protecting and enhancing the environment
- The tourism sector and communities work together for mutual benefit.'

(Tourism New Zealand 2007, pp. 6-7 l

In order to steer tourism towards achieving these outcomes and measure the success of NZTS 2015 a number of targets have been set. Interestingly the strategy stresses that the targets focus on not only increasing volume but also improving quality and value. In terms of volume NZTS 2015 assumes that international visitor arrivals will increase by forecasted 4% every year. In terms of quality and value additional targets are set across five key areas:

- "Increasing visitor satisfaction
- Increasing the amount that visitors spend
- Reducing seasonality
- Delivering environmental best practice
- Creating positive community outcomes."

In some cases existing data sources are used to identify and measure specific targets. For example success in increasing visitor satisfaction will entail an "increase by four percentage points the number of international travellers who rate their overall experience of New Zealand as 8 or more on a 10-point scale." (ibid., p. 64) Similarly the target for increasing visitors spend is raised from $130 to $160 per night by 2015. However for targets 4 and 5, NZTS 2015 identifies the need to develop ways of measuring environmental performance, and community benefit and to define and implement measurable targets in these areas.

The meaning of strategy

Strategy: The planning of a desirable future and the design and testing of suitable ways of bringing it about.

According to Ghemawat (2010, p. 2), the word 'strategy' is Greek in origin (*strategos*) and this term was used to designate a military commander-in-chief. The context of war therefore offers an initial understanding of strategy as a master plan for achieving victory. However strategy is now a key focus of business schools and used widely in the tourism sector.

From the case on New Zealand's Tourism Strategy a number of key features about strategies emerge. For example it can be seen that at the heart of a strategy is an overall aim or end – in this case that tourism becomes a leading contributor to the economy. A strategy also contains a means to its end. For NZTS 2015 these are identified in four outcomes encompassing the visitor experience, investment, the environment and partnership between the tourism sector and communities. A strategy also uses medium to long term planning horizons, setting its sights on a time in the future which in the case of NZTS is the year 2015.

The following examples illustrate a range of definitions of strategy by key writers in the study of strategy. Quinn defines strategy as:

> *the pattern or plan that integrates an organisation's major goals, policies and action sequences into a cohesive whole. (Mintzberg et al., 1998, p. 5).*

One of the main integration challenges for NZTS 2015 is to ensure a good working relationship or partnership between the public sector and private sector. According to Johnson *et al.* (2008, p. 3):

> *Strategy is the direction and scope of an organisation over the long term which achieves advantage in a changing environment through its configuration of resources and competences with the aim of fulfilling stakeholder expectations. (Johnson et al., 2008, p. 3).*

The long term nature of strategy is demonstrated by the fact that NZTS 2015 was published in 2007 – a planning horizon of 8 years. Mintzberg identified the five Ps for strategy noting:

> *"five definitions of strategy ... - as plan, ploy, pattern, position and perspective." (Mintzberg et al., 1998, p. 13).*

To some extent NZTS 2015 can be seen as a ploy and a way of outperforming other competing destinations.

An article that researched the views of a range of strategy researchers and senior practitioners came up with the following broad agreement on the term:

> *The field of strategic management deals with the major intended and emergent initiatives taken by general managers on behalf of owners, involving utilization of resources, to enhance the performance of firms in their external environments. (Nag et al., 2007, p. 944).*

Because of the range of tourism strategies (including organisations and destinations) examined in this book it should be noted that the term 'organisation' or 'firm' is not always appropriate. So the term 'entity' will sometimes be used to refer to the strategic decision making unit.

From the above it can be seen that a strategy is akin to a master plan which has certain key features. It is medium to long term and is concerned with aims. But what then is an aim? To aim is to look towards and try to hit something – a target – and so an important part of a strategy is the careful identification of a target. It needs to be clear to everyone involved in the strategic process exactly what it is they are aiming for, so the target needs to be carefully defined and described.

Consequently the idea of an aim and target is central to a strategy but does not fully explain the term. Targets can look quite different from one another and can be placed in different places, so we need to consider the form which a particular target will take. The process of considering strategic options and deciding which is the most appropriate one (strategic evaluation) is essentially the choosing between different targets.

However merely having a target is necessary but not sufficient for a strategy. Part of strategy is the formulation of a plan of how to hit our target. For a simple target, like an archery target this is straightforward. We take aim, we fire, and we can see if we have hit the target by observing where our arrow has landed. But for a complex business target this process is far from simple. How do we know if we have hit the target? We need to express clearly what hitting the target means – it could be sales, or profit or market share or customer satisfaction or a combination of these or other things. It might take some time for us to find out how well we have hit the target since we have to collect, process and present complex data. So that is a key problem for strategists. Another problem is aligning or aiming a complex entity so that all of its workforce and component parts are heading in the right direction to hit the target. This may be a particular difficulty if our strategy has involved identifying a radically new target or if the entity in question is a large and cumbersome one.

Summarising the above a strategy needs to address the following questions:

- ◊ Where are we trying to go?
- ◊ How can we get there?
- ◊ How do we know if we've got there?

There are also a number of terms that cover similar ground to strategy. These are 'business planning', 'organisational strategy' and 'strategic management'. The characteristics common to all these forms of analysis are that they involve decisions which:

- ◊ Are complex rather than simple
- ◊ Are integrated rather than isolated
- ◊ Are long-term rather than short-term
- ◊ Are proactive rather than reactive
- ◊ Have an impact on the whole rather than a part of the entity
- ◊ Involve major rather than minor change
- ◊ Involve grand design rather than marginal tinkering
- ◊ Are made by those in positions of power in the entities rather than subordinates.

Another way to understand the meaning of the term strategy is to consider what it is not. Strategy is not 'flying by the seat of your pants', for this implies reacting to events as they happen, without a long-term plan. This approach is sometimes termed ad-hocism, luck, or muddling through. For example the original development of the Spanish Mediterranean resort of Torremolinos lacked a clear strategy. The resulting somewhat chaotic development embraces an inharmonious juxtaposition of buildings.

Is a tactical approach the same as a strategic approach? It certainly implies more planning than ad-hocism, and more thinking things out in advance. But a strategy is more comprehensive than tactics. Tactics represent a way of dealing with a particular problem facing an entity and generally refers to focused small-scale interventions. Strategy, on the other hand involves a blueprint for the whole entity.

Finally there are some similar terms to strategy such as policy, goal, objective programme and plan. It is worth examining the distinctions between these for analytic clarity. Policies generally designate broad rules or guidelines that direct behaviour. For example a hotel might have a 'buy local' policy, or an airline might have a policy of 'green at the gate' (meaning that all passengers have their seat allocations finalised before they reach the departure gate). Of course such policies may often support a strategy. Goals and objectives spell out the detail of what needs to be achieved in order to deliver a strategy. For NZTS 2015 these are identified as targets and in the case of visitor spending, a specific target is designated of increasing expenditure from $130 to $160 per night by 2015. A programme or plan identifies a blueprint or set of actions that identify how objectives will be achieved.

In summary the definition of strategy used in this text is:

the planning of a desirable future and the design and testing of suitable ways of bringing it about.

The process of strategy

Figure 1.1 illustrates in schematic form the four key elements of tourism strategy:

- ◊ Strategic purpose
- ◊ Strategic analysis
- ◊ Strategic choice, and,
- ◊ Strategic implementation.

What do each of these stages mean and how do they relate to New Zealand's Tourism Strategy?

Strategic purpose

We start by considering the mission and purpose of an entity in chapter 2. The mission can be thought of as a concise statement of:

- ◊ What the entity is trying to achieve
- ◊ What its purpose or aim is
- ◊ Where it is trying to head for in the medium to long term.

In the case of NZTS 2015 the mission (in this case called vision) is that:

In 2015, tourism is valued as the leading contributor to a sustainable New Zealand economy. (Tourism New Zealand, 2007, p. 5).

This statement guides and integrates the New Zealand Tourism Strategy. All of its subsequent detail should support and help to achieve this vision. But mission begs two other key questions. The first of these is *who* does the entity seek to serve and the second is *what* is the general purpose of the entity.

NZTS 2015 is not the output of a single organisation. Three parties, the Tourism Industry Association, the Ministry of Tourism, and Tourism New Zealand were involved in the preparation of the document. The people who have key interests in an entity are called its stakeholders and these groups will help to fashion its mission. In this case three main stakeholder groups are identifiable. The Tourism Industry Association is a trade association that represents mainly private sector organisations for whom profitability would be of prime importance in mission. A marketing organisation such as Tourism New Zealand would generally seek to increase visitor numbers. On the other hand the Ministry of Tourism will wish to satisfy other objectives such as social responsibility and good governance. In this case the interests are not necessarily compatible and the NZTS 2015 mission reflects an amalgam of interests. This explains why it stresses the contribution of tourism to a *sustainable* economy. This encompasses not just economic considerations but also environmental and social ones too. A fuller range of stakeholders are identified in relation to the specifics of NZTS 2015. For example in order to promote 'actions to protect and enhance New Zealand's environment' the following groups are deemed to be key stakeholders:

- ◊ Ministry of Tourism
- ◊ Tourism Industry Association
- ◊ Tourism New Zealand
- ◊ New Zealand Maori Tourism Council
- ◊ Maori regional tourism organisations
- ◊ Regional tourism organisations
- ◊ Tourism operators
- ◊ Ministry for the Environment
- ◊ Department of Conservation
- ◊ Ministry of Transport
- ◊ Local Government New Zealand.

(ibid., p. 49)

Stakeholders and missions exist within entities which in turn exist within societies. They therefore reflect the cultural and political norms that exist both within entities and society at large. One challenge therefore for entities which wish to be innovative is how to escape the tendency for cultural reproduction where entities induct, train and reward staff to conform to current corporate and political thinking. The relationship between culture and mission is addressed in Chapter 3.

Strategic analysis

This involves understanding the major influences upon the entity's success in terms of the:

- ◊ Environment that it operates in
- ◊ Its use of resources
- ◊ Products and services offered.

Strategic analysis is concerned with studying the opportunities and threats posed by an entity's external environment and the strengths and weaknesses of its internal resources. This is sometimes called situational analysis enabling an entity to understand both its operating environment, its own capability and the degree of match between the two.

The external environment is typically analysed in terms the competitive, political, economic, socio-cultural and technological environments (C-PEST) factors. Chapter 4 concentrates on PEST factors. NZTS 2015 identifies three significant threats in its PEST environment. The first of these relates to concerns about the impact of travel on climate change. This is both a socio-cultural factor reflecting changing perceptions and attitudes and a political factor reflecting the likelihood of government actions to curb the impact of tourism on climate change. The second external change noted by NZTS 2015, located in the technological environment, is the greater use of IT by consumers. The final factor, in the economic environment, is the trend towards higher fuel prices. The competitive environment is covered in Chapter 5. Here the NZTS 2015 (ibid., p. 13) notes the highly competitive nature of the global tourism industry where the popularity of different destinations is heavily influenced by marketing spend and product development.

Chapter 6 investigates the internal environment or capability with an emphasis on resource deployment and products. Here NZTS 2015 identifies three weaknesses which need to be addressed by recruitment of skilled staff, developing a more environmentally sustainable product and the provision of tourism infrastructure.

Strategic choice

This is concerned with:

- ◊ Generation of strategic options
- ◊ Identifying strategic direction and methods, and
- ◊ Evaluation of strategic options.

In simple terms an entity seeks to gain advantage over its competitors either by offering a cheaper product than the competition, or a better product than the competition, or a cheaper and better product. These are the main generic strategic options available.

The subject of Chapter 7 is strategic options and those available to NZTS 2015 are featured in answer to the question 'what kind of tourism is best for New Zealand?'. Box 1.1 contains an extract from NZTS 2015 that addresses this.

Box 1.1 What kind of tourism is best for New Zealand?

"The best kind of tourism for New Zealand is sustainable tourism, that is, tourism that delivers maximum value — economic, social, cultural, and environmental — with as few unwanted effects as possible. Twenty years ago, the debate about what kind of tourism would be best for New Zealand largely centred on how many international visitors would be appropriate."

Source: Tourism New Zealand (2007, p.15.)

It can be seen from Box 1.1 that the strategic option favoured by NZTS has moved from mass tourism (where price is a major consideration) to quality/differentiated tourism (where visitor and host experience is a major consideration). Of course this change represents a big shift in thinking and has important implications in terms of changing business culture throughout the sector (see Chapter 3).

Chapter 8 looks at the directions and methods that are available to pursue a given strategy. A number of pointers are given to these in NZTS 2015. In terms of product development the '100% Pure New Zealand' brand (p. 10) remains a central part of the strategy and the notion of appealing to the 'Interactive Traveller' (p. 19) is introduced. Other product initiatives include the opportunities for developing Maori tourism, the need to tailor the tourism product to the domestic market and the potential of the Conferences and Conventions niche to counter seasonality. With regard to markets the overriding concern is to retain and grow market share but within this some specific opportunities are noted. For example:

China .. is now New Zealand's fastest–growing international visitor market, and it is projected to be our fourth largest market by 2010. (ibid. p.24).

Chapter 9 focuses on strategic evaluation. During any phase of strategic review a number of strategic options will be generated from strategic analysis. Here the tests of suitability, feasibility and acceptability are often used to test the robustness of a range of possible strategies in order to arrive at a preferred option. Suitability asks whether a strategy is appropriate in view of the entity's situational analysis. NZTS 2015 does not specifically include the process of strategic evaluation. However it does include an analysis of its external and internal environments and since its strategy is consistent with the findings of this analysis it would appear to be suitable. Feasibility tests whether a strategy can be achieved in terms of resources, finance and capability. Again NZTS 2015 does not explicitly review the feasibility of its strategy and there is little mention of its financial implications or other resource or organisational implications. Acceptability judges a strategy in terms of its endorsement by its major stakeholders. NZTS 2015 takes a strong stakeholder approach throughout. The process of consultation is evidenced as follows:

"Many people have contributed to this Strategy. They include the 400 delegates at the Tourism Industry Conference held in August 2006, as well as the many hundreds who attended meetings to discuss the Strategy between October 2006 and January 2007. More than 100 individuals and organisations provided substantive feedback on the draft Strategy when it was released in May 2007. They include representatives from the private sector, local and central government, the education and training sector, and related organisations. (ibid. p. 2).

Acceptability is enhanced by this kind of comprehensive consultation.

Strategic implementation

This is concerned with issues of operationalising a strategy, particularly:

- ◊ Organising and resourcing
- ◊ Managing and monitoring
- ◊ Strategy articulation.

Organising and resourcing for strategic implementation is covered in Chapter 10. This aspect is not covered in NZTS 2015. Instead the strategy refers to the development of a separate document:

"The next step is to develop a detailed implementation plan. This will be led by the Ministry of Tourism, the Tourism Industry Association, and Tourism New Zealand, in consultation with all relevant stakeholders. (p. 7).

Typically an implementation plan will address, roles and responsibilities, timeframes, financial implications and any organisational structure changes that need to be made.

Chapter 11 address issues of managing and monitoring strategies. Box 1.2 shows some of the key issues here for NZTS 2015. For example it offers some clear measurable targets to be achieved to monitor the success of the strategy. But interestingly it states that for some of the strategic objectives new methods of measurement will need to be devised. Also NZTS 2015 contains an appendix which monitors achievements of its previous strategy (NZTS 2010). For example:

> *Total tourism expenditure grew from $13.7 billion in 2000 to $18.6 billion in 2006. (ibid., p. 66).*

Box 1.2: Performance targets for NZTS 2015

Increasing visitor satisfaction

Target: Increase by four percentage points the number of international travellers who rate their overall experience of New Zealand as eight or more on a 10–point scale...

Increasing the amount visitors spend

Target: Increase the average amount that visitors spend per night from $130 to $160 by 2015.

Reducing seasonality

Target: Increase the number of international visitors who arrive in the shoulder season ... at a rate that is 25% faster than the overall annual forecast growth rate every year between now and 2015.

Delivering environmental best practice

We must develop ways of measuring the amount of carbon emitted by the tourism sector ...

We must develop ways of measuring how satisfied visitors are with New Zealand's environment performance.

Creating positive community outcomes

We must develop ways of measuring how local government accommodates and promotes tourism and how residents feel about the tourism activities taking place in their communities. (p. 64, 65)

Source: Tourism New Zealand (2007)

Finally, Chapter 12 looks at strategies in action. It sets out the fundamentals of strategy articulation, addressing the structure and content of a typical strategy document. NZTS 2015 is a good example of strategy articulation. Its contents page demonstrates a structured and comprehensive approach to the document and extracts from this are reproduced in Box 1.3.

Box 1.2 The elements of New Zealand's tourism strategy

1. Executive summary (a one page summary of the key points)
2. Tourism in New Zealand (offering an understanding of the context)
3. Sustainability — the way ahead (articulating the vision)
4. The challenges facing tourism In New Zealand (analyzing the key external and internal factors)
5. Strategy to 2015 (articulating the objectives and steps needed to be taken to deliver the strategy)
   - Outcome One: New Zealand delivers a world–class visitor experience
   - Outcome Two: New Zealand's tourism sector is prosperous and attracts ongoing investment
   - Outcome Three: the tourism sector takes a leading role in protecting and enhancing New Zealand's environment
   - Outcome Four: the tourism sector and communities work together for mutual benefit
6. Setting Targets (offering metrics to measure and monitor success).

Source: Tourism New Zealand (2007, p. 1)

The importance of strategy

Without strategy, tourism entities are susceptible to strategic drift, particularly in today's turbulent environments and fragmentation which might be likened to the headless chicken syndrome. Each of these ideas is now addressed.

Strategic drift

Strategic drift (Johnson, 1988) occurs when an entity has failed to monitor and keep pace with its changing external environment. This is illustrated in Figure 1.2.

Strategic drift: When an entity has failed to monitor and keep pace with its changing external environment.

An organisation without a strategic view is likely to replicate current policy with perhaps a few minor changes. This is not a problem when environments are fairly stable, thus for example between time periods 0 and 1 there is very little change in organisational policy, but this is not necessarily a problem since the environment has also witnessed little change either. However between time periods 1 and 2, the environment has changed substantially from H to K. A tourism organisation without a strategic view is likely to make only marginal change to its policy from J to L. Thus a gap opens up between the position of the tourism organisation and its environment. This gap, KL in the figure, represents strategic drift. Given the eight-year planning cycle of NZTS 2015 there is a danger that strategic drift might occur in the later years. However perhaps in an attempt to avoid this pitfall the authors of NZTS 20015 provided for an update of the strategy in 2012.

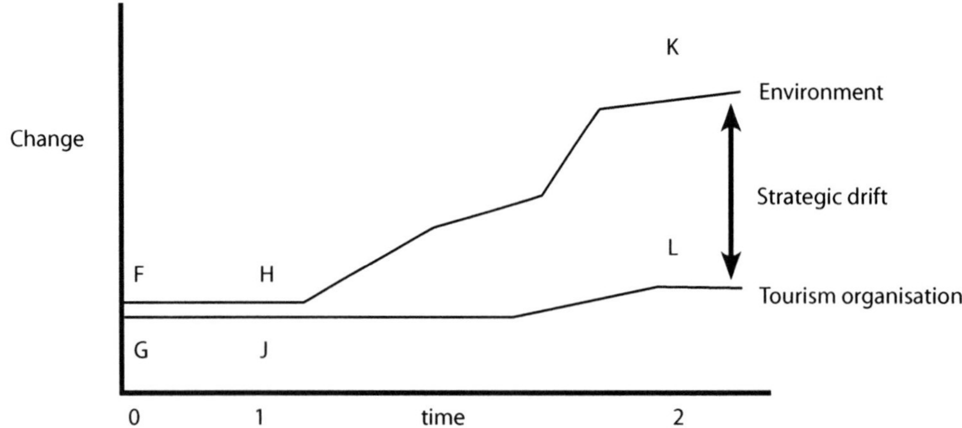

Figure 1.2: Strategic drift

Turbulent environments

Turbulent environments: Dynamic, diverse, difficult and dangerous.

The changing nature of the operating environment within which organisations work has also underlined the importance of strategic planning. It is possible to characterise business life as being relatively straightforward perhaps up to the end of the 1960s. Under this reading of things the external environment could be expressed by the time period from 0 to 1 in Figure 1.2. It was essentially static. Thus for example New Zealand Tourism faced a fairly predictable market and competition and the economic and political environments were generally stable. Technology advanced relatively slowly. Additionally many entities tended to specialise in a one product or service. Airlines, for example tended to stick to the job of transporting passengers, and thus they operated in a single environment. Planning in these environments was a relatively simple exercise and this combination of features provided safe operating conditions for organisations.

Contrast this with the turbulent conditions that face New Zealand Tourism today. The static environment has given way to the dynamic one where the pace of change is fast. Economies move from boom to recession, exchange rates and interest rates are volatile. Internet developments and widespread access to the Web have revolutionised distribution and information channels in the tourism sector. The rise of multi-stakeholder interests means that entities have moved from a single focus to a diversity of interests and thus have to operate in diverse environments. Terrorism and the threat of terrorism has cast a deep shadow over all tourism activities. The new condition that tourism entities find themselves in is therefore one of danger. Thus the environment previously characterised by the four Ss (static, single, simple and safe) is now characterised by the four Ds (dynamic, diverse, difficult and dangerous).

Fragmentation

Fragmentation is another symptom of lack of effective strategy. The larger the organisation, or the more complex the strategic network, the more pronounced

Fragmentation: When the constituent parts of an entity do not serve a common goal.

this problem may become. For a small tourism organisation, such as a family-run hotel, most functions will be run or co-ordinated by one or two people. It is therefore relatively easy to ensure that the different functional areas of management are complementary to one another and are pulling in the same direction. Thus a hotel that is seeking expansion will ensure that it has sufficient room capacity, a supporting marketing campaign, is able to field an increase in customer enquires, and is able to service a higher occupancy rate.

For larger organisations, the danger is that functional areas take up a life of their own and can therefore pull in different directions and frustrate each other's plans. The human body serves as a powerful metaphor here. Each of its constituent parts needs to be fulfilling the same objective. If different limbs, organs and senses do not act in concert, chaos results. The challenge is even greater for a strategic entity such as that encompassed by NZTS 2015. For New Zealand Tourism consists of a complex network of destinations, host communities, special interest groups, hotels, attractions, operators, transport providers, and various layers of government. Each of these may have very different aims and it is the job of NZTS to attempt to bring direction and cohesion to these independent forces. An example of the difficulties and tensions that present themselves to national tourism strategies is that between welcome and security. On the one hand, tourism strategies generally stress the importance of creating a welcoming environment with efficient arrival procedures at international borders. But dif-

Figure 1.3: How a strategy can acts as a powerful magnet

ferent agencies are responsible for border security and they have different aims. Customs exist to ensure that prohibited or untaxed goods do not enter a country. Immigration exists to ensure that those without visas do not enter a country. Airport security exists to ensure that bombs and explosives are detected.

Figure 1.3 illustrates how a strategy can acts as a powerful magnet to pull the different parts of an organisation together. The top part of the figure represents organisational fragmentation with different functions often operating in different directions. This is a caricature since in reality a typical hierarchical structure will impose some discipline over the organisational structure. The bottom part of the diagram shows corporate strategy as a unifying theme. A corporate plan offers a goal to which all the functional areas become oriented.

A range of strategies emanate from government and other organisations and entities that are part of the tourism sector. So another challenge faced by strategies such as NZTS 2015 is to ensure that they are aligned with other major strategies, that vital connections are made, that they are mutually supportive and do not propose outcomes that would contradict them. NZTS 2015 refers to a number of key related strategies such as:

- The New Zealand Emissions Trading Scheme
- The New Zealand Energy Strategy
- The Biosecurity Strategy
- The New Zealand Transport Strategy
- The New Zealand Waste Strategy

Contexts and uses of strategy in tourism

Athiyamen and Robertson (1995) found that the level of commitment to strategic planning in the tourism industry was at least as strong as that in the manufacturing sector. However their analysis concentrated on large firms. The use of strategy in tourism is not confined to large firms and in this section the question of where strategies are being used in tourism is examined. Several key contexts can be indentified:

- Destinations
- Governments
- Trade associations
- Supra-government entities
- Private sector profit making organisations
- Special events
- Not for profit organisations
- Non-governmental organisations (NGOs)
- Strategies for specific defined ends

NZTS 2015 offers an interesting example of the first three of the above contexts. Here strategy is being used at the national destination level. But NZTS 2015 is a complex strategy. As we have noted it is led by the Ministry of Tourism (a government department) and directly supported by the Tourism Industry Association (the industry's peak trade association which is a private sector, membership-based organisation) and Tourism New Zealand (the public sector national tourism organisation for New Zealand). NZTS 2015 is therefore also a good illustration of a public/private strategic partnership. Zhang (1999) also describes strategy at the destination level examining the development of tourism for Altay Prefecture, Xinjiang, China.

Supra-national strategies are conceived by entities such the European Union (EU) or the United Nations World Tourism Organization (UNWTO). The EU tourism strategy addresses issues of common concern to member countries whilst the UNWTO offers strategic guidance to achieving global tourism goals such as poverty alleviation. Strategies are common in larger private-sector profit-making organisations such as the Walt Disney Company. Strategy can also provide the organising framework for special events such as the Olympic Games or special sectors of tourism such as wine tourism (Lockshin and Spawton, 2001). Increasingly, strategic planning is also undertaken by organisations outside the public sector such as not-for-profit organisations and NGOs as illustrated by Tourism Concern, an organisation which exists to promote just and ethical tourism. Finally, strategies may be employed to deliver specific defined ends such as accessibility in tourism or sustainable tourism. For example, Hosni (2000) outlines a strategy for sustainable tourism development in the Sahara and Ashley *et al.* (2001) analyse the effectiveness of strategies designed to achieve of the goals of pro-poor tourism.

We also need to distinguish between those organisations whose strategies are largely internally-focused (e.g. an organisation's own strategy which is a blueprint for how that organisation will act) and those which are externally focused (e.g. a strategy which is designed to co-ordinate or influence the strategies of others). Thus profit-seeking organisations such as Kingfisher Airlines (India) and the Hilton Hotels Corporation tend to have internally focused strategies, whereas organisations such as the pressure group Tourism Concern and national tourism organisations tend to have externally-focused strategies.

Despite the fact that there are some important differences between the elements of strategies used by, for example, private sector organisations and destinations, this book will attempt to cover the broad range of strategies used across the tourism sector.

Competing approaches to strategy

The explanation of strategy as presented so far in this text is designed to be clear and uncluttered. The purpose of this is to offer a relatively simple view for introductory purposes. But in reality it would be wrong to portray strategy as being such a simple process or one about which there is universal agreement. There are in fact many different accounts of what strategy is. Whittington (2001) refers to four main approaches to strategy which are categorised as the classical approach, the evolutionary approach, the processual approach and the systemic approach. Johnson *et al.* (2008) distinguish between the content and process approaches to strategy. Capon (2008) divides strategies into prescriptive and emergent ones. These various approaches reflect two different underlying philosophies about how strategy works. In the first, strategy is seen as a challenging yet achievable task of identifying and implementing a suitable plan whilst in the second, issues of fallibility, fluidity and complexity are seen to frustrate the neat execution of strategy in practice. These two positions might be further refined under the headings of strategy as prescription and the contested nature of strategies.

Strategy as prescription

The approach outlined so far in this chapter tends to follow the classical approach as developed by Ansoff (1965), Sloan (1990) and Porter (1990). This approach has a strong belief in the importance of strategy. It endorses a strong link between survival and profitability, on the one hand and the effective application by managers of the key strategic tools of analysis, policy choice and implementation, on the other. It considers that an informed strategy can be formulated and will be important in determining the success of the organisation. In a similar way the prescriptive approach holds that strategy is a logical and sequential set of actions and under the content approach, the key is to find the best strategy to suit the conditions at hand. This grouping of approaches believes that a strategy can be formulated using knowledge about an entity's situation and that the strategy can be effectively put into action. Here strategy is straightforward and certain.

The contested nature of strategy

Other approaches underline the messiness of the world that entities operate in, the difficulties of obtaining correct knowledge, the sometimes overwhelming power of the external environment on entities and the effects of humans on the whole process. For example, process approaches to strategy emphasise the lived realities of strategy in action. Emergent strategies stress the interconnectedness of the elements of strategy, the lack of chronological, linear progression from one phase to the next and the difficulty of dealing with the huge information demands of a strategy. Further, under emergent strategies, aims and missions are not necessarily front-loaded but develop in response to events.

Evolutionists include writers such as Alchian (1950), Friedman (1953), and Williamson (1991). They down-rate the power of strategic managers to have much influence. Rather they stress the power of market selection and the fact that corporate survival is at the mercy of the market. Market selection can be likened to biological selection – the fittest survive. Thus we might envisage dinosaur-type organisations which are unable to adapt fast enough to changing environments. These organisations give way to those best adapted to survival in particular market conditions.

Processualists are also sceptical about classical planning. They stress that humans are imperfect cogs in the corporate machine in contrast to the classical model of the organisation as a perfect machine. Processualists such as Cyert and March (1963) stress that humans operate in 'bounded rationality' by which they mean that they cannot see a complete picture and only have the ability to process a number of factors. Thus they challenge the power of classical analysis which tends to assume that a comprehensive strategic picture can be composed and items within it readily manipulated to a strategic end. Furthermore they see the labour force as being motivated by a range of factors, only one of which may be the corporate plan. Thus they challenge the ability of managers to effectively operationalise a strategic plan (which they have already discounted as being flawed by the limited perspective of its authors).

The systemic school emphasises that an organisation's labour force cannot be understood as simple automatons programmed to maximise the organisation's well-being. It also stresses that there is no universal corporate goal shared by organisations across the globe. Rather, human resources have to be understood through their human-ness, and as members of a particular cultural group. Granovetter (1985) refers to this as the 'embededness' of economic activity within a social system. So for this school of thought, psychological and sociological factors are important.

Review of key terms

- Strategy: the planning of a desirable future and the design and testing of suitable ways of bringing it about.
- Four key elements of tourism strategy: strategic purpose, strategic analysis, strategic choice and strategic implementation.
- Strategic drift: when an entity has failed to monitor and keep pace with its changing external environment.
- Turbulent environments: dynamic, diverse, difficult and dangerous.
- Fragmentation: when the constituent parts of an entity do not serve a common goal.
- Competing approaches to strategy: strategy as prescription vs the contested nature of strategies.

Multiple choice questions

1 Which of the following is NOT one of the five Ps identified in Mintzberg *et al.* as significant for strategy?
   A Politics
   B Plan
   C Ploy
   D Pattern

2 Which is the correct order of activities in the strategy process?
   A Strategic analysis, strategic purpose, strategic choice, strategic implementation
   B Strategic analysis, strategic choice, strategic implementation, strategic purpose
   C Strategic purpose, strategic analysis, strategic choice, strategic implementation
   D Strategic purpose, strategic choice, strategic analysis, strategic implementation

3 Which of the following are NOT characteristics of strategic planning and actions?
   A Complex rather than simple
   B Reactive rather than proactive
   C Involve grand design rather than marginal tinkering
   D Long term rather than short term

4 The 'C' in the C-PEST factors that are part of an entity's external environment refers to
   A Competition
   B Costs
   C Culture
   D Choice

5 Which of the following best reflects the meaning of the Greek word *strategos*?
   A Eagle-eyed
   B Far-reaching
   C Power
   D Military general

Discussion questions

1 Define the term strategy in your own words. Use examples, explain the essential features which distinguish a strategy from similar concepts and use counter-examples to clarify what strategy is not.

2 Explain the relevance of the terms strategic drift, turbulent environments and organisational fragmentation to a named tourism entity.

3 Map out the four key elements of strategy for a named tourism entity.

4 Explain, using examples, what Mintzberg *et al.* (1998) meant when he described strategy as "plan, ploy, pattern, position and perspective". Do you think his definition is an appropriate one?

5 What factors can make strategy a contested concept?

References

Alchian, A. (1950) Uncertainty, evolution and economic theory. *Journal of Political Economy*, **58**, 211-221.

Ansoff, H.I. (1965) *Corporate strategy: an Analytic Approach to Business Policy for Growth and Expansion*. New York: McGraw-Hill.

Ashley, C., Roe, D., and Goodwin, H. (2001) *Pro-poor Tourism Strategies: Making Tourism Work for the Poor: A Review of Experience*. London: International Institute for Environment and Development.

Athiyamen, A. and Robertson, R. (1995) Strategic planning in large tourism firms: an empirical analysis. *Tourism Management*, **16**, 447-453.

Capon, C. (2008) *Understanding Strategic Management*. Harlow: Pearson Education.

Cyert, R. and March, J. (1963) *A Behavioral Theory of the Firm*. Englewood Cliffs, NJ: Prentice Hall.

Friedman, M. (1953) *Essays in Positive Economics*. Chicago: University of Chicago Press.

Ghemawat, P. (2010) *Strategy and the Business Landscape*. London: Pearson.

Granovetter, M. (1985). Economic action and social structure: the problem of embededness. *American Journal of Sociology*, **91**, 481-450.

Hosni, E. (2000) *Strategy for Sustainable Tourism Development in the Sahara*. Paris: United Nations Educational Scientific and Cultural Organization.

Johnson, G. (1988) Rethinking incrementalism. *Strategic Management Journal*, **9**, 75-91.

Johnson, G., Scholes, K. and Whittington, R. (2008) *Exploring Corporate Strategy*. Harlow: Prentice Hall.

Lockshin, L. and Spawton, T. (2001) Using involvement and brand equity to develop a wine tourism strategy. *International Journal of Wine Tourism*, **13**, 72-81.

Mintzberg, H., Quinn, J. and Ghosal, S. (1998) *The Strategy Process*. London: Prentice Hall.

Nag, R., Hambrick, D.C. and Chen, M.J. (2007) What is strategic management, really? Inductive derivation of a consensus definition of the field. *Strategic Management Journal*, **28**, 935-955.

Porter, M.E. (1990) The competitive advantage of nations. *Harvard Business Review, March and April*, 74-91.

Sloan, A.P. (1990) *My Years with General Motors*. New York: Doubleday.

Tourism New Zealand (2007) *The New Zealand Tourism Strategy 2015*. Wellington: Tourism New Zealand.

Whittington, R. (2001) What is Strategy – and Does it Matter? London: Thomson Learning.

Williamson, O. (1991) Strategizing, economizing and economic organization. *Strategic Management Journal*, **12**, 75-94.

Zhang, C. (1999) Division and development strategy of tourism in Altay prefecture, Xinjiang. *Arid Land Geography*, **22**, 20-26.

2 Mission and Purpose

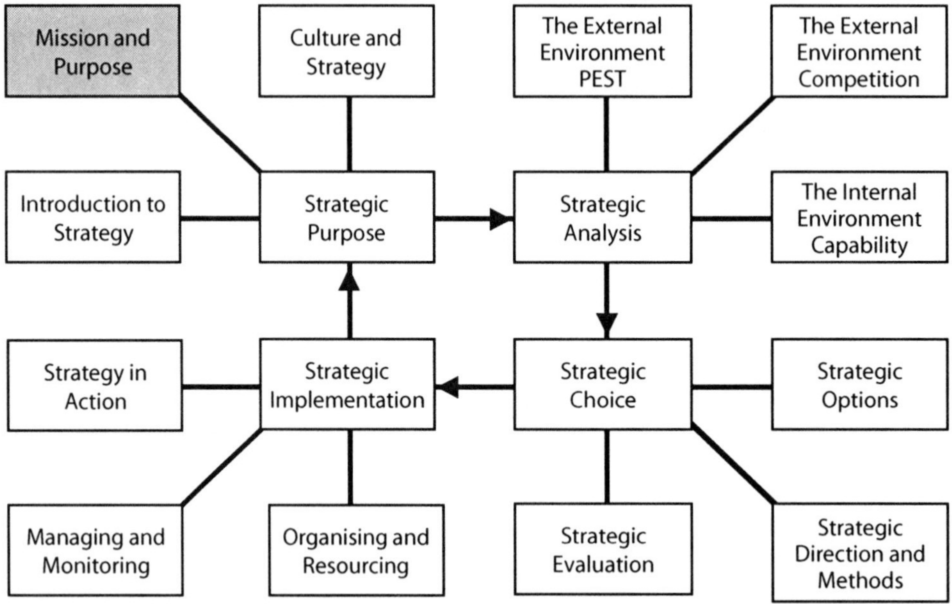

Figure 2.1

Learning outcomes

After studying this chapter and related materials you should be able to understand:

- Vision, mission and objectives
- Mission types such as profit and growth and quality of life
- Governance and social responsibility
- Stakeholders and stakeholder power

and critically evaluate, explain and apply the above concepts.

Introduction

The study of the purposes of tourism entities must necessarily precede any further analysis of strategy since it is difficult to have a strategy without having an idea of what the strategy is designed to achieve. A strategy is a means to an end, thus we need to state that desired end at the outset.

At first glance the aims of tourism entities appear to be straightforward. Surely the owners of most organisations simply want the highest possible return on their investment so that profit maximisation is the universal aim. However, two considerations make a further study of aims worthwhile. First, the concept of 'stakeholders' is an important one, particularly for large organisations and complex entities. A stakeholder is any person or group which has an interest in an organisation, and the concept of stakeholders is a much broader one than that of owner or shareholder. This makes the study of aims a more complex issue since stakeholders do not necessarily have identical aims. Second, many tourism entities are non-profit making and so if their aims are not profit-maximisation, we need to investigate what other aims are pursued, and who decides them. Related to this is the issue of governance which describes how an organisation should conduct its affairs.

Missions and objectives are by no means static, and indeed the whole idea of strategy is to engage in regular reassessment of them to ensure that they remain appropriate. Thus mission and aims need to be understood as part of the circular nature of strategic planning. Figure 2.1 illustrates this cycle of planning. The starting point of this diagram is mission and objectives. Strategic analysis is then undertaken to test their continuing appropriateness. Such analysis may lead to a reformulation of mission and objectives in a new strategy for implementation over the next few years. The cycle of strategic planning will then recommence. Case study 2 uses the British Airports Authority to introduce the terms 'mission', 'stakeholder' and 'governance' in the context of an airport operator.

Case Study 2: British Airports Authority

The British Airports Authority (BAA) runs major airports in the UK including London Heathrow, one of the world's busiest international airports. It was set up by the Labour government in 1965 as a government-owned organisation. However in the 1980s the Conservative government had a policy of privatisation, designed to transform government organisations into innovative, profitable, efficient and service-orientated enterprises. As part of this, BAA was floated on the London Stock Exchange in 1987. It was thereby transferred from government ownership in the public sector to shareholder ownership in the private sector. Some ten years later, in 2006, BAA was purchased by Ferrovial, a Spanish company with interests in construction and infrastructure. BAA's vision statement for Heathrow airport is to 'Become Europe's hub of choice by making every journey better' (BAA, 2009, p. 2) and it describes its strategic intents to achieve this vision as follows:

- Make Heathrow the preferred choice for passengers
- Improve airport operations every day
- Succeed through airline success
- Run our airport responsibly, safely and securely
- Focus people and teams on service and results
- Deliver the business plan
- Transform the airport
- Win support for our airport vision.

London Heathrow Airport – Generating noise as well as profit

However Heathrow faces intense competition from Schiphol (Netherlands), Paris, Charles de Gaulle (France) and Frankfurt (Germany) airports which also wish to be Europe's hub of choice and for example, Schiphol has five main runways in contrast to Heathrow's two. So part of BAA's long term strategy is to develop a third runway at Heathrow in order to become more competitive and generate increased profit to its parent company's (Ferrovial) shareholders. Runway 3 is a controversial strategy. Heathrow is situated in a busy residential area to the West of London and a new runway will mean loss of residential housing, extra air noise, increased road traffic and an expansion to air capacity which appears to contradict government policy to reduce CO_2 emissions. Runway 3 therefore demonstrates the extent of stakeholder interests in BAA's strategy. Stakeholders extend beyond the company's shareholders to include:

- Employees
- Customers (including passengers, airlines, retailers, car hire and other tenants)
- TheAviation industry (including other airports, aircraft and engine manufacturers and air navigation service providers)
- Government (including national and local government) which affects BAA through, border control, legislation and policie.
- Local communities which are affected by airport operation.
- Non-governmental organisations (NGOs) (including Greenpeace and Plane Sense) especially those which campaign on environmental issues.

- Regulators (including the Civil Aviation Authority (CAA) and the Competition Commission)
- Suppliers (including banks, construction companies and IT support)
- Public transport operators (including bus, coach, taxi and rail).

Large organisations such as Ferrovial and its subsidiary BAA are required to demonstrate good governance and corporate social responsibility and there are two publications that report on each of these. BAA's Annual Report focuses on governance. It is primarily aimed at shareholders and shows how the company is run and reports on financial and other achievements. BAA's Corporate Responsibility Report focuses on social responsibility. It is aimed at the wider community of stakeholders covering issues such as the integration of a responsible approach into everyday business, economic and social benefits of the business, and the main environmental impacts of BAA.

Vision, missions and objectives

Vision and mission

Vision: signals what an entity would like to become.

Many tourism entities work to a vision and/or mission statement (David, 1989). Visions and missions consist of concise statements which generally preface a strategy document and Boxes 2.1 and 2.3 show examples of these. The terms 'vision' and 'mission' are often used interchangeably but there is a subtle difference between them. A vision signals what an entity would like to become. It carries with it connotations of aspiration and inspiration. On the other hand a mission sets out in more concrete terms the general aims of an entity, what it is trying to achieve and what it is in existence for.

Mission: sets out in more concrete terms the general aims of an entity, what it is trying to achieve and why it is in existence.

A useful mission statement should have the following characteristics:

- ◊ Succinct
- ◊ Future-oriented
- ◊ An umbrella statement which can cover more detailed objectives
- ◊ Realistic and achievable
- ◊ Describe the main aims of the organisation.

Sidhu (2003, p. 443) addressed what he perceived as a waning in interest in mission statements. He noted that:

> *management practitioners have become increasingly sceptical of investing valuable organisational resources in developing mission statements when the returns from these are uncertain.*

His empirical study sought to investigate whether mission statements were of benefit and investigated the relation between mission statements and performance. His findings underlined the importance of mission statements concluding that their existence was associated with superior performance.

Objectives

Objectives: spell out the goals that have to be achieved to realise a mission.

Objectives spell out the goals that have to be achieved to realise a mission. In this way objectives set out in more detail how a mission is to be achieved. There are two main levels at which objectives are set out. At one level there are general objectives. These tend to be framed at a fairly broad level.

Pearce and David's (1987) study found that effective mission statements included comments on the following nine objectives:

- ◊ Customers
- ◊ Products/services
- ◊ Location/markets
- ◊ Technology
- ◊ Profitability
- ◊ Philosophy
- ◊ Self-concept
- ◊ Concern for public image
- ◊ Concern for employees.

Kemp and Dwyer (2003) followed this with a study that investigated the mission statements of international airlines. These were analysed to determine the extent to which they conformed to the Pearce and David (1987, p. 637) view of an effective mission statement. They found that:

> *the three components most prevalent in the airline mission statements are self-concept (88%), philosophy (80%), and customers (72%) ... The components least prevalent in the mission statements were technology (22%), concern for employees (22%), and concern for public image (30%).*

Typical general objectives for the tourism sector might include financial return, safety and security, customer satisfaction, employment conditions and sustainable practices.

Box 2.1 shows the five key ways in which British Airways sets out to achieve its mission in terms of customers' needs, improved margins, airline of choice, differentiated service, presence in key global cities and leadership position in London. But general objectives do not generally offer much guidance as to how an entity will know whether it is fulfilling its mission. For this reason operating objectives or performance indicators may be used. These are much more specific and set out targets for operating units within an entity. Again Box 2.1 shows these for British Airways. It identifies four key performance indicators of operating margins, customer recommendations, punctuality and colleague involvement which relate to finance, customers, operations and colleagues. Box 2.1 additionally shows the missions of the Schiphol Group and Singapore Airlines.

Box 2.1 Missions: Mainly for Profit

Schiphol Group

Schiphol Group is an airport operator based in The Netherlands.

Vision

To rank among the world's leading airport companies.

Mission

To create sustainable value for our stakeholders by developing AirportCities and by positioning Amsterdam Airport Schiphol as the leading AirportCity.

Source: www.schipholgroup.com

Singapore Airlines

Singapore Airlines is a member of the Star Alliance

Mission

Singapore Airlines is a global company dedicated to providing air transportation services of the highest quality and to maximising returns for the benefit of its shareholders and employees.

Source: www.singaporeair.com

British Airways

British Airways is a member of the One World Alliance

Mission

To be the leading global premium airline

Objectives

- Meet our customers' needs and improve margins through new revenue streams
- Be the airline of choice for long-haul premium customers
- Deliver differentiated service for all customers at key touch points
- Grow our presence in key global cities
- Sustain and build on our leadership position in London

Key Performance Indicators

- KPI1: Financial. Indicator: Operating margin
- KPI2: Customers. Indicator: Customer recommendation
- KPI3: Operations. Indicator: Punctuality (Ready to Go)
- KPI4: Colleagues. Indicator: Colleague involvement

Source: www.ba.com

Framing of objectives and missions

Objectives and missions may be framed as open or closed statements. Closed statements are written as a quantifiable target. This might be a financial target or an operating target. For example British Airways has set a goal of achieving

SMART objectives: should be specific, measurable, agreed with those who must attain them, realistic and time-constrained.

a 10 per cent operating margin. This is a closed operating target. It is readily measurable. Closed objectives should conform to the SMART principles, that is they should be:

- ◊ Specific
- ◊ Measurable
- ◊ Agreed with those who must attain them
- ◊ Realistic, and,
- ◊ Time-constrained.

Open objectives are written in more qualitative terms. Missions are generally written as open statements and targets such as 'the most successful' are not measurable without further definition. Notice from Box 2.1 that Singapore Airlines' mission to 'achieve highest quality' and 'maximising returns' is couched in qualitative rather than quantitative terms.

Types of mission

The aims and missions of organisations can be classified according to a number of types, where classification depends upon the significance of profit as against other aims. The following classification illustrates five main types.

Profit-maximisation

Many tourism organisations are exclusively profit-driven. If an activity does not contribute directly to profitability it will not be pursued by an organisation in this grouping. Profit-maximisation is assumed by neo-classical economic theory to be the key objective of private sector firms, a point underlined by the economist Milton Friedman (1970, p. 122) whose view was that 'the business of business is business'. Friedman argued that:

> *In a free enterprise, private property system a corporate executive is the employee of the owners of the business. He has direct responsibility to his employers. That responsibility is to conduct the business in accordance with their desires, which generally will be to make as much money as possible while conforming to the basic rules of the society.*

Tempered profit maximisation

The next group of organisations may be termed 'tempered profit maximisers'. These organisations generally seek to maximise profits but their missions include some features which do not directly generate profits. For example, in Box 2.1, Singapore airlines includes employee benefits along with shareholder returns in its mission. Tempered profit maximisation often includes community aspects. In practice, a community aspect of a mission may be viewed in several ways. It might be considered as a purely altruistic policy which is followed solely on ethical grounds. Alternatively it might be viewed as good public relations with no instant payback, but improving the general image and attractiveness of the entity, and thus adding to profitability in an indirect way.

Indirect profit maximisation

Trade associations which promote the interests of their members may sometimes have their missions categorised in this group. Their missions are not to maximise their own profits, but to enhance the interests of their members. The Universal Federation of Travel Agents' Associations (UFTAA), for example, aims to protect its members' interests through collective negotiation with principles. Similarly, the International Hotel and Restaurant Association (IHRA) exists to promote the interests of, and provide services for, its members in the hotel and restaurant industry world-wide. Its aims are set out in Box 2.2.

Box 2.2 The aims of the International Hotel and Restaurant Association

- Monitor issues that are raised by major international organizations involved in tourism.
- Represent the collective industry interests before policy makers.
- Lobby for better recognition of the hospitality industry worldwide.
- Lobby against damaging or costly attempts to regulate the industry.

Source: www.ih-ra.com

Some tourism trade associations and coalitions seek to promote 'good practice' in conjunction with profits. For example, the World Travel and Tourism Council (WTTC) is a forum for business leaders in the travel and tourism industry. Its membership includes the chief executives of about 100 leading travel and tourism companies. It exists to promote the travel and tourism industry on behalf of its corporate members, but also promotes environmental tourism.

Social and other aims

For some organisations, profit is not a major consideration. Instead their mission is to serve some other end. An important grouping of organisations under this heading are those run or financed by national and local government. Their missions generally embrace more general economic or social aims (O'Hagen *et al.*, 1986). For example the Kenya Wildlife Service is a state corporation. It was established by an Act of Parliament with a mandate to conserve and manage wildlife in Kenya and this is reflected in its mission which is shown in Box 2.3. Box 2.3 also shows the visions and goals of the Aboriginal Tourism Strategy for Western Australia, a strategy produced by a government agency – Tourism Western Australia – in conjunction with a range of stakeholders. This has the specific aim of increasing the opportunities for Aboriginal people to become more involved in and benefit from tourism.

Box 2.3: Missions for Social Aims

Kenya Wildlife Service

The Kenya Wildlife Service conserves and manages Kenya's wildlife.

Vision

To be a world leader in wildlife conservation.

Mission

To sustainably conserve and manage Kenya's wildlife and its habitats in collaboration with other stakeholders for posterity.

Source: www.kws.go.ke

Tourism Concern

Tourism Concern is an independent charitable organisation

Vision

A world free from exploitation in which all parties involved in tourism benefit equally and in which relationships between industry, tourists and host communities are based on trust and respect.

Mission

To ensure that tourism always benefits local people.

Source: www.tourismconcern.org.uk

Ecumenical Coalition on Tourism (ECOT)

The Ecumenical Coalition on Tourism is an advocacy and lobby network of ecumenical, church, other faith-based, and secular groups working for justice and humanity in tourism.

Mission

ECOT will play a lead role in advocacy for a Just and Equitable Tourism for all.

Objectives

1 ...promote a tourism that assists the quest for a just, participatory, and sustainable society.
2 Focus on tourism and the effect it has on the lives of the people of the Third World and their natural environs.
3 Provide opportunities for the local people displaced and otherwise affected by tourism to express their views and concerns.
4 Work for gender justice and child protection in tourism.
5 Empower indigenous peoples in their efforts to critique tourism as is presently structured, and support them in their attempts to get a fair price for their exposure to tourism.
6 Draw attention to unfair practices in tourism and encourage action to change them.
7 Lobby against the violation of human rights related to tourism development projects at national and international level.

8 Provide research and information on the impact of tourism.

9 Engage in analytical study on the implications of globalization for the tourist trade and offer alternative paradigms for justice.

10 Advocate for just practices in the tourist trade and to ensure that international mechanisms are in line with values of justice for the host communities.

11 Protect the rights of workers in the formal and informal sectors of the industry.

Source: www.ecotonline.org

An Aboriginal Tourism Strategy For Western Australia 2006 – 2010

Vision

Western Australia will be the premier destination for authentic Aboriginal tourism experiences. In the future...

- innovative Aboriginal tourism operators will respond to market needs
- industry partnerships will form to add to or create new opportunities for tourism development
- visitors will receive great experiences found nowhere else in the world.

Goals

- To ensure sustainable Aboriginal participation in the tourism industry
- To provide Aboriginal people with ongoing opportunities to add cultural and commercial value to the WA tourism industry, for mutual benefit.

Source: www.tourism.wa.gov.au/publications%20library/polices%20plans%20and%

Recall also from Case Study 1 that the mission of the New Zealand Tourism Strategy is that 'In 2015, tourism is valued as the leading contributor to a sustainable New Zealand economy'. This is about benefit to the wider population of a country rather than narrow profit to shareholders and it is a vision which it would be difficult for a private sector organisation to justify, since it is difficult to pinpoint clear private profit streams.

The UN World Tourism Organization (UNWTO) is a specialised agency of the United Nations funded by member states (national governments) and affiliates. It provides a forum for tourism policy issues and a source of tourism expertise. One of its key aims is to promote the development of responsible, sustainable and universally accessible tourism. The UNWTO is another example of an entity seeking wider economic benefits rather than private profit in tourism.

The missions of voluntary and non-governmental organisations may take a number of forms. For example, for some organisations, like Tourism Concern (UK), ethical considerations are paramount. Tourism Concern is able to sustain its social mission through its ownership and finance. It is an independent, non-industry based, UK charity. Its income derives from a subscription membership of around 900 people as well as a series of fund-raising activities. The prime aim of Tourism Concern (see Box 2.3) is 'to ensure that tourism always benefits local people' (Tourism Concern, 2008, p. 5)

The mission of the Ecumenical Coalition on Tourism (ECOT) (see also Box 2.3) is to provide 'just and equitable tourism for all'. The International Council on Monuments and Sites (ICOMOS) is a professional association with a membership of around 9500 throughout the world. Interestingly its aim is cultural rather than social since it works 'for the conservation and protection of cultural heritage places' (www.international.icomos.org).

Organisations in communist states

Many organisations operating under communist systems such as Cuba and China are also not primarily profit maximisers. Their role is to fulfil part of the state plan and these organisations' missions are therefore subordinate to the general aims of state or local planners. Such organisations might be required to have employment provision, or regional development as a key objective. However private enterprise is firmly established in China and permitted in Cuba and such organisations increasingly exhibit profit maximising or tempered profit maximising missions.

Figure 2.2 locates a sample of tourism organisations on a grid which depicts the significance of profit on the vertical axis against social aims on the horizontal axis. It can be seen that there is a trade-off between profit missions and social missions. Tourism Concern is able to sustain a pure social mission because it is funded through donations and does not therefore need to resort to profit making. A sex tourism operator is positioned at an extreme part of the grid as the business ignores any social or ethical concerns. British Airway's position reflects the fact that there is some social dimension to its mission but that profit is paramount.

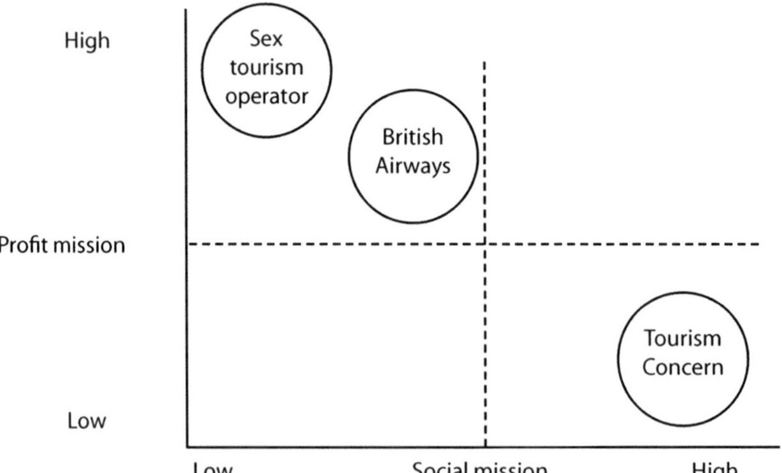

Figure 2.2: Classification of missions

Mission types and mission agenda

Each of the five main mission types outlined above can be roughly matched to a more particular agenda. This is illustrated in Table 2.1 where a distinct pattern emerges. Profit maximising organisations have a well focused agenda which is not diluted by any social responsibility. Tempered profit maximisers incorporate a wider agenda which includes a range of possible social considerations. Those organisations which are not essentially profit maximisers have a mission which focuses on issues of social benefit, community activity and ethical considerations.

Table 2.1: Mission types and mission agenda

	Mission type				
Mission agenda	1	2	3	4	5
Maximising profits	✓	✓	✓		
Corporate success	✓	✓	✓		
Customer satisfaction	?	✓	?		
Employee welfare		✓			
Environmental sensitivity		✓		✓	
Product safety		✓	?		
Employment policy		✓			
Community activity		✓		✓	
Ethical considerations			?	✓	
Benefits to society			?	✓	✓
Political considerations					✓

Notes:
1 = Profit maximiser
2 = Tempered profit maximiser
3 = Indirect profit maximiser
4 = Social welfare maximisers
5 = Communist organisations

Mission and reality

The discussion of mission is concluded with two critical views of missions. Both views suggest that they are a side issue and that, to see their real goals, what we really need to consider is the actual track record of organisations. The first view is that mission statements are just a good public relations front which put an acceptable face on the cut-throat world of the activities of organisations in modern markets. This view would suggest that cost reduction and revenue enhancement are the universal unspoken missions of most private sector organisations, but that such a frank mission would make rather alarming reading.

The second view stresses the divorce between ownership and control in the division between owners (shareholders) of large organisations and the professional managers who run them (Baumol, 1959). Whilst the shareholders will favour a mission which generates a good rate of return on their capital, managers (who may not necessarily have a significant shareholding) may actually pursue a different mission which maximise their own benefits, irrespective of the published mission. In this way they may seek remuneration packages, and a series of perks including cars and travel which detract from profitability. At other times they may seek to maximise particular targets such as sales at the expense of profit because of the personal prestige that is gained. However the adoption of profit-related bonuses for directors may have lessened the significance of this point.

Governance

Governance: describes the rules that determine how an entity is directed and controlled to discharge its responsibilities to its owners and to the law.

The crisis of capitalism centred around corporate and bank scandals, bail-outs and collapses of 2008 brought the issue of governance to front stage. Governance is concerned with authority, accountability and responsibility. It describes the rules and ways that determine how an entity is directed and controlled. Good governance exists to ensure that too much power is not vested in one or a few individuals and that the actions of those responsible for controlling entities are subject to proper scrutiny. At the most extreme case, good governance prevents corrupt, fraudulent or illegal activity. Governance is generally delivered through some kind of regulatory framework which provides a system of checks and balances. In practice, systems of governance are highly developed in some countries and less sophisticated in others. Box 2.4 shows two examples that illustrate governance in action. The first is for VisitBritain, the National Tourism Organisation for the UK and the second is for Singapore Airlines. These examples illustrate the public sector and private sector respectively.

Box 2.4 Governance in tourism in the public and private sectors

VisitBritain

The guiding principles that govern how VisitBritain is to be run were outlined by the UK government in the Development of Tourism Act 1969. There are also legal and administrative requirements for how public sector bodies such as VisitBritain use public funds. The VisitBritain Board has the responsibility for ensuring that VisitBritain operates within these principles and requirements as well as having responsibility for its overall strategic direction. The Board is comprised of a Chairman and six other members appointed by the government. It also has responsibility for two other key governance issues. These are audit (making sure that the accounts are true and fair) and remuneration (reviewing salaries). Two sub-committees report to the Board on each of these matters.

Singapore Airlines

Large shareholder-owned enterprises such as Singapore Airlines are generally required to include a statement of corporate governance in their annual reports. The Singapore Airlines' report uses the Code of Corporate Governance issued by the Ministry of Finance in Singapore (July 2005) as a framework for setting out its corporate governance processes. For Singapore Airlines, responsibilities for governance including strategic direction, planning and monitoring performance and ensuring compliance with relevant laws and regulations, are the responsibility of the Board of

Directors. There is a strong independent contingent on the Board, consisting of seven out of nine of the members. Other governance issues that the Board is responsible for include ensuring that board members have access to relevant information, reviewing remuneration, ensuring accountability (generally demonstrated through the Annual Report), making provision for a robust system of internal controls and internal audit and communication with shareholders.

It can be seen in each of these examples in Box 2.4 that a board is constituted and used as an overseer of the entity's operations. Johnson *et al.* (2008) identify two broad types of governance structures – the shareholder and the stakeholder models. The shareholder model is typical for large organisations in the UK and USA where shareholder interests are paramount. Here a single board has both an executive role for improving company performance and a supervisory role on behalf of the shareholders. On the other hand in the stakeholder model, shareholders are seen as one of a number of interested parties that might include banks and employees. Boards of large companies in Germany, France, Sweden and Japan are more likely to include representatives of such interests and may have different boards for supervisory and business interests. Tourism entities such as national tourism organisations and destination management organisations as well as NGOs are likely to favour the stakeholder model although for national tourism organisations the government is likely to be the major stakeholder. Finally it should be evident from this discussion that principles of governance will necessary override any other considerations of strategy and mission.

Social responsibility

Social responsibility: actions that appear to further some social good, beyond the interests of the firm and that which is required by law.

Where governance defines the ways in which an entity must act in relation to the law and its stakeholders, social responsibility is an area that is more discretionary. Social responsibility refers to a commitment to avoid negative impacts and deliver benefits to the wider society in which an entity operates. It is defined by McWilliams and Siegel (2001 p. 117) as:

> *actions that appear to further some social good, beyond the interests of the firm and that which is required by law.*

Henderson (2007) investigated social responsibility practices in the hotel sector in the light of the 2004 Indian Ocean tsunami. She found that several hotel companies represented in Phuket acted in ways that demonstrated clear social responsibility after the tsunami.

The very nature of tourism offers many opportunities for practising (or avoiding) social responsibility and many organisations adopt the term 'responsible tourism' to describe their efforts in this direction. Box 2.5 shows responsible tourism initiatives undertaken by the Adventure Company.

Box 2.5 The Adventure Company

The Adventure Company offers worldwide tours based around four themes of discovery, wildlife, adventure and trekking. It has a well-developed responsible travel policy which includes the following initiatives:

- Local group leaders/staff welfare – local group leaders are employed on more than 90 per cent of trips.
- A porter protection policy is in place.
- Use local services – by using local transport and as many local businesses as possible, money stays in-country and local enterprise is encouraged.
- Everyone who travels with the company gets a copy of its responsible travel policy .
- It audits all of its trips to ensure their environmental impact is minimised.
- 55 per cent of the company's trips support a local project. Examples include a school in India and a community centre in Tanzania.
- The company offsets all staff carbon emissions from work-related flights and travel to work, and also office-generated emissions.
- The suppliers used by the company and the practices adopted in its offices are constantly reviewed.

Source: www.adventurecompany.co.uk/responsible-travel.aspx

In tourism, social responsibility encompasses issues such as employment, the environment, human rights, services and suppliers, the community and ethical marketing. For example, social responsibility in employment might extend to working conditions, sick leave, recruitment practices, and the hiring and training of local labour. Here the cruise ship industry has come in for particular scrutiny regarding social responsibility in employment practices. This is also true of the working conditions for porters who support mountain trekking expeditions. Environmental considerations include provision for reducing waste, energy use and carbon emissions as well as preventing ecological damage. Human rights issues include child labour, union rights and whether tourism should be encouraged in countries with oppressive political regimes. Fair trade is a responsible tourism term that promotes among other things, fair prices for those who provide tourism services and supplier audits can be used to ensure that responsible practices are in place all along the supply chain. Responsible tourism marketing should ensure that consumers are given a true picture of the services that are advertised and that advertising is not offensive or exploitative. Finally Pro-Poor tourism (Ashley *et al.*, 2000) is a movement that seeks to maximise the potential economic benefit of tourism on the host community and especially as a vehicle for alleviating poverty in developing countries.

Stakeholders and stakeholder power

Stakeholder: person or grouping with an interest in the operation of a particular entity.

Stakeholder analysis (Friedman *et al.*, 2002) is a useful way of identifying the variety of different forces that act on an entity's mission. The term 'stakeholder' refers to a person or grouping with an interest in the operation of a particular entity. For example Sautter and Leisen (1999) identify the generic stakeholders involved in tourism planning as tourists, activist groups, national business chains, competitors, local businesses, employees and residents. Yuksel *et al.* (1999) examined stakeholder views on the implementation of a preservation and development plan for Pamukkale, a World Heritage Site in Turkey. They identified four broad stakeholder groups as central and local government officials, managers of local hotels or pensions, nearby residents and other interested organisations.

Figure 2.3 shows key stakeholders mapped out for the British Airports Authority under ten main groupings. It can be seen that the community is a stakeholder as it is affected by noise and air pollution from the airport as well as traffic congestion. The interests of the community may be taken up by NGOs such as environmental groups. Similarly as key suppliers, BAA's bankers have an interest in the financial health of its airport to protect their loan exposure. Shareholders are also stakeholders with a keen interest in BAA's fortunes by virtue of their ownership and financial stake in the company. Employees have a range of expectations from the organisation with a particular interest in salaries, working conditions and job security. The airport's passengers too have an interest in the way in which the organisation is run and managed as do its other major customers – airlines and retail operations. BAA's operations have to fall into line with government transport policy and UK airports also come under the scrutiny of two regulatory bodies – the Civil Aviation Authority (CAA) and the Competition Commission. Because of the huge volume of passengers passing through Heathrow Airport, BAA also has to work in close association with transport providers.

Figure 2.3: BAA stakeholder map

We may further categorise stakeholders as those external to the organisation and those internal to it. In the example of BAA, the aviation industry, government, local communities, non-governmental campaigning organisations, regulators, suppliers and public transport operators are external stakeholders whilst employees are internal stakeholders.

Stakeholder power

Interest alone is insufficient to explain the relative influence of stakeholder groups on mission. We need to add another dimension – that of stakeholder power – to get the full picture of stakeholder influence (Mendelow, 1991). Power may be defined as the ability to influence policy and Figure 2.4 maps the key stakeholder groups identified in the BAA case study on a power/interest matrix.

Stakeholder power: the ability to influence policy.

The area in the top right of the matrix represents the domain of most influence since here there is a concentration of both power and interest in the organisation. Major shareholders occupy a dominant position in this sector. Shareholders derive power from their ability to support or veto board policy, and shareholders with large holdings can muster considerable muscle. Individual shareholders on the other hand have little power, as their votes are fairly insignificant in comparison with large shareholders. They probably have a variety of different shareholdings and thus little interest in any one organisation and can be seen to occupy a position of minimal influence in Figure 2.4.

Senior managers can exert considerable power especially the Chief Executive Officer (CEO). This results from his or her position at the top of the managerial hierarchy. This position gives unrivalled access to information in addition to the power of control and patronage of managers in subordinate roles. Turning to the

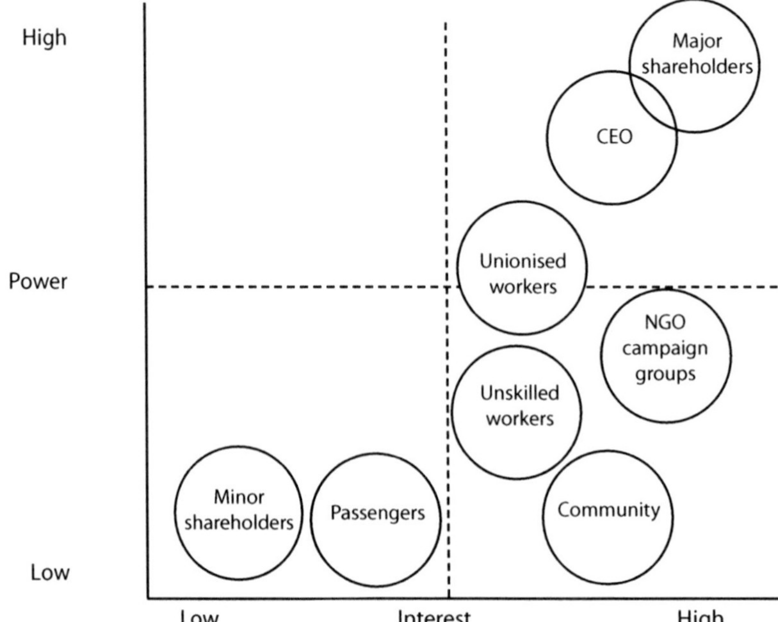

Figure 2.4: Power/Interest matrix

BAA's customers, passengers can exercise little power as individuals, since their isolated decisions about spending have little effect on the overall revenue of the airport. Unskilled workers are in a similar position of limited power although they clearly have a significant interest in the organisation as it represents their livelihood. However trade union membership (a form of coalition) can substantially enhance the power of workers. Being affected by the airport, community stakeholders are going to have some interest in its strategy but notice that NGO campaign groups can exert considerably more power than individuals in a community by virtues of their membership, networks and acquired expertise.

Returning to Yuksel *et al.*'s (1999) study on Pamukkale the authors note that despite the interest expressed by the stakeholders groups that were interviewed:

> *it is likely to be difficult to introduce real shifts in the planning process for Pamukkale as it is not easy to break out of hierarchical centralism with a strong presumption that decisions and power are anchored within central government. (p. 359)*

In this case the power of centralised government is seen to be overriding.

The power/interest matrix also offers a useful tool in determining how an entity should prioritise and respond to different stakeholders (Mendelow, 1991). Clearly the stakeholders in the top right box (high power/high interest) are key stakeholders and should be at the centre of an entity's strategic planning. Working round clockwise, those in the next box (high interest/low power) need to be kept informed of strategy. Stakeholders in the next box (low power/low interest) need perhaps the least effort. Finally those in the top left box (high power/low interest) should be kept satisfied.

The power of internal stakeholders is enhanced by:

- ◊ Position in hierarchy
- ◊ Charisma
- ◊ Comprehensive intelligence about the organisation
- ◊ Specialist knowledge
- ◊ Patronage
- ◊ Control of resources
- ◊ Formation of coalitions.

On the other hand external stakeholder power is enhanced by:

- ◊ Control of resources (e.g. finance)
- ◊ Constitutional role (e.g. shareholders' voting rights)
- ◊ Public relations skills
- ◊ Control of distribution links (e.g. outlets)
- ◊ Formation of coalitions.

Figure 2.5 shows four competing stakeholder groupings for BAA – shareholders, employees, customers (airlines) and NGO campaign groups. Each arrow contains within it key objectives that each group might wish to incorporate in the organisation's mission. However the objectives are conflicting. The owners and airlines wish to have a new runway but the campaign groups object to this. Similarly higher wages conflict with lower landing charges and higher profits. Clearly, the success in incorporating the objectives of particular stakeholders will depend on their relative power. The mission statement of the British Airports Authority (BAA) illustrated in Case Study 2 makes interesting reading in this respect. Its mission appears to appeal mainly to owners/shareholders (to deliver the business plan) with an additional aim to win support for the airport vision (i.e. counteract objections to runway 3 from campaigning groups).

Profit satisficing: not profit maximisation but a level of profit which is sufficient to satisfy an organisation's key stakeholders.

Many missions represent a compromise between the conflicting demands of different stakeholders. The term 'profit satisficing' is used to describe organisational goals resulting from such a compromise. It is not profit maximisation but rather it represents a level of profit which is sufficient to satisfy an organisation's key stakeholders. Owners may therefore have to forgo some profit in order to accommodate the demands of other powerful stakeholders. This acceptable compromise (Cyert and March, 1963) represents a kind of bargaining between stakeholder groups.

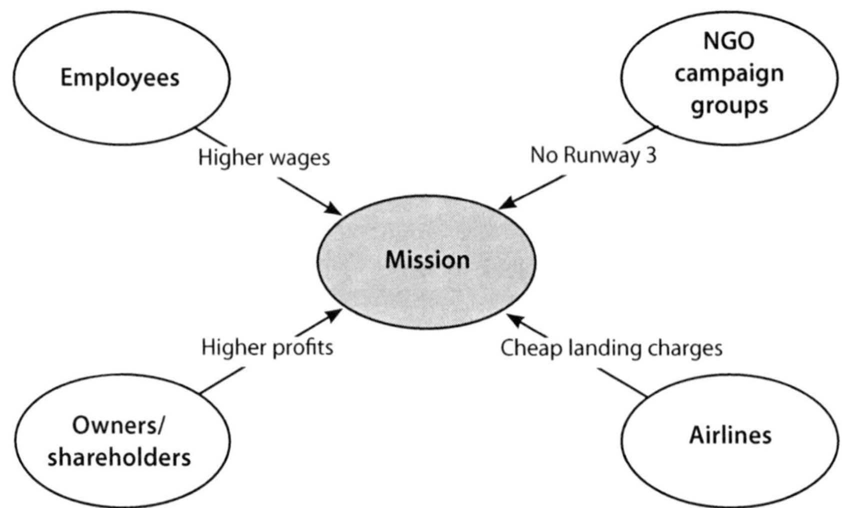

Figure 2.5: Inter-stakeholder dynamics

Review of key terms

- Vision: signals what an entity would like to become.
- Mission: sets out in more concrete terms the general aims of an entity, what it is trying to achieve and what it is in existence for.
- Objectives: spell out the goals that have to be achieved to realise a mission.
- SMART objectives: should be specific, measurable, agreed with those who must attain them, realistic and time-constrained.
- Governance: describes the rules that determine how an entity is directed and controlled to discharge its responsibilities to its owners and to the law.

- Social responsibility: actions that appear to further some social good, beyond the interests of the firm and that which is required by law.
- Stakeholder: person or grouping with an interest in the operation of a particular entity.
- Stakeholder power: the ability to influence policy.
- Profit satisficing: not profit maximisation but a level of profit which is sufficient to satisfy an organisation's key stakeholders.

Multiple choice questions

1 Which of the following statements is true?
  A Vision guides mission
  B Mission guides vision
  C All stakeholders are shareholders
  D The main aim of Tourism Concern is increasing visitor numbers

2 Which of the following is not a SMART principle?
  A Specific
  B Measurable
  C Realistic
  D Achievable

3 Which of the following would demonstrate social responsibility rather than governance?
  A Promoting Fair Trade in tourism
  B Provision of an internal audit
  C Reviewing remuneration
  D Independent representation on the board

4 Which of the following describes the most appropriate level of action for stakeholders who have high power and high interest?
  A Keep satisfied
  B Keep informed
  C Minimal effort
  D Priority effort

5 According to Kemp and Dwyer (2003) which of the following is least likely to appear in the mission statement of an airline?
  A Self-concept
  B Philosophy
  C Customers
  D Concern for public image

Discussion questions

1 Distinguish between vision, mission and objectives for a named tourism entity.

2 What are SMART objectives and what makes them SMART?

3 Distinguish between governance and social responsibility for a tourism entity.

4 What is the difference between shareholders and stakeholders?

5 Distinguish between external and internal stakeholders. What are the main sources of power for each?

References

Ashley, C., Boyd, C. and Goodwin, H. (2000) *Pro-poor Tourism: Putting Poverty at the Heart of the Tourism Agenda*. London: ODI.

Baumol, W. (1959) *Business Behavior, Value and Growth*. New York: Harcourt, Brace and World.

British Airports Authority (2009) *Corporate Responsibility Report 2008* London: BAA.

Cyert, R. and March, J. (1963) *A Behavioral Theory of the Firm*. Englewood Cliffs, NJ: Prentice Hall.

David, F. (1989) How companies define their mission. *Long Range Planning*, **22**, 90-97.

Friedman, A.L., Miles, S., House, S. and Bristol, B.S (2002). Developing stakeholder theory. *Journal of Management Studies*, **39**, 1-21.

Friedman, M. (1970) The social responsibility of business is to increase its profits. *New York Times Magazine*, **32**, 122-126.

Henderson, J.C. (2007) Corporate social responsibility and tourism: hotel companies in Phuket, Thailand, after the Indian Ocean tsunami. *International Journal of Hospitality Management*, **26**, 228-239.

Johnson, G., Scholes, K. and Whittington, R. (2008) *Exploring Corporate Strategy*. Harlow: Prentice Hall.

Kemp, S. and Dwyer, L. (2003) Mission statements of international airlines: a content analysis. *Tourism Management*, **24**, 635-653.

McWilliams, A. and Siegel, D. (2001) Corporate social responsibility: a theory of the firm perspective. *Academy of Management Review*, **26**, 117-127.

Mendelow, A. (1991) 'Stakeholder Mapping'. Proceedings of the Second International Conference on Information Systems. Cambridge, MA.

O'Hagen, J., Scott, Y. and Waldron, P. (1986) *The Tourism Industry and the Tourism Policies of the Twelve Member States of the Community; Summary of Main Findings*. Brussels: Commission of the European Communities.

Pearce, J. and David, F. (1987) Corporate mission statements: the bottom line. *Academy of Management Executive*, **1**, 109-116.

Sautter, E.T. and Leisen, B. (1999) Managing stakeholders. a tourism planning model. *Annals of Tourism Research*, **26**, 312-328.

Sidhu, J. (2003) Mission statements: is it time to shelve them? *European Management Journal*, **21**, 439-446.

Tourism Concern (2008) *Strategic Business Plan 2008-2011*. London: Tourism Concern.

Yuksel, F., Bramwell, B. and Yuksel, A. (1999) Stakeholder interviews and tourism planning at Pamukkale, Turkey. *Tourism Management*, **20**, 351-360.

3 Culture and Strategy

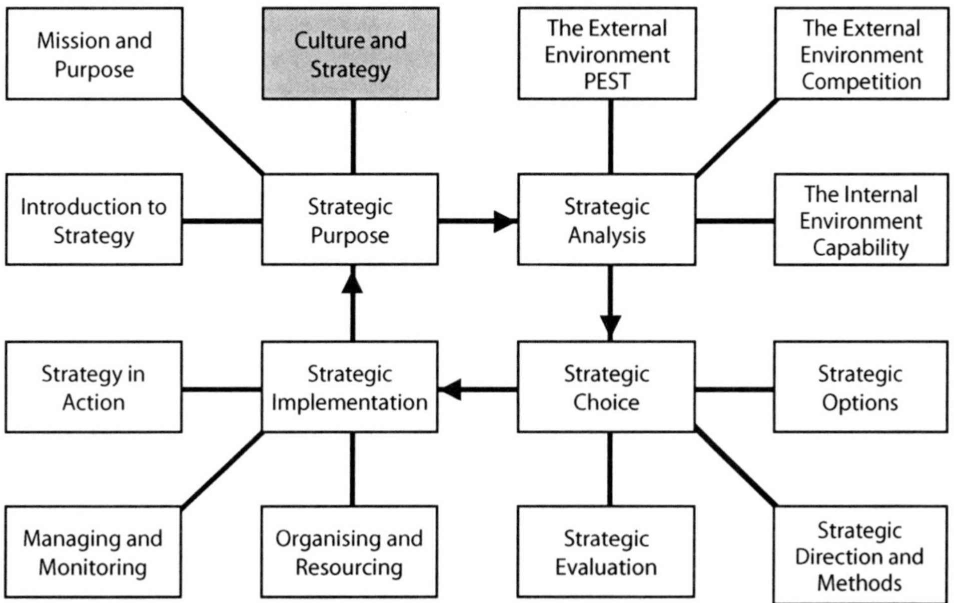

Figure 3.1

Learning outcomes

After studying this chapter and related materials you should be able to understand:

- Culture, difference and reproduction
- Organisational culture
- Cultural web
- The cultural environment

and critically evaluate, explain and apply the above concepts.

Introduction

At the end of Chapter 1 the complexity of strategy was emphasised. In particular it was stated that there are no universal goals shared by organisations and entities across the globe. Rather the human dimension of strategic planning was underlined. This human aspect draws attention to the fact that people operate as members of particular cultural groupings. Their behaviour patterns are moulded and formed by culture. So it is important to understand how individuals are embedded within organisations and entities which are prone to create cultural norms. Additionally, organisations themselves are embedded within a broader social system which sanctions and normalises certain behaviours and ideas.

Culture: a set of shared values, attitudes, goals, and practices that characterise a group of people.

To help understand these aspects of strategy this chapter initially studies the concept of culture and cultural reproduction at a general level. It then focuses on culture at the organisation level before widening its analysis to consider the cultural environment within which tourism entities operate. One of the key reasons to study the effects of culture is the challenge of strategic change. For if organisations cultivate a particular culture, and culture performs a role in determining behaviour, then culture may present a conservative pull that inhibits strategic change and innovation. This is the challenge of cultural reproduction (Bourdieu, 1973), or path dependency, where organisations and entities are prone to reproduce existing ways of doing things. Case Study 3 identifies the corporate culture of the Walt Disney Company, discusses how it is maintained and transmitted and looks at the cultural challenges of a US company operating in China.

Case Study 3: The Walt Disney Company

The Walt Disney Company (WDC) with headquarters in the USA was founded by Walt Disney in 1923 and has grown to its present position as a leading global entertainment and media company with interests in the four key areas of media networks, parks and resorts, studio entertainment and consumer products. The mission of WDC is to be one of the world's leading producers and providers of entertainment and information.

WDC demonstrates a strong and distinctive corporate culture. Walt Disney, the founder of WDC had, and still has, a significant influence on the company's mission. He was always keen to promote a wholesome image for the company and the enduring WDC culture can be seen from a number of angles. For example the value statement of WDC is arranged over seven key ideas:

Innovation

- We follow a strong tradition of innovation.

Quality

- We strive to follow a high standard of excellence.
- We maintain high-quality standards across all product categories.

Community

- We create positive and inclusive ideas about families.
- We provide entertainment experiences for all generations to share.

Storytelling

- Every product tells a story.
- Timeless and engaging stories delight and inspire.

Optimism

- At The Walt Disney Company, entertainment is about hope, aspiration and positive resolutions.

Decency

- We honor and respect the trust people place in us.
- Our fun is about laughing at our experiences and ourselves.

These core values are emphasised by Marty Sklar, Vice Chairman and Principal Creative Executive, Walt Disney Imagineering in the following statement:

> From the beginning, starting with Walt Disney, we have had five things that make me proud to be part of this Company: high-quality products, optimism for the future, great storytelling, an emphasis on family entertainment and great talent, passion and dedication from our Cast Members.
>
> The designation of theme park employees as cast members promotes a strong cultural cue that they should emphasise performance and cultivate audience relationships. Visitors are called guests and creativity and innovation are central the WDC culture.

But how is company culture transmitted to new staff? Larry Lynch of the Disney Institute, Walt Disney World, Florida, explains the role of the WDC 'university' in inducting new staff:

> ... it all begins the day new Cast Members arrive for orientation at Disney University, the company's internal training operation. The timing couldn't be better to show them how our company thinks, to offer concrete examples of how creativity and innovation have helped us grow, and to emphasize how our ongoing traditions have been the steady hand that guides us. Those traditions are pointed out again when new Cast Members are introduced to their assigned workplaces. As they learn the culture of the company, they recognize the traditions in the standard operating procedures and established norms of their work areas. They see how the company has succeeded by placing a high value on creativity. They understand that their ideas can add new insights and improve accepted practices … our Cast Members learn from day 1 that Disney expects – and values – their input on how to make our best ideas even better. Idea generation becomes an integral part of the culture.

Of course this also demonstrates some possible tensions. On the one hand the company wishes to ensure standardisation whilst on the other hand to encourage creativity and innovation. Indeed there are criticisms that WDC employee induction can be stifling. As one observer commented:

> Attend Disney U as a professional staffer and or senior employee: HR will instruct you as to what is expected in the 'employee visual package' the company is looking for. Briefly, it feels like Mattel Barbie Doll think, but that does sell.

A key mechanism for maintaining corporate values is through an organisation's reward and recognition programme. For WDC these are based upon quality of work, length of service, community volunteering and an Employee of the Month scheme. Employee of the Month can be a useful device for signalling and rewarding those attributes that the organisation values in its employees.

More general cultural issues have surfaced through some of the new theme park openings of WDC. For example, Disneyland, Paris opened in 1992 with the traditional WDC prohibition on the selling of alcoholic drinks. The idea that the Disneyland package could be successfully implanted, lock stock and barrel, into France, a country with a very distinct culture proved to be problematic. However the strategists at the Walt Disney Company, like most of us, demonstrated an ethnocentric view of the world. They saw France as if it were populated by Americans, rather than as if it were populated by the French. They were considerably surprised at the lack of enthusiasm by French visitors for a US inspired cuisine of soft drinks and fast food.

More recently the £1bn Disneyland, Hong Kong opened in China in 2005 with an entry fee of HK$350 (£33) which translates to two weeks' wages for an average family from mainland China. The opening ceremony was attended by Chinese Vice President Zeng Qinghong, Hong Kong Chief Executive Donald Tsang, WDC CEO Michael Eisner, WDC CEO-elect Bob Iger, Mickey Mouse, Minnie Mouse and Goofy the Dog. Commenting in *The Guardian* (12 September 2005) Jonathan Watts observed:

> The meeting of the world's biggest Communist party and the planet's best-known entertainment corporation would have been unthinkable to their founders. Walt Disney was a fervent anti-communist; Mao launched deadly purges of rightists and blocked Hollywood films … [The scene] highlights the hybrid nature of modern China, where the desire to make money is now the dominant ideology. Often condemned as a vehicle for US cultural imperialism, Disney is now being embraced for the cash it can bring in. The park's economic spin-off is put at HK$148bn [$15bn] over four decades.

Watts quotes a professor of economics at Hong Kong University of Science and Technology, Francis Lui, who also observes the huge shift in China's communist cultural values:

> Ideology is totally unimportant in China now. All that matters is business. And Disney is no threat to the Communist party. Both are very conservative in their outlook.

The opening of Disneyland, Hong Kong shows the huge cultural change evident in post-Mao China. It also demonstrates other cultural challenges and adjustments. Learning from initial problems at Disneyland Paris, local adjustments were made. A Chinese restaurant competes against regular US menus and offers more leisurely dining as opposed to fast food. The Chinese zodiac was consulted for a propitious opening date and the ancient Chinese system of Feng shui was used to ensure the project used the laws of Heaven and Earth to capture positive energy flows. On the other hand, local cast members have been shown by their supervisors how to smile, wave and great guests in the American way. There is some discussion about whether Disney is a key cultural referent for the younger generation of Chinese who may rather empathise with Asia-grown cartoons.

Culture, difference and reproduction

Culture

Chapter 2 investigated the influence of stakeholders on mission and analysed the significance of stakeholder role (i.e. owner, banker, employee, customer) in determining the type of mission and the form of the organisation's more detailed objectives. However, the systemic school of strategic theorists (see Chapter 1) emphasise that organisations and stakeholders need to be understood as part of the wider culture. Stakeholders are products of a particular culture and we therefore need to consider not just their roles, but also the values that they hold, which in turn have been fashioned by their cultural upbringing. Thus stakeholders in different cultures will hold differing values, which in turn will affect their expectations of an organisation's mission. So what is the meaning of culture?

The term 'culture' has a number of meanings. For example, in one sense it describes the arts with an emphasis on theatre, galleries and books. Opera in particular is sometimes referred to as 'high culture'. This has a special resonance in tourism where cultural tourism is defined by Richards (1996, p. 24) as:

> *movements of persons to specific cultural attractions, such as museums, heritage sites, artistic performances and festivals outside their normal place of residence.*

In this sense, culture represents either the artefacts or products generated by different cultures or performances associated with them. However the meaning of culture which is most relevant to this chapter is a slightly different one. It is:

> *A set of shared values, attitudes, goals, and practices that characterise a group of people.*

We might also understand culture as part of the means (along with nature) by which we have come to be the persons that we currently are. Since we are all shaped by culture we may not be alert to its existence. Indeed we may fall into the trap of ethnocentrism and think that the cultural values that we hold and practices that we perform are *the* way of doing things rather than just *a* way of doing things. Of course one of the benefits of tourism is that by coming into contact with different cultures we become more aware of the diversity of values, attitudes and practices. These differences may range from quite fundamental ones in religious beliefs between for example Christians, Muslims and Buddhists, to different food preferences and different attitudes to work and leisure.

Difference

Business culture varies considerably between different countries. Japanese business practices are closely identified with the concept of *kaizen* or continual improvement, as well as having a holistic and comprehensive approach to the long-term care of employees. Business in some parts of Latin America exhibits 'the mañana culture' which describes an unhurried world where action can be readily postponed until tomorrow. Eastern European countries sometimes retain lengthy bureaucratic procedures for business transactions. This can be evident in the tourism sector in long queues at airports for immigration clearance and visa control. In Cuba, some businesses are still under the influence of attitudes of indifference which are a characteristic of state-run enterprises. The existence of shortages and the lack of employee incentives do little to encourage a culture of customer service in Cuba. This may be contrasted with the cultural values of the United States where the capitalist ethic has been closely embraced and where making profits has been seen as a laudable aim. Tipping and other employee incentives underpin a strong culture of customer service. In Israel a culture of security and defence permeates tourism as every other activity, meaning that some incoming tourists face lengthy questioning about their purposes, their previous travel and their identity. The photograph below shows cross-cultural accommodation with Ronald McDonald adopting a Thai gesture of greeting.

Ronald McDonald greets Thai customers

Cultural variance between countries in which tourism organisations operate can be understood by reference to differences in:

- Attitudes to authority
- Attitudes to work and leisure

- ◊ Beliefs including religion and materialism
- ◊ Traditions
- ◊ Pursuit of individual or community goals
- ◊ Definitions of good and bad, worthy and unworthy (the moral and ethical system)
- ◊ Sources of status.

Stakeholders will tend to adopt different values in different countries as the above influences vary from culture to culture, and research studies have been carried out into the effects of different national cultures on organisations (Schneider and De Meyer, 1991).

Hofstede

Hofstede: studied the relationship between national cultures and organisational cultures.

The relationship between national cultures and organisational cultures has been analysed by Hofstede and Hofstede (1991) and Hofstede (2001) and these studies uncovered national and regional cultural groupings that affect the behaviour of societies and organisations that work within them. Hofstede found five dimensions of culture in his study of national work related values:

- ◊ Low vs. high power distance (PDI)
- ◊ Individualism vs. collectivism (IDV)
- ◊ Masculinity vs. femininity (MAS)
- ◊ Low vs. high uncertainty avoidance (UAI)
- ◊ Long vs. short-term orientation (LTO)

Power distance: willingness to accept an unequal distribution of power by those who have less power in organisations.

Power distance (PDI) measures the expectations and willingness to accept an unequal distribution of power in organisations by those who have less power. Here Hofstede identified countries such as Australia, New Zealand, Austria and Denmark as having low power distance cultures. In these cultures, workers relate to one another more as equals regardless of their position in an organisational hierarchy. Those in less powerful positions expect to, and feel comfortable to criticise the decisions of those in more powerful positions. They expect and accept power relations to be democratic and consultative. In contrast countries like Malaysia and Russia demonstrate high power distance. Here those in less powerful positions accept and expect power relations that are less consultative and more autocratic and do not feel comfortable in criticising their superiors. They accept the power of superiors based on their hierarchical formal, positions in an organisation.

Individualism: the pursuance of individual goals as opposed to adherence to group goals and norms.

The dimension of individualism vs. collectivism (IDV) measures how much members of a culture define themselves in terms of the pursuance of individual goals as opposed to adherence to group goals and norms. The USA is a classic individualist culture where people are strongly competitive, expected to act alone and use their initiative. Individual personalities are strong and choice of affiliations and groups to join are personal and independent. China illustrates a collectivist culture and here group membership and adherence to group norms and goals are important. In collectivist cultures, individual identity often gives way to group identity and the kinds of groups that are influential may include the family, a political party, a region or a religious group.

The dimension of masculinity vs. femininity (MAS) measures the importance and significance of traditional male or female values to members of a culture. Here it should be noted that masculinity and femininity are defined and understood from a Western cultural perspective. The dimension of masculinity vs. femininity has often been adapted by later followers of Hofstede's work to quantity of life vs. quality of life. The characteristics of masculine cultures such as the USA include an emphasis on accumulation of wealth and material possessions, ambition, competitiveness, strength, assertiveness, and ambition. On the other hand in feminine cultures such as Thailand, people value co-operation, nurture, compassion, mutuality, relationships and quality of life. Analysis of this dimension also points to differences between gender roles being more clearly demarcated and less fluid in masculine rather than in feminine cultures.

Femininity stands for a society in which social gender roles overlap: Both men and women are supposed to be modest, tender, and concerned with the quality of life. (Hofstede, 2001, p. 291)

Low vs. high uncertainty avoidance: measures a society's tolerance for uncertainty and ambiguity.

The dimension of low vs. high uncertainty avoidance (UAI) measures a society's tolerance for uncertainty and ambiguity. Low uncertainty cultures feel uncomfortable in situations which are different from usual ones, novel, unknown, surprising and unexpected. Cultures which favour uncertainty avoidance try to circumvent these situations by comprehensive laws and rules which define behaviour in most situations. In contrast, in uncertainty accepting cultures people prefer less rules and guidelines and a high degree of flexibility. Employees in uncertainty accepting cultures tend to change jobs more frequently.

Short-term orientation: the importance a society attaches to the past and present rather than the future.

Finally the dimension of long vs. short-term orientation (LTO) relates to the importance a society attaches to the past and present versus the future. For long-term oriented societies actions and attitudes that are valued include thrift persistence, perseverance, and shame. For short-term oriented societies actions and attitudes that are valued include protection of 'face', stability, tradition, and reciprocity of favours.

Table 3.1 illustrates Hofstede's scores across his five dimensions for a range of countries, illustrating the considerable diversity of cultural norms. For example it can be seen that Thailand has a both a Power Distance Index and Uncertainty Avoidance Index of 64. This indicates a high level of inequality of power and a low level of tolerance for uncertainty. It has a low score in its Individualism Index at 20 reflecting a tendency to collectivist rather than to individualist behaviour and the importance of the family and the community. Thailand has a Masculinity Index of 34 indicating a society with a low propensity for assertiveness and competitiveness. On the other hand the USA has a high Individualism Index of 91 showing a society with stronger individualistic than communal attitudes. Its Masculinity Index is 62 reflecting a country with a high gender differentiation of roles and prevalence of masculine values. The Power Distance Index of 40 for the USA indicates less deference to persons by virtue of their position in organisational hierarchies and a willingness to criticize those in positions of power. The Uncertainty Avoidance Index of 46 indicates a society that tolerates variety, exists with informal rules and can deal with unusual situations.

Table 3.1: Country scores for Hofstede's cultural dimensions. Source: www.geert-hofstede.com

	PDI	IDV	MAS	UAI	LTO
Arab world	80	38	52	68	
Austria	11	55	79	70	
China	80	20	66	30	118
Japan	54	46	95	92	80
Malaysia	104	26	50	36	
Slovakia	104	52	110	51	38
Thailand	64	20	34	64	56
United Kingdom	35	89	66	35	25
United States	40	91	62	46	29

It should be noted that the Hofstede cultural differences are generalised descriptions of cultures and not deterministic. That is to say that there may be considerable variance between individuals within a culture. Criticisms of Hofstede should also be noted. These include that culture is conceptualised by Hofstede as static and essential and the tendency for his analysis to seek out a uniform national culture and ignore diversity and hybridity.

Mok *et al.* (1998) used Hofstede's work to understand the work values and leadership preferences of Chinese hotel managers in Hong Kong. They used Hofstede's (1980) Values Survey Module to develop a questionnaire which was completed by 120 ethnic Chinese hotel managers working in Hong Kong. Their findings indicated that Chinese hotel managers in Hong Kong valued good working relationships with superiors and peers highly, as well as good monetary rewards. The study found that respondents did not highly value quality of life or quality of the external community. Under the heading of leadership style, the hotel managers' preference was mostly for paternalistic leadership and it was found that the majority of them worked under autocratic superiors.

In a more recent study King-Metters (2007) compared the personal values of hospitality service employees in China to the national culture dimensions that were first published by Hofstede in 1980. Her study suggests important differences between today's Chinese workers and those measured by Hofstede. For example the masculinity index moved from an 'above average' masculine score (Hofstede) to an above average, strongly feminine culture (King-Metters). The individualism scores swung from strongly collectivist (Hofstede) to strongly individualistic (King-Metters). The King-Metters' distance score was almost half of Hofstede's high power distance score and found to be very close to the US power distance score. Finally King-Metters found a strong short-term orientation in contrast to Hofstede's findings.

Lee-Ross (2005) undertook a study to compare the attitudes and work motivation between hotel workers in Australia and Mauritius using Hackman and

Oldham's Job Diagnostic Survey. He notes an increasingly participative style of management is currently popular in Western organisations but cautions that managers should avoid a parochial perspective arguing that this would be unsuitable for Mauritian workers because autonomy is a 'foreign' concept which they find difficult to work with.

Reproduction

Critical theorists alert us to the existence, importance and often overlooked understanding of culture. Critical theory was developed by the Frankfurt School and its key figures included Horkheimer, Adorno, Marcuse, and Habermas. Its development was largely a reaction to the unreflexive nature of scientific research in the United States. Three of the central aims of critical theory are the uncovering of the operation of taken-for-granted ideologies, the operation of power and an emancipatory interest. So what is an ideology? It is, according to Tribe (2007, p. 248):

Ideology: a system of beliefs that directs the policies and activities of its adherents.

> *a system of beliefs that directs the policies and activities of its adherents. Ideology, then, frames thought and guides action, and its presence may lead to the suppression and partial exclusion of other world views. But the operation of an ideology can remain hidden from view, for the deeply embedded nature and long tradition of a particular ideology can serve to camouflage its existence ... so that it becomes the taken for-granted way of thinking and doing. It becomes the accepted or common sense view of the world. The job of critical theory is to identify ideological influences at work.*

So ideology can be seen as a constellation of ideas that infuses and permeates a particular culture. Ideologies may be deeply internalised and so frequently performed by so many people that we cease to notice their existence. It could be said that an central, taken-for-granted aspect of ideology in Western culture is the dominance of the free market and the primacy of the interests of profitability for firms and satisfaction for consumers. These aspects of ideology are also predominant in the management of tourism.

Cultural reproduction: the way in which culture is maintained over time and transmitted from one generation to the next.

Cultural reproduction (Bourdieu, 1973) refers to the way in which culture (including values, attitudes, goals, and practices) is maintained over time and transmitted from one generation to the next. Indeed the terms 'socialisation' or 'acculturation' refer to the process by which new members are inducted into the value systems of a culture. Socialisation mechanisms include those of family, education, media, language and peer group influences, but interestingly adherence to social norms is generally obtained not by use of force but by human tendencies and preferences to fit in and to conform.

Language is also an important aspect of cultural transmission and here Foucault's (1971) notion of discourse offers an interesting explanation of how cultural conformity is encouraged. A discourse is described by Hall (1997, p. 44) as:

> *a group of statements which provide a language for talking about ... a particular topic at a particular historical moment.*

Foucault was interested in how statements were given meaning by rules and practices and that the formation and solidifying of these rules and practices regulated what could be said. Discourses regulate the bounds of what is sayable and it is possible to identify a range of discursive formations such as professionalism, managerialism, health and safety, efficiency, profitability and sustainability amongst others. Each of these favours certain values over others, encouraging certain moves and suppressing others and each of these discourses can be observed in operation in the field of tourism.

Path dependency

Path dependency: when certain decisions and events create paths or routes into the future and exert long-term effects on subsequent decisions and events.

Related to the idea that cultures have a tendency to reproduce themselves is the concept of path dependency (Liebowitz and Margolis, 1995). This illustrates another way by which organisations and entities can be constrained and subject to conservatism and inertia. Path dependency occurs when certain decisions and events create paths or routes into the future and exert long-term effects on subsequent decisions and events. Location and technological adoption choices can be important sources of path dependency. For example London's Heathrow Airport is located about 20 km west of central London. It was based on an existing aerodrome. Over the years it has attracted new terminals, new motorways and rail links. Each of these additional investments adds to the importance of the site, increases its path dependency and makes it almost impossible to consider resiting the airport. However were the airport to be built from scratch today it would be unlikely to be located on its present site. For the site is in an area of dense residential housing and this causes conflicts especially in terms of noise, other pollution and congestion. Another way to think about path dependency is the existence of significant sunk costs in tourism resorts and facilities. Papatheodorou (2006, p. 6) notes that:

> *Tourism is characterised by substantial fixed costs in transport, accommodation and in some cases technological infrastructure; airports, hotels and electronic reservation systems are good examples. These costs are largely sunk.*

Path dependency is also evident in destinations. Some destinations have accumulated a built environment dominated by large hotels catering for mass tourists. It would be difficult in such places to radically deviate their destination tourism strategy from mass tourism given the durability of the built environment and sunk costs in such developments. Similarly, as an example, Antigua, in the Caribbean, has made decisions and established a deeply entrenched path that means that its economy is highly tourism-dependent and that over 80 per cent of GNP is attributable to tourism. Climate change induced changes in travel patterns may mean that Antigua suffers a reduction in tourist arrivals. But path dependency suggests that the destination will find it difficult to make the significant change in strategy that would abandon its accumulated tourism assets.

Organisational culture

Organisational culture: organisational beliefs, values and attitudes.

Organisational culture refers to organisational beliefs, values and attitudes (Schein, 1985; Martin and Siehl, 1983). It describes the way things are done in a particular organisation or entity and forms the basis for the rules of acceptable and unacceptable behaviour. Organisational culture is the arbiter of organisational norms and it acts as a powerful force in encouraging or frustrating the emergence of new missions and strategies. This is particularly so where culture is deeply embedded. Schein (1987, p.17) defines culture, as it relates to organisations, in the following way:

> *a pattern of shared basic assumptions that was shared by a group as it solved its problems of external adaptation and internal integration, that has worked well enough to be considered valid and, therefore, to be taught to new members as the correct way to perceive, think and feel in relation to those problems.*

Drennan (1992, p.3) offers a similar definition explaining that:

> *culture is 'how things are done around here'. It is what is typical of the organisation, the habits, the prevailing attitudes, the pattern of accepted and expected behaviour.*

Scholz's (1987, p.80) definition of organisational culture underlines the two-way exchange in organisations with culture both affecting and affected by individual behaviour. Here it is understood as the:

> *implicit, invisible, intrinsic and informal consciousness of an organisation which guides the behaviour of the individuals and shapes itself out of their behaviour.*

Dwyer *et al.* (2000) examined the importance of organisational culture as an influence on strategy and performance in a hospitality organisation on Bintan Island, Indonesia. They analysed a number of characteristics associated with organisational culture and their findings are summarised in Box 3.1. They concluded that the presence of these characteristics is important for the socialisation of employees as well as for establishing strategic links with employee performance and the development of a coherent organisation.

Box 3.1 Main conclusions from Dwyer et al.'s (2000) study on organisational culture in an Indonesian resort hotel.

- Individual initiative: the authors noted that the staff at various levels in the hotel had a considerable degree of responsibility and independence.
- Risk tolerance: the study concluded that management's encouragement of employees taking initiatives and being innovative, was evident.
- Direction: the study found that managers had strong beliefs that the hotel should create objectives and performance expectations,
- Integration: the study found that that there was considerable inter-departmental communication at the managerial level.

- Management support: Dwyer *et al.* note that management support was visible and clearly communicated to employees and that this extended to on-the-job and off-the-job employee behaviour.
- Control: it was observed that the hotel had a relatively flat organisational structure, and management control was for the most part to be characterised by 'soft' rather than 'hard' control.
- Reward system: according to the researchers, managers had established a reward system that included career orientation and career possibilities and included an intention to eventually replace expatriate managers with Indonesian staff.
- Conflict tolerance: the authors found that a Works Council had been set up through which employees were able to express their grievances, criticisms, and suggestions.
- Communication patterns: the report found that formal channels of communication were complemented by communication which attempted to minimise hierarchy and authority. Additionally a Works Council had been established.

The Cultural Web

Cultural web: the different strands of an organisation's culture.

Figure 3.2 illustrates a cultural web (Johnson *et al.*, 2008) which is a useful device for highlighting the different strands of an organisation's culture. These include:

- ◊ Symbols
- ◊ Rituals and routines
- ◊ Stories
- ◊ Power structures and organisational structures
- ◊ Control systems.

These aspects of a cultural web add up to a paradigm, or an agreed way of going about things.

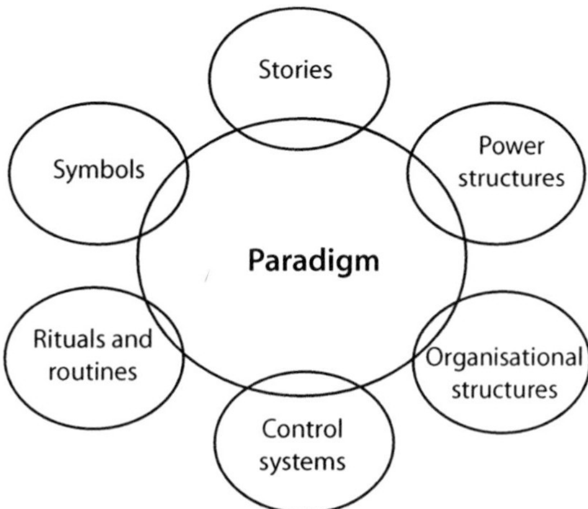

Figure 3.2: The Cultural Web

Symbols

A powerful symbol for an entity is its logo. British Airways (BA) has the Union Jack (the national flag of the United Kingdom) on its tail fin. But at one stage it felt that the flag symbolised some negative features of UK culture (such as lack of fun, formality, being old fashioned, class rigidity, etc.) It therefore replaced the tail fin with a series of designs inspired by different world cultures. The change resulted in some loss of recognition and identity for the airline and provoked a lot of opposition which included that of Prime Minister Margaret Thatcher. Eventually the flag was reinstated – but in a softer more fluid version.

Destinations associate themselves with images and brands which are important cultural symbols. For example 'Texas is for lovers', 'What happens in Vegas stays in Vegas', 'Incredible India'. Uniforms are also powerful symbols and cabin crew on the low-cost UK-based airline easyJet wear black jeans and orange T-shirts in contrast to the formal uniforms of airlines such as Qantas. Again this symbolises a less formal, more easy-going organisational culture. Calling Disneyworld staff 'cast members' is a symbolic gesture. Other symbols include titles, office size and location, secretarial support and IT resources all of which can indicate the value placed on particular employees.

Rituals and routines

The flight crew on US-based South West Airlines are encouraged to vary the established routines when making announcements on flights. They use humour and have used rapping to underline the difference between South West and other airlines. On the other hand, the rituals and routines at airport security stations are designed to underline the seriousness of security and portray a culture of safety and 100 per cent attention to detail. Rituals include periodic body searches, removal of shoes and belts, and special tests for explosives' residues, all of which create a culture designed to encourage passenger confidence and discourage potential terrorists.

Stories

'There are armed plain clothes Sky Marshalls on El Al flights'. 'I know someone who was interrogated for 2 hours when they arrived at Ben Gurion Airport in Tel Aviv'. 'El Al flights have missile interception systems'. These are some of the stories that circulate about the levels of security associated with travel to Israel. Stories are powerful ways in which cultures are transmitted and established. They articulate and reconfirm acceptable and unacceptable behaviour and establish organisational heroes and anti-heroes. Similarly, stories about drunkenness, drugs, nakedness, wild parties and carefree sex circulate about destinations such as Ayia Napa in Cyprus and Faliraki in Greece, emphasising these as destinations of youth culture.

Power structures and organisational structures

The most powerful groups within an organisation are likely to be associated with the key values of an organisation and be responsible for transmitting and managing organisational culture. However in some instances, in tourism destinations for example, power structures are often ineffective. This is because a destination comprises of a whole range of enterprises – hotels, attractions, government, transport providers, restaurants and a destination management organisation does not have direct power over any of these. This makes the whole issue of developing and nurturing a destination culture (and a supporting destination brand) a challenging one.

Organisational structures tend to fall into two major types. Hierarchical, top-down structures indicate a culture of regimentation, rule-following and obedience to orders. More devolved structures are indicative of a culture of a listening, possibly rule-questioning organisation and one where collegiality, collaboration and teamwork are encouraged.

Control systems

Control systems include those for management, measurement and reward within an organisation. In tourism, management systems range from the necessarily rigid and formal in the flight operations of airlines to the flexible and hedonistic orientation of running clubs. Many business organisations are increasingly subject to detailed measurement and performance monitoring with targets reflecting a culture of command and control and erosion of professionalism. Reward systems both reflect and create culture. For example, reward based on length of service alone may discourage initiative or extra effort. Employee of the month schemes can be used to reward and signal behaviour which supports key elements of an organisation's culture and these are sometimes linked to customer nominations or ratings to encourage good service.

Cultural typologies

Miles and Snow (1978) distinguished between defender and prospector types of cultures in organisations. Their characteristics are summarised in Table 3.2.

Table 3.2: Defender and prospector type cultures

Defenders	Prospectors
Conservative	Outward-looking
Seek security	Responsive to environment
Cautious	Daring
Avoid change	Opportunistic
Inflexible	Flexible
Set in their ways	Adaptive
Reactive	Proactive

Defender type cultures may represent a barrier to effective corporate strategy, since by their very nature they guard the status quo and thus seek strategies not on the basis of their suitability for the future of the organisation, but based on how well they fit the current paradigm. Thus they are likely to seek cautious and conservative strategies. On the other hand, the very nature of a prospector type culture is its open-mindedness. Organisational culture under this type is adaptive and flexible. A difficulty for defender type cultures is that they may not be aware of the fact that there is any problem, because the problem is not visible through their particular cultural spectacles.

The cultural environment

The broad political system within which entities operate should also be considered as an important aspect of the cultural environment. Here the cultural effects on tourism entities of a number of competing ideologies will be briefly discussed. These are:

- ◊ Communism
- ◊ Democratic Socialism
- ◊ Neoliberalism and
- ◊ Third Way politics.

Communism

A Communist system outlaws private enterprise in favour of state control and ownership of the means of production. Sofield and Li (1998) analysed tourism development and cultural policies in China with specific reference the communist era and post-Mao modernisation. In their article they refer to the intricate interrelationships between socialism, modernization, and traditional culture. They note that the communist government of Mao Zedong:

> *Was confronted with conflicting tensions generated by their desire to introduce a more egalitarian society through socialism, their desire to modernize rapidly, and their need to rebuild China's sense of national identity. Paradoxically, the rigidity of socialist ideology was their greatest obstacle to modernization, while traditional culture was the single greatest obstacle to socialism. (p. 367)*

The authors explain how Mao Zedong's regime suppressed both traditional culture and freedom to travel and note the paradox of socialist ideology and modernity. They point out that while socialist ideology wished to embrace modernity it was too rigid and inflexible to encompass many of the values that would encourage modernisation. So here was culture as a strong directional force exercising a powerful grip on tourism entities. The authors note that it was Deng Xiaoping's 'open door' policies of 1978 that signalled an important cultural turn. The market mechanism began to be utilised, individual enterprise was encouraged and tourism was identified as a potential contributor to modernisation.

Democratic Socialism

In principle, Democratic Socialism aims for public ownership of industry, workers' control of the production process and redistributive tax policies, all through democratic means. The state, its workforce and social justice are the hallmarks of Democratic Socialism whilst markets and private profit are relegated from centre stage. On the other hand, Social Democracy is more supportive of a mixed economy where social justice is achieved through the combined activities of government and the free market. The effect of this on culture in tourism entities therefore depends where in the 'mixed economy' the entity is located. In some areas, enterprise values are encouraged whilst in others access and equality values are more prevalent.

Neoliberalism

Neoliberalism refers to a package of beliefs and policies which aim to reduce the role of the state in the economy and increase that of the private sector. Promotion of the free market is central to its policies which also include deregulation, trade liberalisation, reduction of government spending, competition and the promotion of incentives and free enterprise. Its impact on culture in tourism entities is to encourage profit, risk, short-termism and individualism and discourage consideration of wider issues of public welfare.

Third Way politics

Third Way politics was conceptualised by Giddens (1998) as an alternative to the two extremes that dominated the post-war political landscape. Those alternatives were Neoliberalism which depended on the unregulated outcomes of the free market and Democratic Socialism with its emphasis on active demand management and belief in the importance of the state in the economy. According to Giddens, the Third Way supports the growth, entrepreneurship, enterprise and wealth creation that arises from markets but wishes to marry these with greater social justice that needs to be facilitated by the state. Burns (2004) has addressed what Third Way politics means for tourism planning arguing that:

> *The emerging political climate in which people negotiate globalization, personal and civic transformations and the relationship with nature – namely the 'Third Way' approach – has a place in destination development. (p. 40)*

The culture nurtured by the Third Way tempers individualism, incentive, enterprise and self-help with a communal responsibility for social justice and the particular encouragement of social mobility.

Review of key terms

- Culture: a set of shared values, attitudes, goals, and practices that characterise a group of people.
- Hofstede: studied the relationship between national cultures and organizational cultures.
- Power distance: willingness to accept an unequal distribution of power by those who have less power in organisations.

- Individualism: the pursuance of individual goals as opposed to adherence to group goals and norms.
- Low vs. high uncertainty avoidance measures a society's tolerance for uncertainty and ambiguity.
- Short-term orientation: the importance a society attaches to the past and present rather than the future.
- Ideology: a system of beliefs that directs the policies and activities of its adherents.
- Cultural reproduction: the way in which culture is maintained over time and transmitted from one generation to the next.
- Path dependency: when certain decisions and events create paths or routes into the future and exert long-term effects on subsequent decisions and events.
- Organisational culture: organisational beliefs, values and attitudes.
- Cultural web: the different strands of an organisation's culture.

Multiple choice questions

1 Which of the following is not one of Hofstede's dimensions of culture?
   A Low vs. high uncertainty avoidance (UAI)
   B Masculinity vs. femininity (MAS)
   C Low vs. high incentive importance (INI)
   D Low vs. high power distance (PDI)

2 Which of the following is not part of the meaning of culture?
   A Values
   B Attitudes
   C Genetics
   D Goals

3 Which of the following is a high power distance culture?
   A Malaysia
   B Austria
   C Australia
   D Denmark

4 Which of the following is not an aim of critical theory?
   A Uncovering of the operation of ideologies
   B Uncovering the operation of power
   C Uncovering the meaning of culture
   D Promoting emancipatory interest.

5 Which of the following statements is true?
   A Symbols are part of an entity's cultural web.
   B Defender type cultures are open-minded
   C Path dependency means high adaptability
   D Foucault was a critical theorist

Discussion questions

1 Analyse the cultural issues that relate to the Walt Disney Company in relation to its strategy.

2 Construct a cultural web for a tourism entity of your choice giving examples of the components.

3 Explain the uses of Hofstede's dimensions of culture for understanding the culture of a tourism entity.

4 What causes reproduction and path dependency? Explain why these are problems for tourism entities that you are familiar with.

5 Explain the interrelationship between socialism, modernisation, and traditional culture in China and its relevance for the study of the culture of tourism entities.

References

Bourdieu, P. (1973) Cultural reproduction and social reproduction. *Knowledge, Education, and Cultural Change: Papers in the Sociology of Education*, 71–112.

Burns, P.M. (2004) Tourism planning: a third way? *Annals of Tourism Research*, **31**, 24–43.

Drennan, D. (1992) *Transforming Corporate Culture*. New York: McGraw-Hill.

Dwyer, L., Teal, G., Kemp, S. and Wah, C.Y. (2000) Organisational culture and human resource management in an Indonesian resort hotel. *Tourism, Culture and Communication*, **2**, 1–11.

Foucault, M. (1971) *L'ordre du Discours*. Paris: Gallimard.

Giddens, A. (1998) *The Third Way: the Renewal of Social Democracy*. Cambridge: Polity Press.

Hall, S. (1997) *Representation: Cultural Representations and Signifying Practices*. London: Sage.

Hofstede, Geert. (1980). *Culture's consequences: International differences in work-related values*. Newbury Park, CA: Sage.

Hofstede, G. (2001) *Culture's Consequences: Comparing Values, Behaviors, Institutions, and Organizations Across Nations*. London: Sage.

Hofstede, G. and Hofstede, G. J. (1991) *Cultures and Organizations: Software of the Mind*. London: McGraw-Hill.

Johnson, G., Scholes, K. and Whittington, R. (2008) *Exploring Corporate Strategy*. Harlow: Prentice Hall.

King-Metters, K. (2007) A shift in loyalties: How do the personal values of hospitality service employees in the People's Republic of China compare on Hofstede's national culture dimensions over time?, PhD dissertation, Capella University.

Lee-Ross, D. (2005) Perceived job characteristics and internal work motivation. *Journal of Management Development*, **24**, 253–266.

Liebowitz, S.J. and Margolis, S.E. (1995) Path dependence, lock-in, and history. *Journal of Law, Economics, and Organization*, **11**, 205–226.

Martin, J. and Siehl, C. (1983) Organizational culture and counterculture: An uneasy symbiosis. *Organizational Dynamics*, **12**, 52–64.

Miles, R. and Snow, C. (1978) *Organizational Strategy, Structure, and Process*, New York: McGraw-Hill

Mok, C., Pine, R. and Pizam, A. (1998) Work values of Chinese hotel managers. *Journal of Hospitality and Tourism Research*, **21**, 1–16.

Papatheodorou, A. (2006) Corporate rivalry, market power and competition issues in tourism: an introduction. In A. Papatheodorou (ed.), *Corporate Rivalry and Market Power: Competition Issues in the Tourism Industry*, London: I.B. Tauris, pp. 1–18.

Richards, G. (1996). *Cultural Tourism in Europe*. Wallingford: CAB International.

Schein, E.H. (1985) *Defining Organizational Culture*. San Francisco: Jossey Bass.

Schein, E.H. (1987) Organizational culture and leadership. In J.Shafritz and J. Ott (eds), *Classes of Organizational Theory*, 2nd edn, Chicago: Dorsey Press, pp. 381–393.

Schneider, S.C. and De Meyer, A. (1991) Interpreting and responding to strategic issues: the impact of national culture. *Strategic Management Journal*, **12**, 307–320.

Scholz, C. (1987) Corporate culture and strategy: the problem of strategic fit. *Long Range Planning*, **20**, 78–87.

Sofield, T.H.B. and Li, F.M.S. (1998) Tourism development and cultural policies in China. *Annals of Tourism Research*, **25**, 362–392.

Tribe, J. (2007) Tourism: a critical business. *Journal of Travel Research*, 245–255.

Part II
Strategic Analysis

The next stage of tourism strategy is strategic analysis. Strategic analysis utilises techniques for situational analysis. This involves reporting on the current and future opportunities and threats and strengths and weaknesses facing the organisation.

Opportunities and threats summarise the external environmental factors that a tourism organisation faces. The key elements of the external environment may be summarised as C-PEST factors which refer to the:

- Competitive
- Political
- Economic
- Socio-cultural, and,
- Technological environments.

Of these, PEST factors are analysed in Chapter 4, whilst the competitive environment is considered in Chapter 5. Strengths and weaknesses analysis summarises the state of the internal resources of an organisation. Resource analysis is undertaken in Chapter 6. All these factors are brought together in a comprehensive SWOT analysis at the end of Chapter 6, thus concluding strategic analysis and Part II.

4 The External Environment: PEST

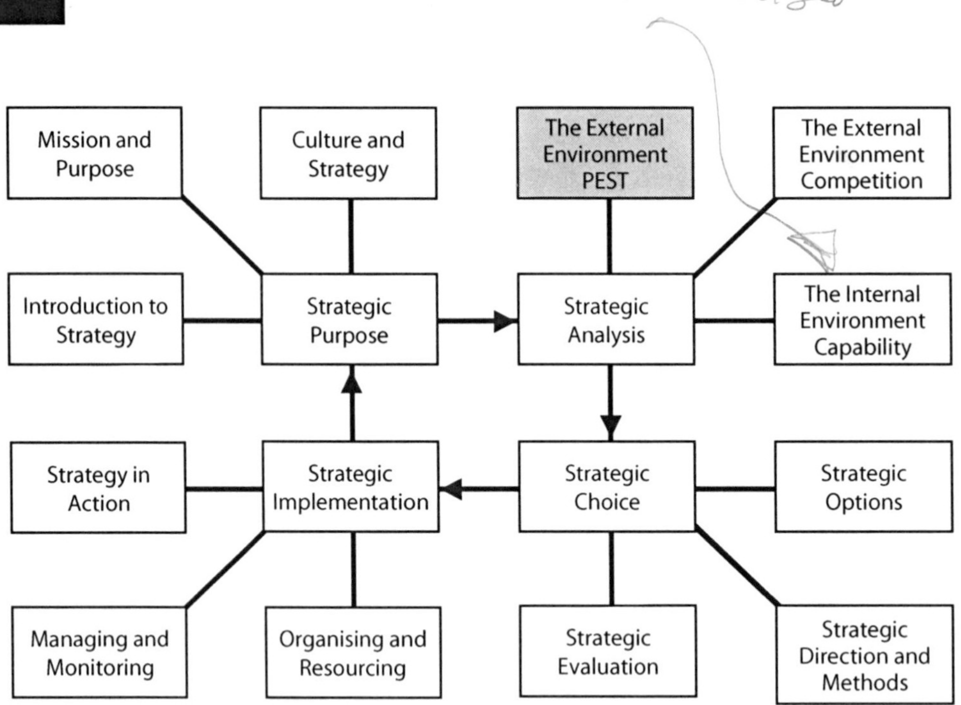

Figure 4.1

Learning outcomes

After studying this chapter and related materials you should be able to understand:

- The political environment
- The economic environment
- The socio-cultural environment
- The technological environment

and critically evaluate, explain and apply the above concepts.

Introduction

Political analysis: the effects of government policy and laws.

Tourism entities do not operate in a vacuum. They operate within an external environment which can have a significant impact on their operations and strategy. This chapter identifies and analyses four domains in the external environment. These are the political, economic, socio-cultural and technological environments. Political analysis identifies the effects of government policy and laws. Economic analysis seeks to understand what economic factors will affect tourism entities and how these economic factors are changing. Socio-cultural analysis plots changes in population size and structure as well as changes in consumer tastes, preferences and broader cultural shifts. Technological analysis charts changes in science and technology to understand how these will impact on tourism entities.

Case Study 4 analyses the economic crisis of 2008 and plots its effects on a range of tourism organisations.

Case Study 4: Tourism and the 2008 Economic Crisis

The year 2008 can be added to the list of significant economic crises which include the Great Depression (1929–35) and the Asian Economic Crisis of 1997–98. The period prior to 2008 was a time of relative economic stability. For example the UK and US economies were enjoying 2–4 per cent per year growth, China's economy often grew at 14 per cent per year and the continued growth of tourism was evidenced by the upward path of UNWTO data. But by 2007, an unsustainable set of economic conditions were developing. Property price inflation was particularly evident, fuelled by optimistic expectations and cheap and easy availability of loans. But the property boom faltered in the USA and was soon followed by banking crises in Freddie Mac and Fanny Mae, the Northern Rock and Lehman Bros. In the tourism sector XL Holidays collapsed in UK. A domino effect occurred and the root cause of the subsequent economic crisis is easy to trace. The causes can be attributed to:

- Market madness and unrealistic optimism
- Overpriced assets – particularly property prices
- Bad debt
- Deregulation of the banks
- A change in banking culture from the conservative to the risky
- Short-term pay incentives overshadowing long-term sustainability in the banking sector.
- High oil prices
- Globalization and international connectivity enabling the crisis to spread.

The economic crisis caused a run on the banks, followed by their nationalisation /partial nationalisation in the UK and elsewhere. Two quarters of falling output in 2008 confirmed the arrival of a recession in both the UK and the USA, together with mass unemployment and a feel-bad factor. On the other hand, the period witnessed falling oil prices, exchange rate adjustments and low interest rates.

For tourism, the UNWTO predicted stagnation (0 per cent growth) or even a slight decline (–1 to –2 per cent) throughout 2009. Amongst those most affected were the Americas and Europe as most of their source markets were affected by recession. In Asia and the Pacific, Africa and the Middle East, the industry was expected to grow at a slower rate than in previous years.

The effects of the recession in the tourism sector can be traced with the help of some of the stories that appeared on the Travelmole website (www.travelmole.com). For example, Emirates Airline slowed expansion in 2009 – and the year turned out to be one of consolidation with the increase in the number of flights across its network slowing to 14 per cent, against annual growth of 20 per cent in the previous five years. Virgin Atlantic responded to a drop in demand for air travel by cutting 600 jobs. Ryanair posted a third quarter loss in 2008 of €102 million, compared to a profit of €35 million in the same period a year earlier. February 2009 passenger statistics for British Airways showed a 20.2 per cent decrease in premium traffic and a 5.5 per cent fall in non-premium traffic. Cathay Pacific posted a loss of HK$8.56bn for 2008 and in general IATA figures painted a bleak picture for airline industry which it described as 'drowning in red ink'.

A similar picture was evident in other sectors. The UK Tour Operator Superbreak recorded sales for its hotel breaks division for 2008 at 10 per cent below the 2007 figures. For destinations, Amsterdam illustrated a gloomy picture where 12 per cent fewer British and American visitors arrived via Schiphol airport in November 2008. The knock-on effect on attractions was that the number of people visiting tourist attractions in Amsterdam dropped by 13.3 per cent. In hospitality, occupancy of European hotels fell by an average 10

An economic downturn

per cent in the first quarter of 2009. Of UK hotel executives polled for a hospitality report, 95 per cent predicted hotel chain bankruptcies in 2009 citing the inability to raise capital and the struggling European economy as two main reasons. A significant reduction in business travel was also revealed by the poll. The photo shows the effects of an economic downturn on the demand for air travel.

The political environment

The political environment is concerned primarily with government and its effects. Here it is useful to distinguish between autocratic and democratic systems of government. Autocratic systems exist where government is carried out by one party. Opposition parties are generally not allowed and government is not subject to regular, popular elections. Democratic systems are characterised by political choice where rival political parties seek government through regular elections through which the wider population is able to express its preference by a system of voting. Political systems are generally dynamic, particularly in democracies where elections must be held at regular intervals – typically every four to five years. Autocratic systems tend to witness less change but can be subject to in-fighting between factional groups.

Legislature: the body where laws, regulations and policy are made.

Executive: the arm of government which carries out laws and policies.

Government may also be roughly split between the legislature and the executive. The legislature is the body where laws, regulations and policy are made (the process of enacting legislation). In the UK and Australia this is Parliament, in the USA it is Congress, and in China it is the National People's Congress. The executive is the arm of government which carries out government laws and policies. The executive comprises of a number of government departments (e.g. defence, economic affairs, home security). These are staffed by public sector workers. There is generally some representation for tourism in both the executive and the legislature. In the legislature there may be a minister or government spokesperson for tourism and in the executive, tourism may have its own ministry or government department or it might be part of a larger one.

Since tourism entities are affected by current and new government legislation, it is important to understand the location of political power, how political power may change in the future and the likely effects of this on policy (Burns and Novelli, 2009). It is also important to identify the locus of the political environment where a tourism organisation is working. For example a tour operator situated in Italy will face a political environment at local government level, at national government level and at European Union level. Additionally it will have to operate in the different political environments of the destination countries where it operates its tours.

In democratic countries, it is instructive to know when the next election will take place, the likelihood and implications of a change of government and the alternative manifestos of competing parties. Parties generally publish comprehensive manifestos so that voters can see their plans and how they would change things if elected to government. Pressure-group activity can also be important in influencing policy in democracies, and the activities of such groups as Greenpeace and Tourism Concern attempt to affect government policy as it relates to tourism. In autocratic countries, a careful monitoring of the circle of advisors of the leader may be helpful to ascertain possible successors and subsequent policy shifts.

The political environment also includes activity which falls outside official government channels. For example terrorist activity has become more prominent in the last 25 years and has a particular impact on tourism. Here groupings seek to achieve political ends outside and often in direct confrontation with official government policy. Tourism is one of its main targets and is also one of its main casualties in terms of increased security measures at borders.

The consequences of a change in government

Changes in government can bring about profound change to the political environment. For example in the USA the Republican administrations of President Reagan and each of the Bush presidencies signalled a turn to the political right and a radical package of new policies with less state intervention, lower tax rates, less government spending and an emphasis on deregulation, private enterprise and profitability. On the other hand, the democrat administrations of presidents Clinton and Obama had and currently have more of a focus on social issues.

In China a long period of state communism, was presided over by Mao Zedong where free markets, private enterprise and individual tourism were not permitted. However successive administrations of Deng Xiaoping (Xiao, 2006), Jiang Zemin and Hu Jintao have seen a gradual loosening of strict communist ideology and the flourishing of free enterprise, free markets and tourism.

Table 4.1 distinguishes between policy objectives of typical democratic political parties of the left and of the right. The actual manifestos, speeches and policy documents of political parties can give a clearer guide to the consequences for a particular tourism organisation of the electoral success of a particular party.

Table 4.1: Key differences between political parties

Left wing (e.g. Labour / Democrat parties)	Right wing (e.g. Conservative/Republican parties)
Need to control the free market	Belief in supremacy of the free market
Pro trade unions	Anti trade unions
Some state ownership of industry	Private ownership of industry
Progressive taxation	Proportional taxation
Regulation of industry	Minimal state interference
Higher government spending and taxes	Low taxes and government spending
Reduce inequality of incomes	Inequality of income as incentive
Provision of jobs a priority	Control of state spending a priority
Comprehensive welfare state	Minimal welfare state
Poverty reduction and social mobility goals	Belief in self-help

Opportunities and threats in the changing political environment

Analysis of the political environment in which a tourism entity is operating can lead to the identification of key opportunities and threats. Typical areas of change that can have an impact on tourism include:

- ◊ Competition policy
- ◊ Health and safety
- ◊ Transport and infrastructure
- ◊ Global carbon agreements and targets
- ◊ Taxation and spending plans
- ◊ Disability and access legislation
- ◊ Foreign policy
- ◊ Visa policy and home security
- ◊ Regulation and deregulation
- ◊ Regeneration plans
- ◊ Employment and training policy
- ◊ Travel advisories
- ◊ Minimum wages

Box 4.1 illustrates the effects of changes in the political environment on tourism entities.

Box 4.1 Effects of changes in the political environment on tourism entities

The Berlin Wall which had partitioned East and West Berlin fell in 1989 and was an important step in the reunification of German which was concluded on 3rd October 1990. Berlin is now a popular short break destination in Europe (Timothy, 2006).

There have been increasing terrorist attacks directly and indirectly impacting on tourism (Smith, 2004). These include attacks on airports and the hijackings of planes from the 1970s, the Lockerbie bombing (1983), the 9/11 attacks in the United States (2001), the 7/7 bombings in London (2005), the Bali bombings (2002 and 2005) (Robinson & Meaton, 2005), and the Sharm el Sheik bombing (2005). Each of these resulted in reductions in visitor numbers and tightened security measures.

In the United States the 1980s saw the policy of deregulation of airlines, a policy which has subsequently gained favour worldwide. This made it easier for new airlines to set up and exposed the market to intense competition.

The Iraq war, the Gulf war and the war in former Yugoslavia all had significant impacts in tourist movements. The former in particular led to a reduction in North American tourists to Europe.

Outbound tourism in China was heavily restricted to approved trips in the Mao Zedong era. A gradual liberalising of travel started in 1983 when some trips to Hong

Kong and Macau were permitted. Since then more countries have been given approved destination status (ADS) and by 2005, 90 countries, including Australia, New Zealand and 25 European destinations had ADS. This travel liberalisation saw the scale of outbound travel increase from under one million in 1990 to 41 million in 2007.

The Schengen Agreement treaty, signed in 1985 laid the ground for the abolition of border controls for most countries of the European Union (with the notable exception of the UK) removing an important obstacle to travel.

The Kyoto Protocol (1997), the 'Washington Declaration' (2007) and the Copenhagen Meeting (2009) all represent stages in the United Nations Framework Convention on Climate Change (UNFCCC). The UNFCCC has the goal of achieving stabilization of greenhouse gas concentrations to limit climate change. CO2 targets and limits have a significant impact on tourism – especially destinations and air transport.

The Cyprus tourism industry has had to be sensitive to the political problems between Turkish and Greek Cypriots. Altinay et al. (2005) found that any future planning and development is likely to be a complex undertaking, as the two societies tend to have different sets of objectives and expectations.

The economic environment

The economic environment (Tribe, 2005) affects different types of tourism entities in different ways. For example the success of an international tourism destination such as Mallorca, Spain, will be affected by economic fluctuations in those countries which supply the majority of its visitors (tourism generating countries), as well as its economic attractiveness compared to competitive resorts. In line with this national tourism organisations will seek to market destinations in countries whose economies are expanding. Of course, national tourism organisations themselves are often funded by the government and are therefore directly affected by government spending decisions.

Economic analysis: understanding what economic factors will affect tourism entities and how these economic factors are changing.

Tour operators such as Kuoni (Switzerland) and TUI (Germany/UK), face a number of economic environments. First, domestic economic environments affect the expenditure patterns of their clients. Second, the variety of different international economic environments in which their tourism product is located affects the supply of the tourism package. Providers of tourism services will find the international economic environment affects the demand for their services and the costs of supplying those services. Examples of services include hotels such as Best Western and Inter-Continental, transport operators such as Eurotunnel (UK/France) and Korean Air and attraction owners such as Disneyland, Paris.

The key factors in the economic environment which affect tourism organisations are set out in Figure 4.2 in terms of demand and costs. The main terms used in the figure are as follows:

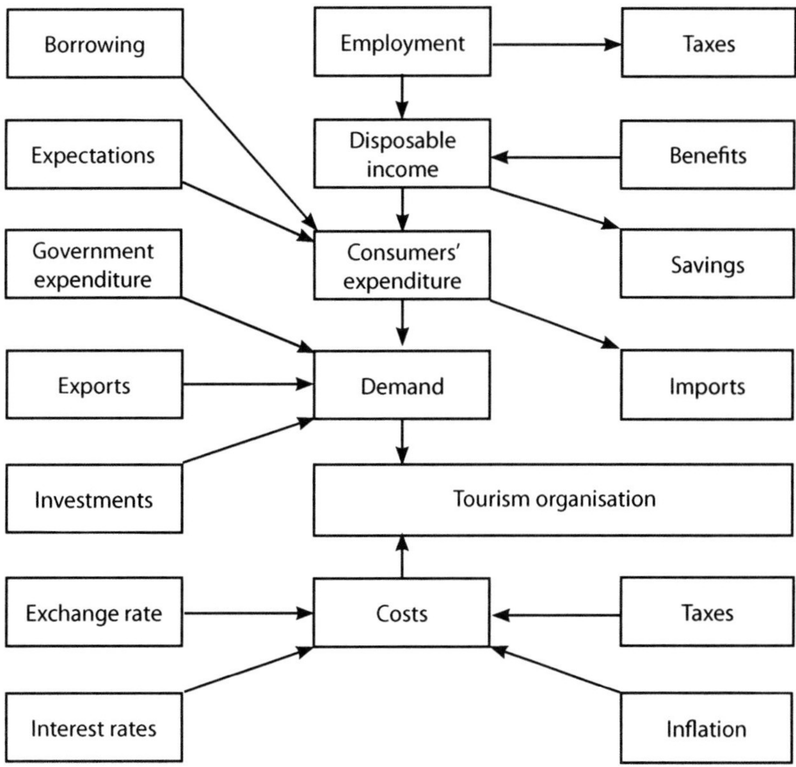

Figure 4.2: The economic environment

- **Consumers' expenditure**: the amount of money consumers actually spend. It is mainly determined by income level, but is affected by savings, taxation and government benefit payments, consumer credit and expectations about the future. We are interested in 'real consumer expenditure', or 'expenditure at constant prices' which is expenditure that has been adjusted to remove any changes which are just due to inflation.
- **Investment expenditure**: expenditure on capital goods such as hotel construction, aircraft and infrastructure such as port facilities.
- **Government expenditure**: including pensions and state benefits.
- **Taxation**: including taxes on income, spending, profits and departure taxes
- **Exchange rates**: the value of a country's currency in terms of others.
- **Interest rates**: the cost of borrowing.
- **Inflation/(deflation)**: the rise/(fall) in the general level of prices.
- **Employment**: the total number of people in work.
- **Expectations**: the way people feel about future economic prospects (optimistic or pessimistic).

Economic growth: a measure of how much better (or worse) off a country is in economic terms over a period of time.

The performance of an economy over time is an important aspect of the economic environment. Here economic growth is a measure of how much better (or worse) off a country is in financial terms over a period of time. It is defined more precisely as the increase in real output per capita of a country and often measured by changes in Gross Domestic Product (GDP). Economic growth is rarely even and most economies are subject to business cycles where an upswing in the economy (or period of economic growth) is followed by a downswing (or period of economic recession). A recession is defined as two consecutive quarters of negative growth. An upswing is marked by rising consumer spending, increasing profits, optimistic expectations, rising employment, increased borrowing, rising inflation and economic growth. During a downswing all of these trends go into reverse. The 2008 recession was particularly marked by a sudden lack of availability of credit (the credit crunch), a deceleration in consumer expenditure and rising unemployment.

Recession: two consecutive quarters of negative growth.

Tourism destinations, NTOs and the economic environment

Figure 4.3 shows how a tourism destination such as Mallorca, Spain is affected by the international economic environment. In general terms it can be seen that the number of visitors to a destination will be affected by changes in economic growth and consumers' expenditure in the tourist-generating economies of its visitors as well as the health of the domestic economy which fuels the number of domestic visitors.

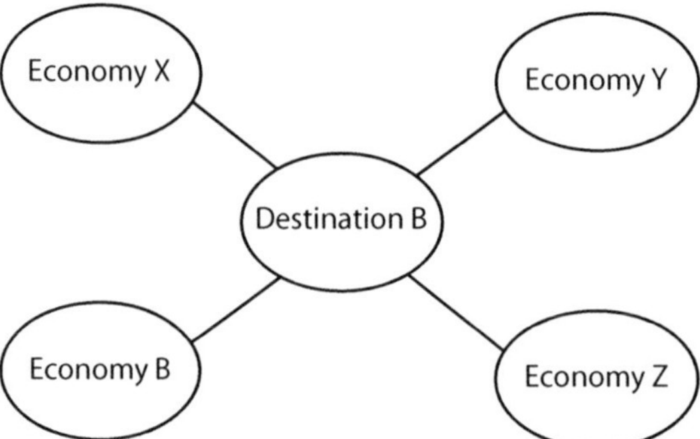

Figure 4.3: The economic environment of destinations

For Mallorca, Spain, the four major sources of tourists are Germany, the UK, Spain itself and France, but August 2009 saw drops in tourists from Germany and the UK of 20 per cent and 16 per cent respectively. These declines reflected the weak levels of demand in both the German and UK economies in 2009. Economic recessions also underline the importance to a tourist destination of its home market. The economy of Spain achieved average growth of around 3 per cent per annum for the years 1980–2007 and is now ranked as a high-income country by the World Bank. Its own population therefore provides a growing source of tourism income. The data for 2009 shows the importance of domestic tourism and for Mallorca domestic tourism arrivals grew by 12 per cent in 2009.

Tourists from abroad are also interested in the exchange rate, for this will affect their spending power in their destination country. Since Spain, Germany and France are all in the Eurozone and use the euro as currency there are no exchange rate effects for tourists from these countries when visiting Mallorca,

Spain. The UK however is outside the Eurozone and so the rate of exchange between the pound and the euro will affect the willingness of UK tourists to visit Spain. The UK economic environment posed a double threat to Spanish tourism in 2009 – not only was the UK suffering from a recession but the exchange rate of the pound against the euro was at a low point, making Spain seem more expensive to UK tourists. Munoz (2007) presents a dynamic model to examine German demand for tourism in Spain. The results suggest that tourism demand in the previous period has an important effect on current tourism demand. They also suggest that the demand for tourism in Spain is a luxury for the Germans and highly dependent on the evolution of relative prices and cost of travel between Germany and the destination.

So the fortunes of tourist destinations are closely tied with those of its tourism-generating countries and the exchange rate can play an important role too. The price level and inflation rate are also significant, since a combination of high inflation and a rising exchange rate can make a destination less attractive than its overseas competitors where such factors might be more favourable. It is therefore important for destinations, and the national and regional tourism organisations which market destinations, to keep a careful watch on economic growth, consumers' expenditure and exchange rates in tourism generating countries as well as the rate of domestic inflation.

A scanning of the international economic environment can alert destinations not only to opportunities and threats in existing markets, but also to opportunities emerging in new markets. In scanning the international environment for such opportunities, Mallorca, Spain might draw a circle to include counties within say three hours' flying time or $500 round trip travel cost and carefully scrutinise the economic prospects of the countries this highlights to identify possible new markets. Indeed a further examination of arrival figures for Mallorca in August 2009 reveal an increase in visitor numbers from Switzerland, Belgium, Austria, Denmark and Portugal and perhaps therefore reveals future opportunities for marketing in these countries.

Finally in this section it should be noted that national tourism organisations are generally funded by governments. Because of this an important consideration in their operating environment is government spending plans. During recessions, spending on national tourism organisations is likely to be cut back as it is easier to cut government expenditure here than in highly visible areas such as health, education, pensions and unemployment benefits.

Tourism firms and the economic environment

Tour operators are complex organisations which are exposed to a variety of economic environments. They face an additional problem of time lags in matching booked capacity and holiday sales. We may classify their activities into client sales and purchase of tour components. On the demand side a tour operator is selling to clients. Figure 4.2 illustrates that the key variable influencing the level of sales is the level of overall consumer expenditure. This in turn will be affected by earnings, taxes, and expectations about the future (if clients fear unemployment, their spending decisions will be more cautious). Interest rates will affect different groups of clients in different ways. Younger clients are more likely to have house and student loan debt, whilst older clients are more likely to have savings. For this reason a rise in interest rates will tend to stimulate expenditure of older groups and curb the expenditure of younger groups. Changes in the exchange rate will also alter patterns of consumer expenditure as different destinations become attractive due to weak currencies.

On the supply side, a tour operator will be affected by interest rate changes where capital is borrowed, and changes in company taxation will also affect it. Tour operators will find the costs they incur for transportation and accommodation affected by general inflationary pressures (wage levels and raw materials costs), as well as changes in interest rates and taxes. Where supplies are purchased from overseas, the exchange rate will also be significant. Since tour operators generally operate in a number of countries, economic data must be sought from these countries.

Figure 4.2 can also be used to analyse the economic environment for other tourism service providers so that the leisure or tourism organisation might be a hospitality provider, attraction, or transport operator. From Case Study 4 it can be seen that the 2008 economic crisis has had a negative effects on hotel occupancy and that visitor numbers at key attractions fell. Airlines such as Emirates, Ryanair, Virgin and British Airways reported negative effects on expansions plans, profitability, employment and load factors – particularly in business class.

BRIC countries: Brazil, Russia, India and China.

It is interesting to note that the economic environment differs from one part of the world to the next. The BRIC acronym is used to identify Brazil, Russia, India and China as economies in the world that are likely to experience higher than average levels of economic growth. China in particular has witnessed rapid economic growth, and with a population of 1.1 billion it is set to become a leading global economy in the 21st century. Also notable is the growth of the economies of South Korea, Malaysia, Singapore and Thailand which have shown strong growth in recent years whereas mature economies such as the USA, and those in the EU grew at a much more modest pace. It should be noted that economic growth figures by themselves, may give a distorted view of the marketing prospects for a particular country. It is important to see what level of economic development a country is growing from and here GNP per capita data is useful. Such data puts China's growth in a more sober perspective. Since average income starts at a low point, even high levels of growth mean that the average consumer will not have an income on a par with those in the most developed countries for some years.

Opportunities and threats in the economic environment

Table 4.2 summarises the main opportunities and threats that stem from the economic environment.

Table 4.2: Opportunities and threats in the economic environment

Opportunities	Threats
Low interest rates	High interest rates
Low unemployment	High unemployment
High consumer expenditure	Low consumer expenditure
Low oil and other commodity prices	High oil and other commodity prices
Low taxes	High taxes
Favorable exchange rate	Unfavourable exchange rate
Stable prices	Inflation
Optimistic expectations	Pessimistic expectations

The socio-cultural environment

Factors in the socio-cultural environment of tourism entities include the size and structure of the population, inter-cultural differences, other factors and tourist motivations

Demographics

Socio-cultural analysis: understanding changes in population size and structure as well as changes in consumer tastes, preferences and broader cultural shifts.

Demographics is the study of population and includes analysis of:

◊ Population size
◊ Age distribution
◊ Sex distribution
◊ Geographical distribution
◊ Income distribution
◊ Health data

Population is significant to tourism entities for two reasons. First, the population is a key factor influencing the demand for tourism services. Second, the labour force which supplies tourism organisations is derived from the population. So for example a country with a large population represents a potential market for tourism services and one where economies of scale may be achieved. The age distribution of the population is also significant. A predominantly older population will perhaps seek less physically demanding holidays, and perhaps more culturally focused ones. This might mean a reduction in the demand for skiing holidays for example. Table 4.3 illustrates the marketing profiles for different age groups.

Similarly, an ageing population will present different problems for training for the labour force than a young population.

Table 4.4 illustrates population data for selected countries. Note that China's population exceeds one billion but that its growth rate is modest. Because India has a higher population growth rate, its population is forecast to exceed that of China by 2050. Ethiopia has a particularly high population growth, which if maintained would triple its population between 2009 and 2050. For Japan, a declining rate of growth of population means that its total population is expected to decline to 100 million by 2050.

Table 4.3: Tourism marketing profiles for different age groups

Life stage	Characteristics	Tourism income	Tourism time
Child	Tourism decisions generally taken by parent	Low	High
Bachelor	High propensity for travel. Independence asserted, budget travel popular, social aspects sought.	Medium	Medium
Partnered	High tourism propensities underpinned by high income and free time.	High	Medium
Full nest	Children become key preoccupation. Tourism must meet children's requirements. Costs per person important	Medium	Low
Empty nest	Children have left home. Opportunities for tourism increase. Exotic destinations and meaning of life sought	High	Medium
Old age	May lack partner, may suffer from infirmity. Safer travel pursuits sought, package holidays popular	Low	High

Table 4.4: Population data

	Population 2009	Population 2050 (projected)	Growth rate %
China	1,341,687,010	1,424,161,948	0.66
India	1,172,368,058	1,807,878,574	1.55
USA	308,259,674	313,020,847	0.98
Indonesia	241,224,577	313,020,847	1.14
Brazil	199,569,074	260,692,493	1.20
Pakistan	176,242,949	295,224,598	1.05
Japan	127,156,225	101,658,573	-0.19
Ethiopia	85,237,338	278,283,137	3.21
World	6,790,062,216	9,538,988,263	1.17

Source: www.geohive.com

Inter-cultural differences

There are important cultural differences between different client groups of tourists. So if economic change demands a change in tourism marketing to new groups, the cultural differences of such groups need to be identified and addressed. For example the alcohol aspect of tourism which is so important to the north European male is a religious taboo for Muslims. Whilst sun-based holidays are an attraction for many North American and North European tourists, it is not so for other groups. For instance the most important motivation for travel for the Japanese is to enjoy nature and scenery, whilst for Eastern European tourists, visiting friends and relatives is the priority. European groups appreciate dining facilities al fresco in warm destinations whilst Asian groups expect air conditioned restaurants. In Bali, where Europeans want discos, Chinese, Koreans and Japanese want karaoke bars. European travellers to China often seek to get off the beaten track. The Chinese seek out crowded places since they equate popularity with quality in an attraction.

Other socio-cultural changes

Other socio-cultural changes include:

- ◊ Attitudes and values about travel
- ◊ Availability of paid leave
- ◊ Unemployment

The work of Greenpeace, Tourism Concern, Friends of the Earth and similar environmental groups continues to raise the public consciousness of the harmful environmental effects of economic growth and development. Changing attitudes to the environment mean that gradually tourists, on the demand side, and host communities on the supply side, require higher standards of impact containment. Similarly the increased concern for healthy lifestyles means that tourists are becoming more cautious about sun-worship holidays. Scientific evidence points up the undesirable effects of exposure to the sun which include increased risk of skin cancer, and premature ageing. The diminution of the ozone layer adds weight to these concerns.

Changes in the duration of paid holidays and hours worked will affect demand for tourism. Europeans have comparatively generous holiday entitlement, whereas two weeks' paid leave is common in the United States and Japan. This may help account for the fact that the Japanese have a lower propensity for overseas travel compared to Britons.

Factors such as income distribution and unemployment can also be important influences. Although for many countries, average living standards have increased, this has often happened in an unequal way. Those who are unemployed or who rely solely on state benefits have generally not benefited from the fruits of economic growth. In some countries this has led to the development of an economic underclass – for example those living in shanty towns in Peru and Bolivia, and those living on the streets in London and New York. This clearly poses a threat to such places as tourism destinations. Tourists to Peru are advised to line their handbags with chicken wire to stop them being slit open – hardly an alluring image for attracting tourists.

Tourist motivations

Poon (1994) identified a change in values in values between 'Old Tourists' and 'New Tourists'. Her thesis suggested that tourism organisations need to be aware of the opportunities and threats resulting from this change in tourists' values, attitudes and aspirations. Old Tourists are characterised by Poon as follows. They find security in large groups and seek a yearly pre-packaged tour to destinations which are not important in themselves but because of their location by the sea and in the sun. They see themselves as culturally superior to their hosts and demand home cooking and home facilities abroad. They often cause high impacts and are seeking relaxation.

On the other hand New Tourists avoid large groups and want something different. They travel more often and more spontaneously to destinations which are chosen because of their differentness from home. The differentness is sought and encouraged and they adapt their behaviour to fit in. They want to experience local cuisine and local life and understand a destination's culture and heritage. They are environmentally sensitive and are seeking new experiences. In many ways Poon's analysis of New Tourists draws on ideas earlier propounded by MacCannell (1999) that a key motivation for tourists is the search for authentic experiences.

Dann (1981) analysed tourism motivation in terms of push and pull factors. He suggested that the conditions prevalent in the tourist's home environment could affect the desire to travel – especially the desire to escape the monotony of work or apparent meaninglessness of modern consumer society. On the other hand, pull factors exerted by destinations might include cultural and climate difference.

The technological environment

Technological analysis: analysing changes in science and technology to understand their impact on tourism entities.

The technological environment offers both opportunities and threats to tourism organisations. The opportunities resulting from technological development may be found in cheaper provision, or improvements in goods and services, in better marketing or easier distribution. However technology may result in an organisation's product or service becoming obsolete, or subject to new forms of competition. The technological environment may be divided into information communication technology and other technology.

Information Communication Technology (ICT)

ICT: information and communication technology

Three significant waves of ICT development can be discerned. In the 1970s, computer reservation systems (CRSs) brought huge efficiencies by better matching of clients with the tourism services on offer. In the 1980s, global distribution systems (GDSs) meant that the market was more easily extended from the local and national to the global. From the late 1990s, the development of the Internet extended access to information technology to a huge range of suppliers and consumers and heralded the networked age. These waves illustrate that as ICT develops, its associated opportunities and threats change. For example in the first wave, CRS offered clear opportunities to travel agents. Labour costs in bookings could be saved, and customers could be offered an improved booking service. However the continued development of ICT posed a significant threat.

The development of the Internet meant that suppliers could directly access their customers increasingly making the travel agent's role redundant.

ICT relevant to tourism encompasses information search, purchase of services, post travel engagement and networking. It includes information and reservation systems for airlines, hotels and attractions, timetables for transport systems, search engines (e.g. Google) online travel services (e.g. Expedia, Orbitz, Lastminute.com, Opodo, Travelocity and edreams), destination management systems (e.g. visitbritain.com), networking and web 2.0 portals (e.g. tripadvisor.com) and price comparison sites (e.g. travelsupermarket.com).

The review of information and communication technology research in tourism by Buhalis and Law (2008) prompted the following observations:

- The Internet has increased consumers choices.
- ICT offers cheap, convenient, immediate and portable access to information, reservation and purchase.
- The Internet provides a channel for consumers to complain about poor service (so-called 'electronic word of mouth')
- Web 2.0 and Travel 2.0 technologies extend the benefits of social networking and virtual communities to the tourism industry. For example, Trip Advisor (www.tripadvisor.com) offers a communal pooling of reviews and ratings of hotels. It therefore offers a participatory and democratic system of updated and independent advice.
- 'Wiki' technologies will enable the creation of more create collaborative and community websites. It is a technology that allows accessible and open creation and editing of interlinked web pages using a simple text editor embedded in the website.
- The Internet allows suppliers to collect data on customers allowing profiling and therefore customisation of offers and personalised recommendations.
- Wireless and mobile networks are increasingly important in ICT.
- The concept of 'info-structure' describes an integrated and holistic system which incorporates an organisation's internal and external communications and operational processes.
- Interoperability (that is the ability of different systems to work together) is a key issue.
- Multimedia can be deployed as a powerful aspect of ICT in tourism where photos, graphics and videos are incorporated into Internet sites to provide a more realistic image of services and destinations.
- Dynamic packaging, where for example airlines up-sell car hire, insurance and hotels, offers a significant opportunity for developing new markets.
- Interactivity, for example, the use of avatars and virtual environments offer the possibilities for visitor immersion in potential destinations.

- ◊ The sophistication and widespread adoption of mobile phones offer new opportunities. Smartphones that incorporate Internet access and global positioning systems (GPSs) enable tourists to access ICT services without any spatial constraints. Downloadable applications (applications and widgets) enable location based services (LBS) to be accessed. These include the locating of persons, provision of routes, searching for local restaurants, shops, hotels, or sights, and the provision of information about travelling conditions, such as traffic and air departure related data and weather.
- ◊ Satellite navigation systems for car users also provide a range of location based services.
- ◊ WiMAX technology can offer wireless broadband access over a 40 km radius as an improvement on cable and DSL. WiMAX is capable of providing Internet broadband wireless access to entire destinations and extending Internet access to tourists away from their usual network providers.
- ◊ Developments in ambient intelligence mean that intelligent interfaces can be embedded in the things we use and places we visit such as furniture, hotels, destinations, vehicles and roads so that they can be enhanced through ICT to be sensitive, proactive and responsive.
- ◊ The Internet is changing the competitive environment of the tourism industry by opening access to distribution channels, reducing barriers to entry, reducing switching costs, enabling greater consumer knowledge about prices and services, stimulating competition, and generating production efficiencies.
- ◊ Yield management systems use records of demand and supply patterns and current booking levels to suggest prices to maximise the yield for a service such as hotel rooms or air or train tickets. Yield management systems allow variable charges which can change by the minute to maximise yield or revenue.

The hotel sector demonstrates a range of recent uses of ICT. These include Internet bookings, dynamic packaging, rapid registration and billing, smart keys, energy management systems, and security management systems. In France the *Hotel Premiere Classe*, has used ICT to provide a low price chain of hotels. Booking, registration, key issue (a PIN number) and check-out are entirely automated, and bathrooms are cleaned automatically, resulting in lower costs and prices.

ICT also poses some possible threats to hotels and transportation in the form of video and computer conferencing. The development of this technology means that it is possible for conferences to take place without participants leaving their homes or offices, thus posing a possible threat to this lucrative source of income.

Other changes in technology relating to tourism

Technological change in transportation has generally lead to faster and cheaper services. In air transport, jet travel and cheap fuel were the original drivers of mass tourism. The development of jumbo and super jumbo jets has resulted in a long-term reduction in the real price of air travel, as airlines have passed on the benefits of economies of scale to consumers. The Airbus A380 which made its first commercial flight in 2007 provides seating for 525 people in a three-class configuration but could seat up to 853 people in all economy class configuration.

These changes have opportunities and threats. Cheap mass air transportation has extended the frontiers of holiday destinations. In terms of European tourists, this may pose a threat to traditional destinations such as Spain, as cheaper fares allow tourists access to more distant destinations, for the same expenditure.

Rail travel has also benefited from technological change, particularly in Europe and Japan. For example the TGV, France's high speed train offers a journey time from Paris to Lyon to under 2 hours. The *Shinkansen* is a network of high-speed railway lines in Japan where trains travel at up to 300 km/h. The system uses tunnels and viaducts to keep the track as straight as possible and an automatic train control system for efficient operations. In the UK Virgin Pendalino trains are able to travel at high speeds on conventional track using a technological system where the train banks into corners.

Other areas where technologies have had a significant impact on tourism include:

- ◊ Construction techniques – allowing faster erection of buildings.
- ◊ Bridge technology – extending access and cutting journey times.
- ◊ Materials – lighter and more durable materials.
- ◊ Glass – especially with better insulation properties.
- ◊ Fuels – e.g. biofuels.
- ◊ Energy – especially alternative sources of energy such as wind and solar power.
- ◊ Security scanning – which enables quicker and more accurate passenger checking at airports.

PEST analysis

PEST analysis provides a framework for tourism organisations to analyse opportunities and threats in part of their external operating environment. The key factors are summarised in Table 4.5.

One of the outcomes of PEST environmental analysis is scenario planning. This technique, pioneered by Shell and the Organization for Economic Co-operation and Development (OECD), sets out a number of different possible scenarios that might unfold in the external PEST environment. The point about scenario planning is that a proactive organisation should plan ahead and have considered a range of strategies suitable to deal with different possible scenarios.

The Forum for the Future (2009) has prepared four possible scenarios that might face the tourism industry in 2023. Each of these would have a distinctive effect on entities in the tourism sector. These are:

1 'Boom and burst' where a huge growth in worldwide travel has been caused by booming economies and high disposable incomes.
2 'Divided disquiet' where violent wars over scarce resources, climate change impacts, and social unrest has created an unstable and worried world.
3 'Price and privilege' where travel has been made punitively expensive by a dramatic rise in oil prices.
4 'Carbon clampdown' where tradable carbon quotas for individuals have restricted access to high CO_2 tourism.

Table 4.5: Summary of PEST features

Political	Economic
Party politics Political stability Terrorism Laws Regulations Change of government	Economic growth Consumers' expenditure Interest rates Taxes Exchange rates Investment expenditure Government spending Unemployment Inflation Budget policy
Socio-cultural	**Technological**
Population growth Age structure Leisure time Income distribution Environmentalism Consumerism Lifestyles Attitudes Values	ICT development Production technology Materials technology Energy technology

Review of key terms

- Political analysis: the effects of government policy and laws.
- Legislature: the body where laws, regulations and policy are made.
- Executive: the arm of government which carries out government laws and policies.
- Economic analysis: understanding what economic factors will affect tourism entities and how these economic factors are changing.
- Consumers' expenditure: the amount of money consumers actually spend.

- Exchange rates: the value of a country's currency in terms of other currencies.
- Interest rates: the cost of borrowing.
- Expectations: the way people feel about future economic prospects (optimistic or pessimistic).
- Economic growth: a measure of how much better (or worse) off a country is in economic terms over a period of time.
- Recession: two consecutive quarters of negative growth.
- BRIC countries: Brazil, Russia, India and China.
- Socio-cultural analysis: understanding changes in population size and structure as well as changes in consumer tastes, preferences and broader cultural shifts.
- Technological analysis: analysing changes in science and technology to understand how these will impact on tourism entities.
- ICT: information and communication technology

Multiple choice questions

1 Which of the following is associated with right-wing governments?
   A Support of trade unions
   B Minimal state interference in industry
   C Poverty reduction and social mobility goals
   D Provision of a comprehensive welfare state

2 Which of the following is likely to cause a rise in consumers' expenditure?
   A A rise in taxes
   B A rise in unemployment
   C Pessimistic expectations
   D A fall in interest rates

3 Which of the following is a characteristic of a downswing or recession?
   A Falling unemployment
   B Rising inflation
   C Optimistic expectations
   D Reduced profits

4 Which of the following is true?
   A Indonesia is a BRIC country
   B The population of Indonesia exceeds that of Brazil
   C The population of Japan is increasing
   D Analysis of an organisation's human resources is part of PEST analysis

5 Which of the following is false?
   A ICT stands for information control technologies
   B LBS stands for location based services
   C WiMAX technology is a type of wireless broadband
   D Interoperability means the ability of different systems to work together

Discussion questions

1. Explain how changes in government or government policy might affect a named tourism entity.
2. Evaluate the economic environment for a named destination.
3. Explain how changes in:

   exchange rates

   consumers' expenditure

   taxation, and

   interest rates

   may affect the business of a named airline. What other economic factors might be relevant to your analysis?
4. What opportunities and threats are destinations facing from changes in ICT?
5. Provide a PEST analysis for the provider of a major theme park, distinguishing between opportunities and threats.

References

Altinay, L., Bicak, H. A. and Altinay, M. (2005) Uncertainty and tourism development: the case of North Cyprus. *Anatolia*, **16**, 27–38.

Buhalis, D. and Law, R. (2008) Progress in information technology and tourism management: 20 years on and 10 years after the Internet – the state of eTourism research. *Tourism Management*, **29**, 609–623.

Burns, P. and Novelli, M. (2009) *Tourism and Politics*. Oxford: Elsevier.

Dann, G. (1981) Tourist motivation: an appraisal. *Annals of Tourism Research*, **8**, 187–219.

Forum for the Future (2009) *Tourism 2023*. London: Forum for the Future.

MacCannell, D. (1999) *The Tourist: A New Theory of the Leisure Class*. Berkeley: University of California Press.

Munoz, T.G. (2007) German demand for tourism in Spain. *Tourism Management*, **28**, 12–22.

Poon, A. (1994) The 'new tourism' revolution. *Tourism Management*, **15**, 91–92.

Robinson, A.J. and Meaton, J. (2005) Bali beyond the bomb: disparate discourses and implications for sustainability. *Sustainable Development*, **13**, 69–78.

Smith, V.S. (2004) Tourism and terrorism: the 'new war'. In J.Aramberri and R. Butler (eds), *Tourism Development: Issues for a Vulnerable Industry*, Bristol: Channel View, pp. 275–290.

Timothy, D.J. (2006) Relationships between tourism and international boundaries. In H.Wachowiak (ed.), *Tourism and Borders: Contemporary Issues, Policies, and International Research*, Farnham: Ashgate, pp. 9–21.

Tribe, J. (2005) *The Economics of Recreation, Leisure and Tourism*. Oxford: Elsevier.

Xiao, H. (2006) The discourse of power: Deng Xiaoping and tourism development in China. *Tourism Management*, **27**, 803–814.

5 The External Environment: Competition

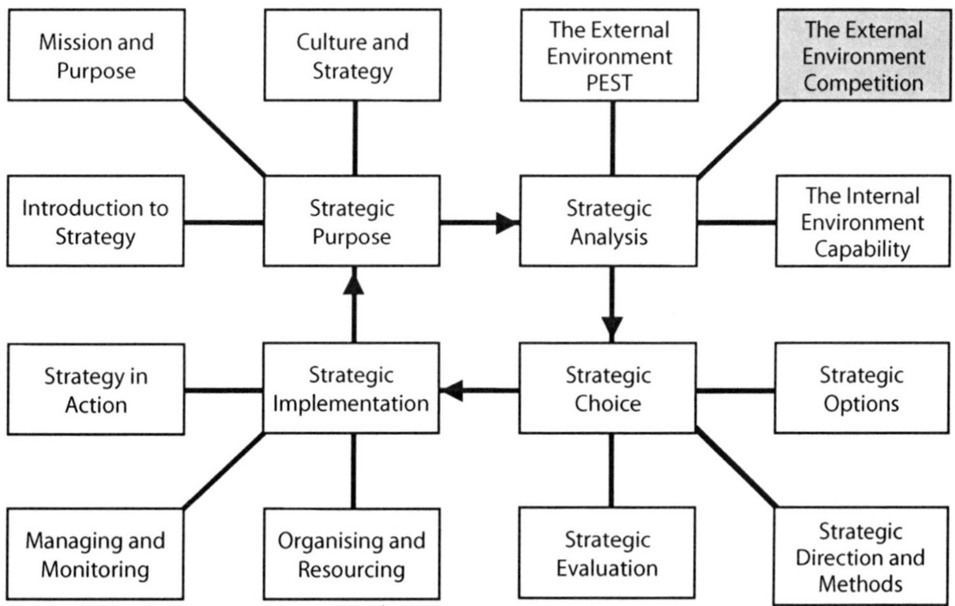

Figure 5.1

Learning outcomes

After studying this chapter and related materials you should be able to understand:

- Industries, markets and strategic groups
- Porter's five forces
- Competitor analysis
- Destination competitiveness

and critically evaluate, explain and apply the above concepts.

Introduction

Competition analysis is used to reveal the opportunities and threats that exist in the competitive environment within the tourism industry. It may be conceived of as the extent of influence of tourism organisations or destinations upon one another as well as the effects of their suppliers and buyers.

The analysis of the competitive environment which follows is divided into a number of sections. First the idea of an industry or market is examined in order to identify the competitive boundaries within which any tourism entity operates. As part of this, the concept of strategic group analysis is introduced to enable a tourism entity to identify its key competitors in specific markets. Next, techniques of competitor analysis are introduced so that profiles of key competitors can be constructed. Following this Porter's five forces framework is used to analyse the competitive forces that act upon tourism entities. This allows a framework for competitor analysis to be introduced and finally the specifics of destination competitiveness are examined. Case study 5 illustrates these points through an analysis of the global airline business where deregulation and the arrival of low-cost carriers led to intensified competition.

Case Study 5: Global Airlines

Competition in the airline industry is intense. But it hasn't always been so. For a long while the 'legacy carriers' (carriers such as British Airways, American Airlines and Lufthansa), which were founded before the deregulation of the airline markets, were protected from competition by regulation that included protective entry barriers and price agreements brokered through the International Air Transport Association (IATA). Consumer choice was limited, markets were stable and prices were relatively high.

But the 1978 Airline Deregulation Act liberalised national aviation markets in the USA opening them up to competition. Subsequently the EU aviation markets were deregulated in the 1980s and 1990s and the USA and EU agreed on the Open Aviation Area in 2008. Other international markets however are still regulated to different degrees.

Deregulation ushered in wave after wave of 'low-cost carriers', notably South West Airlines in the USA and Ryanair in the UK and the airline industry was rocked by the low-cost revolution. Low-cost carriers offer no-frills services and hence not only low costs but also low prices. In fact so low that Ryanair frequently offers free flights from the UK to Europe. The low-cost revolution has meant that whilst many 'low-cost' carriers have reported increased passenger numbers, load factors and profits, several legacy carriers exist precariously on the edge of bankruptcy, and others have been forced into alliances and mergers to survive. KLM was taken over by Air France, and BA has merged with Iberia. Several legacy carriers set up in-house low-cost airlines to compete with the upstart airlines. For example in 1995 Air New Zealand set up a subsidiary, Freedom, which operated between New Zealand and Australia. Freedom was successful in putting out of business, Kiwi Airlines, its new independent low-cost competitor. But Freedom Air was eventually discontinued with

Air New Zealand concentrating on making its core economy service low cost. In Europe low-cost initiatives by legacy carriers, for example Snowflake (SAS), Go (BA) and Buzz (KLM), all proved to be failures as the low-cost arms ate into the parent airlines' core business.

Intense competition continues both in the low-cost and legacy sectors. For instance in the South Pacific, prior to 2009, Air Pacific, owned partly by the Fiji government and partly by Qantas Airways, was the key player for air traffic into Fiji from Australia. But in 2009 two of Australia's low-cost carriers Jetstar (ironically owned by Qantas) and Virgin Blue both intensified competition on this route. Air Pacific posted a loss of 12 million Fiji dollars for 2008–09 compared with a profit of 38.15 million Fiji dollars in 2007–08. Virgin Blue applied to the Australian regulators to approve more capacity, but in response to Virgin Blue's attack on its market share, Qantas also applied for extra capacity seats for Jetstar. Of course this meant that Qantas's Jetstar would intensify competition with its part-owned Air Pacific. All of this put Air Pacific and the Qantas stake in it under threat as its legacy costs, and therefore fares, are much greater than those of the low-cost newcomers.

Meanwhile a fierce competitive struggle has been opened between China's largest airline, Air China and foreign airlines who are trying to increase their market share of the strongly growing Chinese market. In 2004 Northwest Airlines and United Airlines signed an aviation agreement with China. In 2005 Air Europa (Spain) launched a direct Beijing–Madrid flight and British Airways (UK) has commenced five weekly direct flights between Shanghai and London Heathrow Airport. Continental Airlines (USA) launched a daily non-stop air service from Beijing to New York. Continental's return ticket from Beijing to New York was priced at only US$640 and United Airlines' Beijing–New York return ticket was US$590 compared with around US$690 dollars for Air China. Both United and Continental have plans to expand their services to China. The *Asia Times* commented that 'Chinese airlines ... seem a bit humble and passive in facing the aggressiveness of their foreign counterparts'. But a researcher from the China Civil Aviation College explained that:

> Chinese airlines bear greater pressure compared with their foreign counterparts, as the fuel oil prices are higher at China's domestic market, and they also have to spend heavily on importing airplanes. This put them in a disadvantage position in competing with foreign airlines ... Besides, domestic airlines are still less competitive than their foreign counterparts in terms of capacity and management efficiency ... It takes time for Chinese airlines to catch up with their foreign counterparts and learn to compete with them.

One step taken by Air China to compete with its foreign rivals has been to invest US$80 million to upgrade the first-class and business-class of 15 of its long-range aircraft.

Industries, markets and strategic groups

In order for a tourism entity to understand its competitive environment it must establish the boundaries of competitive interaction. Here the terms industry, markets and strategic groups provide useful orientations. Porter (1998) defined

Strategic group: collection of defined suppliers who compete on a similar territory.

an industry as a group of businesses whose products are close substitutes for each other and an industry represents the supply side of the production of goods and services. However it may provide too generalised a picture to be helpful in competitive analysis. For example, we may talk about the tourism industry but it is clear that not all participants in this industry are direct competitors.

Whilst an industry is focused on production, markets are focused on customers and therefore on the demand side. Markets are places where buyers come into contact with a number of sellers and are able to compare prices and products. So a market offers a finer tuning of competition boundaries. Market segmentation provides a further refinement. A market segment is a group of customers who have similar needs which can be differentiated from customer needs in other parts of the market.

It is sometimes the case that the notions of 'industry' or 'market' are too wide to allow for useful consideration of an organisation's competitive position. For example, within the UK package tour industry there is unlikely to be much competitive rivalry between China Travel Service (CTS) and Club 18–30 since their markets are segmented and distinct. It can also be the case that the level of 'an organisation' may be too generalised. For example, the interests of Merlin Entertainments encompass the diverse brands of the London Eye and Madame Tussauds neither of which are direct competitors.

In cases such as these, strategic group analysis can be used to focus on defined business units (which may be part of a larger organisation) which compete on similar territory. The following list of characteristics may be used as a basis for establishing strategic groups which are in competition with each other.

- ◊ Pricing policy
- ◊ Quality of products
- ◊ Product range
- ◊ Extent of branding
- ◊ Geographical coverage
- ◊ Market segment served
- ◊ Distribution channels used
- ◊ Size of organisation.

The choice of characteristics to use varies from industry to industry but two or three sets of key characteristics will generally serve to differentiate between strategic groups. For example, it would be useful to use quality of service (using the national classification system), and pricing policy to differentiate between strategic groups in the hotel industry.

Figure 5.2 considers the strategic groupings that arise from such an exercise in the French hotel market. It enables hotel operators to limit their competitor analysis to competitors in the same strategic group. Thus for example there is considerable competitive rivalry between the Paris Marriott Champs Elysees and the Hotel Ritz Paris, but the Ibis and the Première Classe appeal to a different market segment.

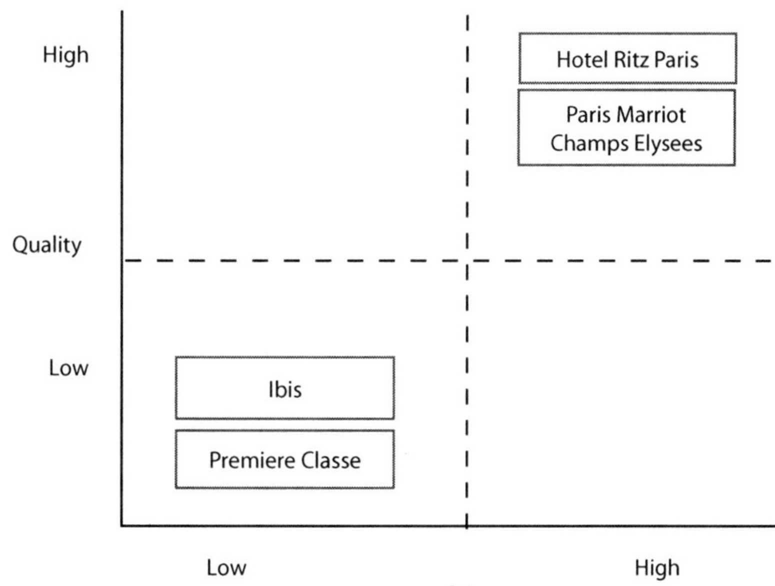

Figure 5.2: Strategic group analysis

Porter's five forces analysis

An increase in competition within the tourism industry generally leads to a loss of a firm's customers and/or a reduction in prices. Either way a reduction in profits is likely. Where an industry approaches the economists' model of perfect competition (no entry barriers, many sellers selling similar products and perfect knowledge of the market) profits will be reduced to a level termed 'normal profits'. This is because any excess profits will attract new firms into the industry. Additional competition will cause prices, and profits, to fall until profits are no longer high enough to attract additional entrants. Profit maximising tourism organisations will therefore seek a position within an industry where competitive threats can be minimised and competitive opportunities exploited.

Porter's five forces: the threat of new entrants, the bargaining power of buyers, the bargaining power of suppliers, the threat of substitutes and the degree of rivalry between competitors.

Porter's (1998) 'five forces' model is used to analyse the competitive environment and these are illustrated in Figure 5.3. The five forces proposed by Porter are:

- The threat of new entrants
- The bargaining power of buyers
- The bargaining power of suppliers
- The threat of substitutes
- The degree of rivalry between competitors.

The purpose of five-force analysis of the competitive environment is so that the corporate strategist can:

> *find a position in the industry where his or her company can best defend itself against these forces or can influence them in its favour.* (Porter, 1998, p. 4)

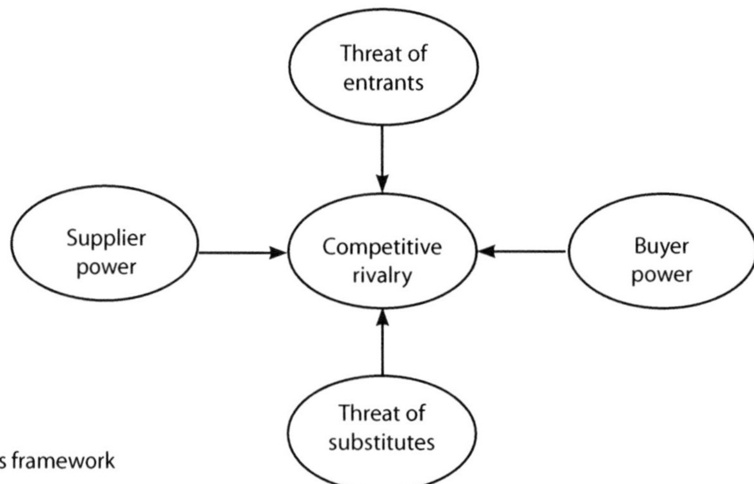

Figure 5.3: The Five Forces framework

The threat of new entrants

The threat of new entrants: the ease with which new firms may enter an industry.

The threat of new entrants determines the ease with which new firms may enter an industry. This largely depends upon the existence of barriers to entry that may exist in an industry and these include:

- ◊ Economies of scale
- ◊ Capital requirements of entry
- ◊ Availability of supply and distribution channels
- ◊ Expected retaliation: price and advertising barriers
- ◊ Product differentiation
- ◊ Government policy.

Economies of scale

Economies of scale occur where average production costs fall as a firm's size increases. Because of this, large airlines should theoretically be able to fight off new entrants because their size confers economies of scale and new entrants will therefore face higher average costs. For example, large airlines may save in fuel costs by bulk purchase. Size can allow sophisticated technology to be utilised (e.g. smart computer systems) and specialist managers to be employed which lead to more efficient operations whilst their costs can be spread against millions of ticket sales. Similarly, advertising costs per ticket become smaller as sales increase. The costs per seat of a jumbo jet are lower than those of smaller aircraft which are associated with smaller airlines.

However some of the large legacy airlines suffer from diseconomies of scale. They are so large that management and co-ordination becomes difficult and small airlines are able to achieve economies in different ways. They are often more adaptable and for example use their labour force more flexibly and have cut out many expenses such elaborate corporate headquarters. By concentrating only on popular routes they achieve higher load factors which cuts the cost per passenger.

Capital requirements of entry

High start-up costs can restrict entry into an industry and so for example the oil refining industry is difficult to enter. The acquisition of aircraft potentially represents a high capital entry requirement for the airline industry but aircraft can be leased enabling potential entrants to spread the high capital costs over a longer period of time and therefore is a way to enter the airline industry.

Availability of distribution channels

Airports and runway slots are key supply channels for airlines. In the relatively uncrowded skies of the USA this is rarely a problem. In the UK however, there are few slots available at London Heathrow Airport (LHR) and this makes entry into the market difficult for newcomers. British Airways has built up rights to key slots over the years (so-called grandfather rights) and this makes it difficult for new operators to establish themselves at LHR. Of course this has meant that new entrants have sought alternative supply channels so that the low-cost airline Ryanair operates out of Stanstead airport and flies to secondary airports where access to landing rights is less competitive (and considerably cheaper too).

It has been the case in the tourism industry that suppliers have sought to restrict distribution channels by vertical integration and the purchase of travel agents. However the widespread adoption of the Internet has meant that new entrants can circumvent such restrictions and distribute their services to consumers directly and very effectively.

Expected retaliation: price and advertising barriers

Small airlines which compete with well established ones may expect a period of sustained price and advertising wars and the aggressive use of loyalty reward schemes. There have been frequent claims (Laker, Virgin) in the airline industry that large established operators have engaged in sustained predatory pricing campaigns in order to prevent new airlines entering their markets. However price co-ordination is illegal in the EU, the USA and many other airline markets.

Product differentiation

Product differentiation occurs where firms can build up customer loyalty to a particular brand. For example, large airlines sell their names strongly and encourage loyalty by frequent flier schemes. The creation of customer loyalty creates a barrier to entry since new firms must incur marketing costs to overcome existing brand loyalties.

Government policy

For much of the immediate post-World War II period the airline industry was heavily regulated making it difficult for new players to enter the market. For example, before deregulation, the Civil Aeronautics Board limited access to the US airline industry, but this barrier to entry was removed in 1978. In Europe, government policies restricted entry in some parts of the EU airline industry but after 1997, it also entered a period of deregulation. Barrett (2009) reports on the outcome of the EU/US Open Skies agreement that became operational in 2008. For example the agreement increased the number of routes and carriers between Ireland and the USA and the increased competition led to lower fares.

Forsyth *et al.* (2006) and Duval (2008) investigated aviation competition and government policy in Asia and found a similar opening of the skies. They noted that China had traditionally restricted competition, but that it had liberalised access to routes since 2005 especially for the USA. They also note a liberalising of air access policies among ASEAN nations beginning in 2003, so that by 2007 an agreement was reached that a regional open skies policy would be phased in by 2015. Also in the region they report on the Multilateral Agreement on the Liberalization of Air Transport (MALIAT) between Brunei, Chile, New Zealand, Singapore and the USA.

The bargaining power of buyers

The bargaining power of buyers: the relative power of customers in relation to the producers.

The bargaining power of buyers measures the relative power of customers in relation to the producers in a particular market. Buyer bargaining power is affected by:

- ◊ Switching costs
- ◊ Large volume purchasers
- ◊ Homogeneous products
- ◊ Buyer knowledge of competition.

Switching costs

Switching costs refers to the costs involved if a buyer of a good or service changes from one supplier to another. Low switching costs increase buyer power as they can readily move from one supplier to another. The UK airline Ryanair has built up a fleet of Boeing aircraft and this unified fleet gives it considerable economies in terms of maintenance, operations and training. However it means that the airline faces switching costs should it wish to acquire aircraft from Airbus and so its buyer power is reduced. In general, customers are not tied to any airline in any way and there are therefore no switching costs involved in moving to a cheaper supplier. However airlines use loyalty schemes to create switching costs (loss of frequent flyer privileges) and reduce buyer bargaining power.

Large volume purchasers

Customers who buy in bulk can exercise considerable buyer power as suppliers will want to attract them to maintain their market share. In the travel industry this means that airlines which have a significant presence at an airport will have greater buyer power over the airport operator than smaller airlines and may be able to negotiate cheaper landing charges. Similarly tour operators who purchase large blocks of hotel accommodation in destinations are able to exercise considerable buyer power over hoteliers.

Homogeneous products

If the goods or services on offer in a particular market are very similar than buyers are able to easily shop around from one supplier to the next. This enhances buyer power since they have wide choice of suppliers, who are supplying basically similar services. Foreign currency is a totally homogeneous product and so buyers are attracted to the lowest price provider. Similarly, despite attempts at product differentiation, there is often little real difference between competing airlines for economy class travel and buyers exercise their power to shop around.

Buyer knowledge of competition

Buyer knowledge refers to the ability of buyers to easily find out about the whole range of potential suppliers and compare services and prices. The Internet has resulted in a significant increase in buyer bargaining power. For air travel, buyers can directly compare prices by visiting a number of supplier sites or use price comparison sites such as travelsupermarket.com or expedia.com. Knowledge increases buyer power.

The bargaining power of suppliers

The bargaining power of suppliers: the relative power of suppliers in relation to producers.

The bargaining power of suppliers is the relative power of suppliers in relation to producers. Suppliers are those organisations which supply tourism entities with raw materials, equipment and other input goods and services. The suppliers to airlines include aircraft manufacturers, oil companies, airport operators, trade unions, banks and in some cases, tour operators and agents. Key factors affecting supplier power include:

- Supplier size and concentration
- Switching costs
- Uniqueness of the supplied resource.

Supplier size and concentration

Where there are only a few large producers which dominate the supply in a particular market supplier bargaining power over buyers will be high. Some airports are able to charge high prices to airlines because of their near-monopoly position especially if they own all the major airports in a particular location.

Trade unions are able to increase their bargaining power in the supply of labour when they have a high level of membership. In the airline industry, trade unions are often more prominent in legacy airlines than in low-cost carriers and this means that trade unions' power and their ability to negotiate better wages and working conditions is higher in these airlines.

Switching costs

It was earlier observed that the switching costs faced by Ryanair in changing its aircraft supplier from Boeing to Airbus reduce the buying power of Ryanair. In this case, buyers and suppliers are opposite sides of the same coin so the same conditions increase the bargaining power of the seller.

Uniqueness of the supplied resource

There are some unique suppliers in the tourism industry. These include cultural attractions such as Venice in Italy or Petra in Jordan and destinations with special natural features such as the Grand Canyon in the USA. Uniqueness bestows high supplier power and this may be felt by tourists who may face high entry charges or by the providers of food or accommodation services who may face high lease charges.

The threat of substitutes

The threat of substitutes describes the likelihood of other services or products being used in place of any existing product or service. When analysing the threat of substitutes the following are of relevance:

- ◊ Price/performance ratio
- ◊ Extra-industry effects.

Price/performance ratio

The threat of substitutes: the likelihood of other services or products being used in place of any existing product or service.

Goods and services which are potential substitutes may not be identical in terms of price or value offered. But it is a competitive price/performance ratio that will increase the threat of substitution. For example Malaysia and Thailand do not appear to be substitutes for established European destination such as Spain or Greece for European tourists since travel costs to them is considerably higher. But the cost of living in these countries is much lower than that in Spain or Greece. So when the full price/performance ratio is considered then Malaysia and Thailand both emerge as potential substitutes for Spain and Greece.

Dwyer *et al.* (2000) examined destination price competitiveness taking account of both travel cost to and from destinations as well as costs incurred within a destination. Using these aspects of a price/performance ratio (ground costs plus airfare) they found that:

> *Australia ranks relatively well for New Zealand, Indonesia, Hong Kong, South Korea, Thailand and Malaysia, but relatively poor for USA, Germany, UK and particularly China. (p.21)*

Elsewhere, a study of Turkey (Kozak and Rimmington, 1999) indicated that France, Spain, Italy, Portugal and Greece are its main competitors in the Mediterranean area whilst Enright and Newton (2004) found that the main competitors for Hong Kong in urban tourism in the Asia-Pacific region are Singapore, Bangkok, Tokyo, and Shanghai.

Extra-industry effects

It is important to look outside of the immediate industry and market for potential threats from substitutes. For example car, coach and rail may create substitutes for some air services. In Europe, the opening of the Channel Tunnel, investment in high speed rail lines and the introduction of direct Eurostar trains between

London, Paris and Brussels has had a considerable impact on airlines operating on these routes. Similarly technological advances in teleconferencing as well as cheap and accessible Skype technologies pose a potential threat to business travel.

The degree of rivalry between competitors

The degree of competitive rivalry: an overall measure of the intensity of competition in an industry.

The degree of competitive rivalry is an overall measure of the intensity of competition in an industry and is broadly determined by the competitive conditions evident in the four forces analysed above. So a persistent threat of entry of new firms, high bargaining power in buyers and suppliers and the threat of substitutes will all mean a high degree of competitive rivalry with much competitor scanning and frequent adjustments to price and service. Additionally the following factors will influence the degree of competitive rivalry:

- Degree of market leadership (dominant firm)
- Industry growth rate
- Perishability of products
- Marginal costs of sales
- High exit costs
- Cross subsidisation.

Degree of market leadership (dominant firm)

The existence of market leadership where there are one or two dominant firms can reduce competitive rivalry as firms in the industry may well operate a 'follow the leader' principle in pricing to avoid retaliation. However the opposite is the case in the US airline industry which is characterised by a substantial number of competitors which means that competitive rivalry is intense. Whilst there are dominant players such as United and American, deregulation and anti-trust laws make it difficult for these airlines to enforce price leadership.

Industry growth rate

Industries that exhibit slow market growth or even decline are generally ones with intense competitive rivalry. Traditional seaside resort destinations in the UK have witnessed market decline over a number of years. This results in overcapacity in accommodation, hospitality and attractions and so there is considerable competitive rivalry resulting in price competition and reduced profits.

Perishability of products

Airline seats along with package holidays and hotels rooms are highly perishable since their capacity cannot be stored. Empty seat prices may therefore fall dramatically as the departure time nears. The existence of such last minute bargains can cause intense competitive rivalry in the industry. Plate 5 shows extreme competitive rivalry with hoteliers competing for customers as tourists disembark from a ferry in Santorini, Greece.

Plate 5: Competitive Rivalry – Hoteliers vying for customers at ferry, Santorini, Greece.

Marginal costs of sales

The extra cost of selling an otherwise empty seat (marginal cost) is small and thus even a low achieved price will benefit an airline as the following example shows. The revenue gained from an empty transatlantic seat is zero. The cost of filling such a seat is perhaps $50 in food, security charges, meals and administration costs. In this case even selling the seat at $100 earns a profit of $50 that would otherwise be permanently lost and such low prices exacerbate competitive rivalry.

High exit costs

Exit costs are those costs that an organisation must bear even if it withdraws from business. These may include the costs of fixed capital and redundancy costs. Exit costs can change according to the phase of the business cycle and when an economy is in recession exit costs may be particularly high. For example selling aircraft or hotels in a recession will be difficult and firms wishing to do so may incur significant losses. So high exit costs may encourage overcapacity in an industry – particularly in recession conditions – and intensify competitive rivalry.

Cross-subsidisation

Cross-subsidisation occurs when an organisation is able to subsidise prices in one area of operations from profits generated in another area. Large firms are able to cross-subsidise and may use this method to try to drive new entrants from the market. There have been many alleged instances of cross-subsidisation in the airline industry where competitive rivalry has increased as legacy airlines have sought to undercut low-cost carriers.

Competitor analysis

> **Competitor analysis:** an analysis to formulate a strategy in the light of an assessment of key rivals.

Porter's five-force analysis enables the level of competition within a particular industry to be monitored. It is therefore helpful for an organisation in deciding where to position itself in the future taking account of the five forces. However competitor analysis involves a more detailed look at a tourism entity's existing and potential competitors. It enables an organisation to formulate a strategy in the light of an assessment of its key rivals, who have been identified by strategic group analysis.

Porter (1998) set out a framework for competitor analysis which entails the construction of a response profile of competitive organisations. For example, Air China might prepare a response profile for United Airlines in relation to their competing routes between China and the USA. The aim of this profile would be to forecast United Airlines' future plans and consider its likely responses to strategic changes that Delta might put into effect. Porter divides the competitor response profile into two sections and these are illustrated for Air China's response profile for United Airlines.

The first section asks questions about the motives of competitors:

- ◊ What is United Airlines' mission?
- ◊ What are United Airlines' future goals?

The second section asks questions about the competitor's current and future activities:

- ◊ What is United Airlines' current strategy?
- ◊ What are United Airlines' capabilities for future change?

The detailed questions that need to be addressed within the response profile include:

- ◊ Product lines
- ◊ Buyers
- ◊ Prices
- ◊ Quality
- ◊ Differentiation
- ◊ Advertising
- ◊ Market segment
- ◊ Marketing practices
- ◊ Growth and prospects
- ◊ Financial resources
- ◊ Human resources.

Table 5.1 examines what Air China's competitor response profile for United Airlines might look like. From this analysis it would be possible to evaluate United Airlines likely response to strategic moves by Air China such as a reduction in fares, or an upgrading of its business and first class cabins.

Table 5.1: Competitor response profile on United Airlines

Mission	Enhance long-term shareholder value
Future goals	Restructure Focus on core
Current strategy	Emerged from bankruptcy with a solid and competitive platform Sharply focused on improving margins by further improving operations, reducing costs, and realizing revenue premiums Meeting distinct customer needs with differentiated products and services Building on core competitive advantages, including strong brand recognition, leading loyalty program and the best global network Driving performance through continuous improvement Increase on-line penetration
Capabilities	Serves 204 cities Serves 42 international cities Second largest US carrier Eliminated $13 billion in debt and pension obligations Flexibility in work rules and scope

Source: United Airlines Corporate Presentation

Destination competitiveness

Porter's diamond: four factors that could be used to understand the origins of competitive advantage in regions.

Porter (1990) also turned his attention to nations and regions and attempted to discover what made some regions and nations more competitive than others. He developed an analytical framework known as Porter's diamond which encompasses four factors that could be used to understand the origins of competitive advantage in regions or, in the case of tourism, destinations. Porter's diamond framework is illustrated in Figure 5.4. The four factors are:

- Factor conditions
- Market structures, organisations and strategies
- Demand conditions
- Related and supporting industries.

Porter also identified two further factors which could influence regional competitiveness and these were:

- Government
- Chance events.

Enright *et al.* (1997) proposed a different framework for tourism destinations, dividing the drivers of competitiveness into the six categories of:

- Inputs
- Industrial and consumer demand
- Inter-firm competition and cooperation
- Industrial and regional clustering
- Internal organisation and strategy of firms
- Institutions, social structures and agendas.

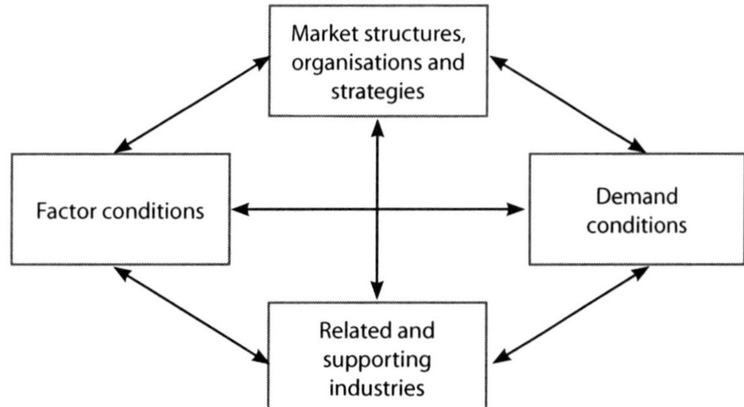

Figure 5.4: Porter's diamond framework

Later Crouch and Ritchie (1999, p. 146) argued for a model where tourism destination competitiveness is determined by four major components:

- Core resources and attractors
- Supporting factors and resources
- Destination management
- Qualifying determinants.

Core resources and attractors include the primary markers of a destination which are important in differentiating one from another. They include landscape, climate, culture, history, links with tourism originating regions as well as accommodation, food services, transportation, tourist attractions and special events.

Supporting factors and resources include the extent and condition of the general infrastructure of the destination and factors that influence its accessibility. Destination management includes destination marketing and the management, co-ordination and maintenance of supporting services, tourism resources and attractors. Qualifying determinants refers to factors that can impinge on the other three components. These include safety, location and overall costs.

Dwyer *et al.* (2003) proposed a modified model of determinants of competitiveness comprising of:

- Inherited resources
- Created resources
- Supporting factors and resources
- Destination management
- Situational conditions
- Demand conditions.

Dwyer *et al.* empirically tested this model using data from Korea and Australia and in 2004 its methodology was applied to evaluate the tourism competitiveness of Slovenia (Gomezelj and Mihalic, 2008). The results of the latter showed Slovenia to be more competitive in its natural, cultural and created resources, but less competitive in the management of tourism and demand conditions.

Enright and Newton (2004) researched tourist views relating to the destination competitiveness of Hong Kong. Their main findings are reported in Box 5.1.

Box 5.1 Enright and Newton's (2004) findings of tourist views relating to the destination competitiveness of Hong Kong

Enright and Newton found that for tourism-specific factors:

> Hong Kong's main strengths lie in cuisine, safety, nightlife, visual appeal, and climate. Its greatest weaknesses are in museums and galleries, music and performances, and notable history.

For Hong Kong's performance in business-related factors they reported that:

> The highest rating for competitiveness was identified as China market potential ... and the lowest rating was ascribed to staff costs ... Hong Kong was seen to have substantial advantages in terms of international access, internal transportation facilities, communication facilities, and in its free port status. The factors where Hong Kong was seen to have disadvantages were staff costs, property-related costs, and other costs.

Source: Enright and Newton (2004, p. 784)

More recently Enright and Newton's (2005) study collected data from tourism industry practitioners in three closely competing destinations in Asia Pacific. It provided strong empirical support for a model that includes both industry-level and destination attributes in studying of tourism competitiveness. Similarly Atomsa and Weiermair (2008) analysed the competitiveness of tourism in Ethiopia focusing on competitive advantages and specialization of tourism-receiving regions vis-à-vis sending regions.

Review of key terms

- Legacy carriers: airlines which were founded before deregulation.
- Strategic group: collection of defined suppliers who compete on a similar territory.
- Porter's five forces: the threat of new entrants, the bargaining power of buyers, the bargaining power of suppliers, the threat of substitutes and the degree of rivalry between competitors.
- The threat of new entrants: the ease with which new firms may enter an industry.
- The bargaining power of buyers: the relative power of customers in relation to the producers.
- The bargaining power of suppliers: the relative power of suppliers in relation to producers.
- The threat of substitutes: the likelihood of other services or products being used in place of any existing product or service.

- The degree of competitive rivalry: an overall measure of the intensity of competition in an industry.
- Competitor analysis: an analysis to formulate a strategy in the light of an assessment of key rivals.
- Porter's diamond: four factors that could be used to understand the origins of competitive advantage in regions

Multiple choice questions

1 Which of the following is not one of Porter's five forces?
   A The threat of new entrants
   B The bargaining power of buyers
   C The bargaining power of suppliers
   D The bargaining power of competitors

2 Which of the following is false?
   A High start-up costs can restrict entry into an industry
   B New entrants to an industry generally face higher average costs
   C Fewer suppliers means they have less bargaining power
   D Switching costs can arise from changing suppliers.

3 For Dwyer *et al.* (2000) destination price competitiveness comprises:
   A The price/performance ratio
   B Travel and destination costs
   C The exchange rate/expenditure ratio
   D Ground costs only

4 Which of the following is most likely to cause increased competitive rivalry?
   A The existence of a dominant firm
   B Low exit costs
   C Difficulties of cross-subsidisation
   D A declining market.

5 Which of the following is a destination core resource and attractor?
   A Safety
   B Landscape
   C Accessibility
   D Destination costs

Discussion questions

1 Distinguish between an industry, markets and strategic groups using a tourism example and explain their usefulness for competitor analysis.

2 Conduct a five-force analysis on the competitive environment for a named tourism firm. Explain how this will enable the director of strategy and planning of that firm to 'find a position in the industry where his or her company can best defend itself against these forces or can influence them in its favor' (Porter, 1998).

3 Conduct a competitor analysis for a tourism firm. Identify its key competitor and prepare a competitor response profile to show how this organisation may react to a low price strategy from your chosen firm.
4 What factors affect destination competitiveness?
5 To what extent can Porter's five forces framework be used to understand destination competitiveness?

References

Atomsa, T. and Weiermair, K. (2008) Raising international competitiveness of tourism in Ethiopia. *Tourism Analysis*, **13**, 181–188.

Barrett, S.D. (2009) EU/US Open Skies – competition and change in the world aviation market: the implications for the Irish aviation market. *Journal of Air Transport Management*, **15**, 78–82.

Duval, D.T. (2008) Regulation, competition and the politics of air access across the Pacific. *Journal of Air Transport Management*, **14**, 237–242.

Dwyer, L., Forsyth, P. and Rao, P. (2000) The price competitiveness of travel and tourism: a comparison of 19 destinations. *Tourism Management*, **21**, 9–22.

Dwyer, L., Livaic, Z. and Mellor, R. (2003) Competitiveness of Australia as a tourist destination. *Journal of Hospitality and Tourism Management*, 60–71.

Enright, M.J. and Newton, J. (2004) Tourism destination competitiveness: a quantitative approach. *Tourism Management*, **25**, 777–788.

Enright, M.J. and Newton, J. (2005) Determinants of tourism destination competitiveness in Asia Pacific: comprehensiveness and universality. *Journal of Travel Research*, **43**, 339–350.

Enright, M.J., Scott, E.E. and Dodwell, D. (1997) *The Hong Kong Advantage*. New York: Oxford University Press.

Forsyth, P., King, J. and Lyn Rodolfo, C. (2006) Open skies in ASEAN. *Journal of Air Transport Management*, **12**, 143–152.

Gomezelj, D.O. and Mihalic, T. (2008) Destination competitiveness: applying different models, the case of Slovenia. *Tourism Management*, **29**, 294 –307.

Kozak, M. and Rimmington, M. (1999) Measuring tourist destination competitiveness: conceptual considerations and empirical findings. *International Journal of Hospitality Management*, **18**, 273–283.

Porter, M.E. (1990) The competitive advantage of nations. *Harvard Business Review*, March and April, 74–91.

Porter, M.E. (1998) *Competitive Strategy: Techniques for Analyzing Industries and Competitors: with a New Introduction*. Glencoe, IL: Free Press.

6 The Internal Environment: Capability

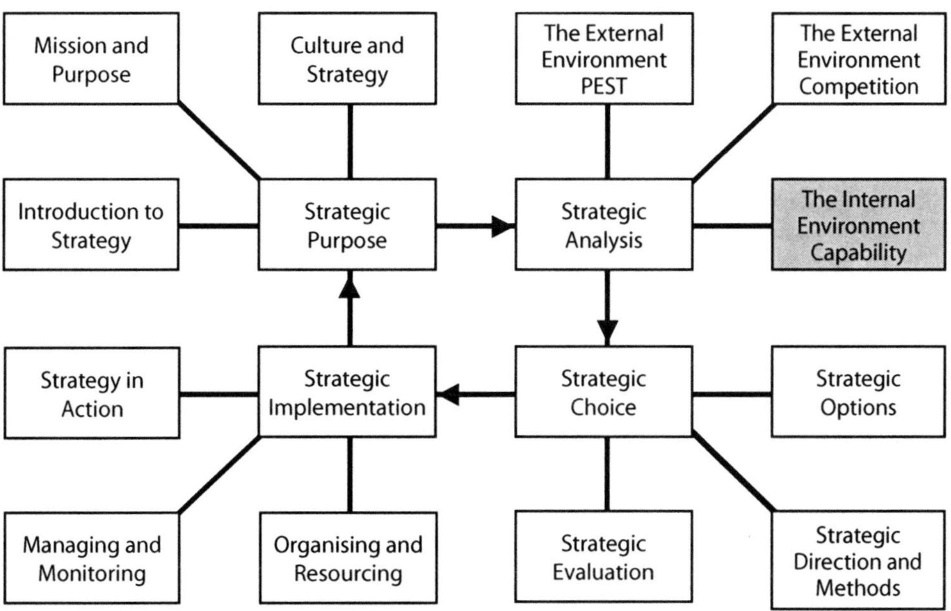

Figure 6.1

Learning outcomes

After studying this chapter and related materials you should be able to understand:

- Resources and competences
- Resource audit
- Performance monitoring and control
- Evaluation of products
- SWOT analysis

and critically evaluate, explain and apply the above concepts.

Introduction

Analysis of the opportunities and threats in the external operating environment is useful in revealing strategic potential for an organisation or destination. The external environment is of course common for all entities. Attention is now turned to the organisation or destination itself where resource deployment analysis considers its strategic capability. Here we are able to discern considerable differences between tourism entities. The main analytical techniques for conducting such a capability analysis include, first, resource auditing. This identifies the level and type of resources that an entity is using. Next, performance monitoring and control asks how well an entity is using its resources. Finally, products and services are subject to evaluation. Capability analysis indicates the organisation's current and potential strengths and weaknesses and reveals its core competences. Capability views of strategy emphasise how competitive advantage can be achieved by effective deployment of resources. Finally, this chapter pulls together the analytical tools developed here and in the previous chapters in the form of SWOT analysis.

Case Study 6 examines the capability of the InterContinental Hotels Group and relates these capabilities to its mission and to its performance analysis.

Case Study 6: InterContinental Hotels Group (IHG)

InterContinental Hotels Group (IHG) is a global hotel company operating seven hotel brands – InterContinental, Crowne Plaza, Hotel Indigo, Holiday Inn, Holiday Inn Express, Staybridge Suites and Candlewood Suites. In 2010 it boasted more guest rooms than any other hotel company in the world with around 4400 hotels across nearly 100 countries. The goal of IHG is 'to create Great Hotels Guests Love' and its mission is 'to grow by making IHG brands the first choice for guests and hotel owners'.

The InterContinental, Goa, India

The strategic priorities of IHG are:

- "Improving the performance of our brands
- Using our insight to make our brands the first choice for guests
- Delivering consistent customer experiences
- Generating excellent returns from our hotels
- Improving hotel revenue by encouraging guest visits
- Improving the efficiency of our hotels and operating processes
- Putting our market scale and knowledge to good use
- Using our worldwide scale and experience to convert more hotels to our brands
- Making the most of our global presence – guests choose brands they know when they travel
- Strengthening our organisation
- Investing in our people and our ability to do business
- Building strong partnerships within our company and with our owners across the world"

Source: www.ihgplc.com

The history of IHG witnessed mergers and diversification before focusing on hotels. InterContinental started in 1946 as part of Pan American Airlines. In 1981, the group was sold to Grand Metropolitan which in turn sold it on to the Saison Group in 1988. The Saison Group subsequently sold InterContinental to Bass, a brewing company, in 1998. Bass sold off its brewing arm in 2000 and changed its name to Six Continents. In 2003 Six Continents plc split into two subsidiaries companies: Mitchells and Butlers concentrated on restaurants and IHG had a portfolio of hotels and soft drinks (Britvic). Britvic was sold in 2005.

In terms of resources, IHG only owned 17 of its hotels in 2010 and its business model, which is increasingly typical in the hotel industry, is to concentrate on the management of hotels which are owned by other parties and on franchising its hotel brands. IHG manages 614 hotels but the largest part of its business is made up of the 3700 hotels that operate under franchise agreements. In other words its key capability is expertise in hotel management, operating systems, and marketing. Hotel property ownership is a capital-intensive business and requires different business capabilities to that of hotel management. For this reason, IHG leaves investment in hotel properties to others.

IHG measures success in three ways:

- Total shareholder returns
- Rooms growth
- A basket of specific key performance indicators (KPIs)

Senior management discretionary remuneration is related to successful performance against combinations of these and other success measures.

Key Results for 2008 included:

- Revenue per available room up 0.9 per cent
- Net room additions up 20 per cent
- Operating profit up13 per cent
- Earnings per share up 26 per cent.

At the heart of IHG is its operating system. This includes an 8000-strong sales force, its marketing and advertising campaigns, 12 international call centres, 13 websites serving local languages and the world's largest hotel loyalty scheme – Priority Club Rewards – which boasts 47 million members.

IHG invests strongly in IT to improve its operating system and management capabilities. Revenue management is an example here where IHG invested in a price optimisation system (POS) to help its hotels determine the best daily price. The POS was designed as an industry leading capability and was the first to continuously measure how guests respond to price changes and use this data together with data on local market demand forecasting, competitive rates and capacity constraints to optimise room rates based upon consumer response,. With this new capability, IHG has minimised the complexity of pricing for their hotels and enabled them to be more responsive to the market.

Another IHG use of IT is the adoption of the Test & Learn software suite. This allows the company to evaluate the effectiveness of promotional offers, capital upgrades, and guest satisfaction by measuring their impact on revenue per available room (REVPAR) and profitability. This system helps IHG to pursue evidence-based strategic decisions using data to enable it to focus resources on initiatives that are proven to work and avoiding ones with little impact on REVPAR or profit.

Given its global reach, geographic diversity, complexity and size, IHG also faces a significant challenge in the management of its human resources. Here it uses an IT software solution called HRM Connect Executive to assist with resourcing, management development, global succession planning and includes an appraisal system. This enables it to collect, analyse, synthesise and integrate information across the whole organisation.

Finally IHG also hosts a virtual Innovation Hotel (http://www.ihgplc.com/innovation/index.asp?pageid=23) to highlight green technologies. The site allows guests to offer feedback on which environmental issues they feel are important especially in the areas of energy, waste, water and community with a view to IHG harnessing these to design, build and operate hotels that are more environmentally responsible.

Resources and competences

Resources: physical resources, human resources, financial resources, and intangibles

Resources are the inputs that are used for the activities of tourism entities. Competences are the skills and abilities used to deploy resources to achieve a given end. Core competences are defined as those which are central to the entity's mission and those which enable it to develop its competitive advantage. Resources used by tourism entities may be divided into tangible and intangible resources. Tangible resources are physical ones such as human resources, buildings and equipment. Intangible resources include knowledge, brand and information. Resources may be classified under four headings:

- ◊ Physical resources
- ◊ Human resources

- ◊ Financial resources
- ◊ Intangibles.

Physical resources include buildings, and fixtures and fittings, machinery and transport fleets. Consideration should be given to age, compatibility, reliability, efficiency and fitness for purpose. Human resources, or an organisation's labour force, may be classified according to skills, costs, and quantity. A probing audit of these will attempt to discover employees' undeclared skills and potential. Financial resources include cash and capital and points of interest here include an organisation's liquidity, its overall debt or credit situation, sources and costs of borrowings and exposure to debt. Intangibles include acquired knowledge and skills, patents and recipes, goodwill, brands and corporate image.

Any initial analysis of an entity's resources should also consider the following:

- ◊ **Flexibility analysis** which considers whether an organisation's resources are flexible enough to deal with the uncertainties of the external environment.
- ◊ **Balance of skills analysis** which considers whether an organisation's team can field a range of types such as innovators, leaders, doers and reflecters.
- ◊ **Reliance analysis** which reveals whether an organisation is over-reliant on key personnel and whether it could manage in the case of their departure.

Performance monitoring and control

Consideration of an organisation's resources may include analysis of the way in which resources are being utilised and should ensure that systems are in place to monitor this aspect of an organisation's activities and oversee performance monitoring and control. Specific techniques are often used for analysing the performance of :

- ◊ Human resources, and
- ◊ Financial resources.

General techniques for such analysis can include:

- ◊ Value chain analysis
- ◊ Balanced scorecard.

An organisation's performance with regard to resource utilisation can be given a useful perspective by way of:

- ◊ Comparative analysis.

Human resources

Monitoring of the performance of human resources is more complex than for other resources and involves qualitative as well as quantitative issues. The IHG Case Study illustrates how IT solutions, specifically HRM Connect Executive software, can be used to provide management information for this purpose.

Key issues for performance analysis include:

- ◊ Succession readiness
- ◊ Performance management
- ◊ Reward management.

Succession readiness is used to identify the ability of an entity to meet its human resource needs of the future – especially in terms of senior managers and chief executives. Key issues here include identification of needs and whether such needs will be met from internal staff development schemes or external recruitment.

Appraisal: setting employee objectives and instigating a periodic system of review.

Performance management of human resources entails the use of a system to encourage and monitor good performance. Appraisal is a common device for managers and this involves line managers setting objectives with their subordinates and instigating a periodic system of review. At the review, success in achieving objectives is discussed as well as any staff training needs that are identified. Appraisal often includes an evaluation of performance in relation to the standards expected for a certain job. Performance management regimes are often tailored to the specifics of jobs and might include targets for customer satisfaction (restaurants/hotel staff), punctuality (transport staff) and accuracy (baggage handling staff).

Reward management systems are designed to identify the most appropriate rewards to incentivise human resources to attain the long-term goals of a tourism entity. These might include commission on sales (aircrew, restaurant staff, sales teams), profit sharing (all staff), profit-related share incentives (senior managers) and bonus schemes.

Financial resources

For profit-making organisations, profitability will clearly be a key indicator of performance. But a broad range of financial indicators are available including:

- ◊ Profit and loss
- ◊ Share prices
- ◊ Earnings per share
- ◊ Price/earnings ratios
- ◊ Return on capital employed
- ◊ Profit margin
- ◊ Revenue per available room
- ◊ Revenue per available seat kilometre (RASK)
- ◊ Efficiency
- ◊ Liquidity.

All these help in the interpretation of the financial health of an organisation. Additionally a range of more specific financial ratios can monitor the use of specific resources, such as the employees' wage ratio and the advertising expense ratio.

Profit and loss

A profit and loss account compares the revenue earned with the costs incurred in earning it.

Profit = Revenue – Cost

Share prices

For companies that are list on stock exchanges, share prices can give a useful guide to how the markets view the profitability of a company. Share prices are determined by demand and supply and will reflect earnings and dividends as well as the future outlook for a company.

Earnings per share (EPS)

Earnings per share is an important ratio used to value shares and represents the average earning per share of a company.

EPS = Total earnings/the number of shares in issue.

Price/earnings ratios (P/E Ratio)

The price/earnings ratio is also useful in the valuation of a company's shares. It is a measure of the price paid for a share in relation to the annual income earned per share (dividend). It therefore also measure how many years a share would have to be held for its dividend to pay for its initial purchase price.

P/E ratio = Price per share/annual earnings per share

Return on capital employed (ROCE)

This measures the return being made on the funds invested in an organisation. It helps determine whether an organisation generates enough returns to pay for the cost of capital employed and can be a useful measure for comparing the performance with other organisations.

ROCE = Earnings before interest and tax/capital employed

Profit margin

Profit margin, or return on sales gives a useful insight into the profitability of a company. It is the ratio of profit per currency unit of sales.

Profit margin = Earnings before interest and tax/total sales

Revenue per available room (RevPAR)

Revenue per available room is a key metric used in the hotel industry to measure the financial performance of a property.

RevPAR = Rooms revenue/rooms available

Revenue per available seat kilometre (RASK)

Revenue per available seat kilometre is used by the airline industry to measure the quality of its revenue stream.

RASK = Operating revenues/available seat kilometres

Efficiency

Efficiency: the ratio of outputs to inputs

Efficiency measures the ratio of outputs to inputs – the fewer inputs that are required to produce a given output, the more efficient an organisation is. Specific indicators of efficiency include sales per square metre; sales per person; sales per outlet as well as output per person. In the tourism sector indicators may include average costs per passenger mile (transport) and average costs per guest day (accommodation), and capacity utilisation.

Efficiency = Work output/work input

Liquidity ratios

Liquidity is the amount of cash in hand, or near at hand, available to a company and a liquidity ratio tests a company's ability to meet its debts or simply to stay in business. The acid test liquidity ratio tests a company's ability to meet its short-term liabilities using liquid assets.

Acid test ratio = Short-term liabilities/liquid assets

Value chain

Value chain: set of connected activities that make up the total service provision

The tendency to analyse organisations by reference to a narrow and visible aspect of its products resulted in analysts such as Porter (1990) developing the idea of the value chain. The product of a scheduled airline for example is not just a seat on an aeroplane. Rather it is a complex set of connected activities that go to make up the total passenger experience – i.e. a value chain exists. Porter's initial model identifies primary activities and support activities in the value chain and is perhaps more appropriate to manufacturing than service industries. Primary activities are those directly concerned with product provision and include:

- ◊ Inbound logistics
- ◊ Operations
- ◊ Outbound logistics
- ◊ Marketing and sales
- ◊ Service.

Support activities are the backroom activities which support product provision and include:

- ◊ Infrastructure
- ◊ Human resource management
- ◊ Technology development
- ◊ Procurement.

For resource analysis the purpose of examining the links in the value chain is to identify where cost savings may be made.

Table 6.1 illustrates the primary activities in the value chain for an airline. Value chain analysis has been instrumental in developing the business model for low-cost carriers. Each part of the value chain has been carefully scrutinised so that unnecessary extras may be stripped out or offered on an optional charged-for basis. Of particular note is the use of IT to reduce booking costs, the use of cheaper secondary airports and the charging for the use of credit cards, food, checked baggage and allocated seats as optional extras. A similar cost-cutting strategy has been deployed for support activities. Head office accommodation of low-cost carriers is characterised by functionality and often located on cheap industrial estates in contrast to the lavish, centrally located HQs of legacy airlines which are often designed to make a corporate architectural statement.

Zhang *et al.* (2009) define what is meant by a supply chain in tourism:

> *A tourism supply chain (TSC) is defined as a network of tourism organizations engaged in different activities ranging from the supply of different components of tourism products/services such as flights and accommodation to the distribution and marketing of the final tourism product at a specific tourism destination, and involves a wide range of participants in both the private and public sectors.*

Table 6.1: Value chain for airline – costs

Element	Activity	Cost questions
Preparation	Routes Airports Advertising Information Reservations Sales	Are any routes unprofitable? Can we use cheap, secondary airports? Is advertising efficient? Can reservation costs be cut? Can IT reduce costs? Charges for use of credit cards Are commissions too high?
Pre-flight	Check-in Baggage Departure Lounge Boarding	Can on-line check-in be encouraged? Can we charge for checked baggage? Use cheap option if available Stairs cheaper than walkways
In Flight	Seat choice Seating Flight attendants Meal Entertainment Other provision	Add as optional cost Maximise seat numbers Wages and commission schemes Optional extra Optional extra Investigate other in flight revenues
Post-flight	Baggage reclaim Airport transfer	Reduce costs by charging for baggage
Follow up	Customer requests Customer complaints	Are passenger refund rules too generous? Can we charge customers for telephone complaint lines using premium numbers?

Yilmaz and Bititci (2006) used a value chain perspective to compare the performance measurement of manufacturing and tourism industries. The authors found that in the manufacturing industry, innovation in value chain management has led to the development of performance measurement frameworks for the supply chain. However they note that the in tourism industry, demand is often met by the joint efforts of the many and various players in the industry. For this reason interdependency in tourism is high and value chains can be complex so there is room for better understanding and measurement of performance of value chains in tourism.

Balanced scorecard

Balanced scorecard: performance data from a range of an organisation's activities.

The balanced scorecard (Kaplan and Norton, 1996) as its name suggests, collects performance data from a range of an organisation's activities. It arose from three criticisms that have been levelled against over-reliance on financial performance indicators. These were first that they are too narrow, second that there is a significant lag between current performance and published financial data and third that they are too distant from direct management intervention to be of immediate practical use.

Advocates of the balanced scorecard approach suggest four areas that should be targeted for review: These are:

- Financial perspective (e.g. profit margins, revenue growth, costs, cash flow, net operating income)
- Customer perspective (e.g., market share, customer satisfaction)
- Internal process perspective (e.g. asset utilisation, supply chain management, customer management, innovation and relations with the external stakeholders)
- Innovation and learning perspective (e.g. human capital, information capital and organisation capital).

Phillips and Louvieris (2005) analysed performance measurement processes within ten small and medium sized enterprises in the UK hospitality industry using the balanced scorecard framework. They found that four key concepts were significant in the measurement and performance evaluation systems of their sample. These were budgetary control as a driver of increased total revenue, customer relationship management to improve service quality and customer retention, strategic management of internal business processes, and collaboration with other parties to enhance innovation and learning. The authors proposed performance indicators for a balanced scorecard template for hotels and these are summarised in Box 6.1.

Comparative analysis

Comparative analysis can be made by reference to:

- Longitudinal analysis
- Best practice.

Longitudinal analysis

Longitudinal analysis: compares data on performance over time.

This uses an organisation's historical record to compare data on performance over time. Typically annual reports compare current figures to those of the previous year but analysis of data over a longer period of time will reveal trends in the data. Care needs to be taken to understand the importance of unusual outside events which can cause short-term deviations in longitudinal figures.

Box 6.1: Phillips & Louvieris's (Phillips & Louvieris, 2005) template of performance indicators for a balanced scorecard for hotels

Financial Indicators
- Gross operating profit
- Net operating profit
- Sales achieved
- Adhering to budget
- Meeting financial targets
- Achieving predicted room and occupancy rates
- Revenue per available room
- Cash flow

Customer Related Indicators
- Guest surveys
- Mystery guest
- Participation in grading schemes
- Anecdotal feedback via staff
- Customer satisfaction levels
- Average spend
- Customer satisfaction levels
- Customer retention rate

Internal Business Indicators
- Meeting financial targets
- Internal auditing
- Completion of capital projects
- Staff satisfaction surveys
- Staff development reviews
- Staff retention rate percentage
- Wages (%) to achieve turnover
- Staff incentive schemes (e.g., performance-related pay)

Innovation/learning Indicators
- Number of new products/services
- Process improvement initiatives
- Networking relationships
- Membership of trade/professional bodies
- Participation in grading schemes
- Courses completed by staff
- Level of multiskilling
- Productivity

Best practice

Best practice: uses data from other organisations in an industry to provide information on the highest performance standards attainable

Best practice uses data from other organisations in an industry to provide information on the highest performance standards attainable. It can therefore be a useful tool for improving an organisation's competitive position. Ideally the choice of organisations to profile for best practice should ensure that they are of an equivalent size, have broadly similar product or service provision and that their customer base is comparable. Best practice analysis can result in the identification of benchmarks. A benchmark is a calibration that specifies the performance standards that an organisation wishes to attain.

Narayan *et al.* (2008) developed scales to measure and benchmark service quality in the tourism industry for destinations. They found that factors such as hospitality, security, food, logistics, and value for money have a significant impact on satisfaction, whilst factors such as fairness of price, amenities, core-tourism experience, hygiene, information centres, culture and personal information do not. The authors note that it is not necessary for a destination to have a natural cutting edge to be successful since good logistics, security, value for money, and quality hospitality and food can offer customer satisfaction.

Other benchmark research in tourism includes Moriarty and Simmons (2007) who conducted research into performance monitoring and benchmarking in tourism in New Zealand. Their studies use financial yield and a variety of operating ratios based on revenue. Min *et al.* (2008) sought to establish a financial benchmark for Korean hotels by developing a set of benchmarks that could demonstrate best practices and inform a successful hotel business model. Finally Hayllar *et al.* (2006) benchmarked caravan and tourist park operations in Australia

Evaluation of products

Part of an organisation's capability review will focus on an evaluation of current products. There are several methods of analysis including:

◊ Effectiveness
◊ Value chain analysis
◊ Portfolio analysis
◊ Product life-cycle analysis.

Whilst effectiveness and value chain analysis focus on current analysis of the product, portfolio and product life cycle analysis consider products in more strategic terms.

Effectiveness

Effectiveness: a measure of how well a particular objective is achieved

Effectiveness is a measure of how well a particular objective is achieved. Measures of product or service effectiveness may include:

◊ Consumer satisfaction with product
◊ Analysis of matching between product and market need
◊ Performance of product
◊ Comparison with competing products.

SERVQUAL: measures the gap between customer expectations and customer experience

SERVQUAL (Parasuraman *et al.*, 1988) is a service quality framework which can form a useful basis for understanding consumer satisfaction. It measures the gap between customer expectations and customer experience. It originally measured ten aspects of service quality. These were reliability, responsiveness, competence, access, courtesy, communication, credibility, security, understanding the customer and tangibles. Later the model was simplified to include the RATER (Buttle, 1996) elements of:

◊ Reliability
◊ Assurance
◊ Tangibles
◊ Empathy, and
◊ Responsiveness.

There have been many applications of SERQUAL and its derivatives in tourism and hospitality research. For example Tribe and Snaith (1998) studied the application of SERQUAL to destinations based on research in Cuba and modified it to arrive at the HOLSAT model. This looked at the specifics of holiday satisfaction and suggested that attributes used are not generic and should be developed for each particular destination. Truong and Foster (2006) studied the potential of Vietnam as a holiday destination for Australian travellers using the HOLSAT model. Fick and Ritchie (1991) examined the operation of the SERVQUAL scale and its management implications in four major sectors of the travel and tourism industry. Ramsaran-Fowdar (2007) investigated whether SERVQUAL dimensions are pertinent to the hotel industry. Results from their study in Mauritius verified SERVQUAL dimensions, but suggested the importance of additional dimensions specific to the hotel sector. Wang *et al.* (2008) analysed Chinese tourists' perceptions of UK hotel service quality using an adapted SERVQUAL questionnaire. Their findings revealed a number of shortcomings leading to negative consumer experiences. These were particularly evident on the empathy, reliability and tangible dimensions.

Value chain analysis

Value chain analysis can also be used to evaluate products and services and determine whether improvements or value added can be incorporated into a product's value chain. Table 6.2 adapts Table 6.1 and uses the value chain to raise questions relating to quality of service.

Table 6.2: Value chain for airline – quality

Element	Activity	
Preparation	Route availability	Is route system comprehensive and timings convenient?
	Advertising	Is advertising helpful for the customer?
	Information	Are queries responded to quickly?
	Reservations	Is the reservation system efficient?
Pre-flight	Arrival at airport	Are there queues?
	Check-in	Are staff helpful?
	Baggage handling	
	Departure Lounge	Are facilities comfortable?
	Boarding	
In flight	Seat location	Are seats comfortable?
	Seat size/comfort	Is there sufficient leg-room?
	Flight attendants	Are there sufficient flight attendants?
	Meal	Is their choice of meals?
	Entertainment	Is there a variety of entertainment?
	Other provision	
Post-flight	Baggage reclaim	Is the destination agent efficient?
	Airport transfer	
Follow up	Customer requests	Are customer requests met?
	Customer complaints	Are complaints dealt with quickly?

Portfolio analysis

Portfolio analysis: evaluates an organisation's range of products in terms of their market share and market growth

Portfolio analysis considers whether an organisation's range of products are well balanced with a particular view to the future. The Boston Consulting Group (BCG) matrix, which considers products in terms of their market share and market growth, may be used to assess the balance of an organisation's portfolio of products and this is illustrated in Figure 6.2.

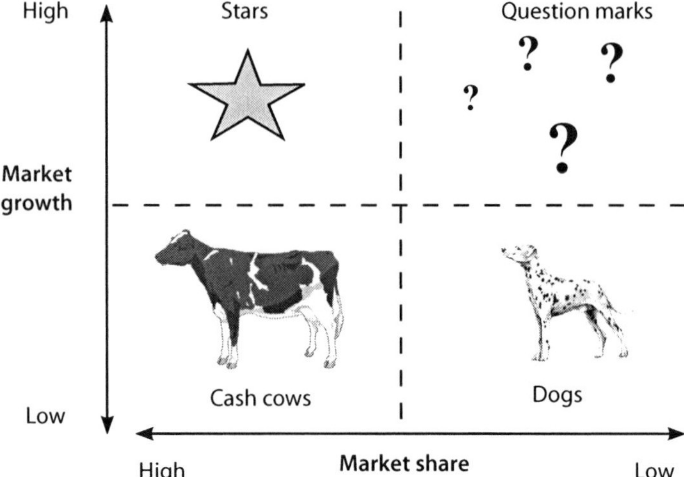

Figure 6.2: The BCG matrix. Adapted from: Boston Consulting Group, (1970)

Star products are those with a high market share in a fast growing market and cash cows have a high market share in a slow growth market. The BCG matrix helps plan the cash cows and stars of the future since in many cases these will be the question marks of today. However the development of question marks (low market share but high market growth) into future stars may require the profits that are derived from current stars and cash cows. Thus a balance of products across these parts of the matrix can represent a strength for an organisation. Products which are dogs exhibit low market share and low market growth and should be withdrawn unless their future prospects are good. It should be noted that profitability is not measured in the BCG matrix. It is thus implicitly assumed that cash cows and stars deliver profits from their high market share.

Product life-cycle analysis

Product life cycle: depicts the four main stages of development as introduction, growth, maturity and decline

Product life cycle (PLC) analysis (Vernon, 1979) is useful in considering the future success of a product, service or destination. Figure 6.3 depicts the four main stages of introduction, growth, maturity and decline, and the characteristics of these stages are tabulated in Table 6.3. Clearly products which are entering decline may need rejuvenation or replacement whereas market development may be appropriate for those in the growth phase.

Tourism services such as flights from London to New York can be located in the mature phase of the life cycle, whereas flights from Beijing to New York are in the growth phase. Other tourism products, such as the cruise holiday for younger age groups, can be placed on the growth phase of their product life cycle.

An organisation's potential strengths and weaknesses in terms of products and services can be identified using PLC and the BCG matrix. There are also clearly links between the PLC and the BCG matrix. In many cases, cash cows will be in the mature stage of the product life cycle, and may be used to finance question marks which will correspond to the introduction phase. However the BCG matrix also serves as a warning that products do not necessarily follow the path into growth and maturity but may end up as dogs.

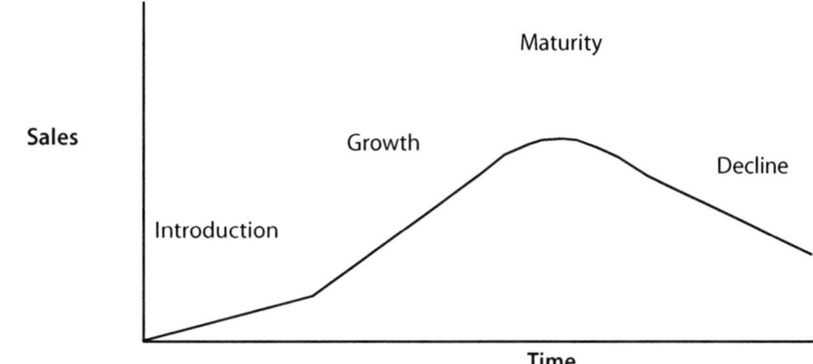

Figure 6.3: Product life cycle

Table 6.3: Characteristics of product life cycle

	Introduction	Growth	Maturity	Decline
Customers	Ignorance of product Scepticism of product	More awareness of product Growing demand	Mass market	Seeking new products Repeat customers
Competition	None or little	Growing	Consumer choice	Market saturated
Products	Changing standards and design Quality unproven	Quality improves	High reliability Standardisation	Overtaken by new products
Production	High costs	Mass production and economies of scale	Low production costs	Over capacity
Marketing	High advertising High prices	Marketing economies Reduce price	Segmentation Competitive strategy vital Reduce price	Seek to re-launch

Tourism area life cycle: exploration, involvement, development, consolidation and stagnation

Butler (1980) applied the PLC model to destinations where he developed the concept of a tourism area cycle evolution, substituting number of visitors for sales on the vertical axis. The stages identified in what came to be known as the 'tourism area life cycle' (TALC) were first exploration, characterised by a few initial visitors, followed by involvement where some facilities are developed. Development involves perhaps more external investment and more sophisticated and comprehensive facilities. A consolidation and stagnation phase represent a destination's journey into maturity where tourism has become a major local industry. Butler suggests that this may be followed by decline, reduced growth, stabilisation or rejuvenation, according to the policy chosen.

Cooper (1995) used the TALC model to place destinations as follows:

- ◊ Parts of Latin America and the Canadian Arctic (exploration phase)
- ◊ The less developed Pacific and Caribbean islands (involvement phase)
- ◊ Parts of Mexico and coastal Africa (development phase)
- ◊ North Mediterranean resorts (consolidation and stagnation phase)
- ◊ Atlantic City (USA) (rejuvenation phase).

Criticisms of PLC analysis are summarised by Witt *et al.* (1995) and include the lack of empirical validation for its shape, and the determinism implied by the cycle (i.e. that maturity and decline are unavoidable). When applied to a destination it is asked whether this is an appropriate level of aggregation since different geographical zones and market segments within a destination may reflect different stages of development. There is also evidence that the length of the PLC is shortening.

The TALC has been frequently examined and applied since it was first proposed by Butler in 1980. For example Agarwal (1997) tested the model in the context of seaside resort tourism along the south coast of Britain. She identified Butler's stages in the historical development of the resort of Torbay. But in trying to apply the model Agarwal found that the 'unit of analysis' was of crucial importance. Zhong *et al.* (2008) examined the applicability of the TALC model to China's Zhangjiajie National Forest Park. They conclude that the park has already experienced the first four stages of the tourist area cycle of evolution and that the park is now in the consolidation stage.

SWOT analysis

SWOT analysis: stands for Strengths, Weaknesses, Opportunities and Threats.

SWOT analysis stands for:

- ◊ Strengths
- ◊ Weaknesses
- ◊ Opportunities
- ◊ Threats.

SWOT can provide an insightful executive summary of the different elements of strategic analysis. Under SWOT, the opportunities and threats of an organisation's external environmental (see Chapters 4 and 5) and the strengths and weaknesses of its internal resource capability (see this chapter) are distilled and summarised into key factors. Figure 6.4 summarises the analytical techniques underlying a SWOT analysis.

Internal (resource) Analysis	Strengths	Weak
Resource audit	●	
Performance monitoring	●	
Evaluation of products	●	●
External (environmental) analysis	**Opportunities**	**Threats**
Competitive environment	●	●
Political environment	●	●
Economic environment	●	●
Socio-cultural environment	●	●
Technological environment	●	●

Figure 6.4: Components of SWOT analysis

Collins-Kreiner and Wall (2007) undertook a SWOT analysis for the potential of ecotourism in the Western Negev, Israel. They organised their analysis into national, regional and local level issues. Figure 6.5 summarises some of their findings at the regional level.

Strengths	Weaknesses
Natural and virgin environment	Peripheral nature of location
Unique desert and rural landscape	Scarcity of accommodation in the area
Crisis in agriculture	Few dining facilities in the area
Novelty of Western Negev	No obvious or distinct ethnic groups in the region
Strong community organization in the region	No direct highway links
Historical and archeological sites of the area (e.g. Tel Sharuchan).	Perceived of insecurity because of location near the Gaza strip
Area lies on major bird migration route	
Opportunities	**Threats**
Raw materials necessary to develop agri-tourism and rural tourism are present	Expansion of ecotourism in the Galilee region presents direct competition
Its isolation could constitute the area's allure	The political situation is a major unpredictable factor
Increased interest in ecotourism	Location near the Palestinian Authority territory
Low-cost carriers expansion into Israel	

Source: Adapted from Collins-Kreiner and Wall (2007)

Figure 6.5: SWOT Analysis for ecotourism in Western Negev, Israel

The strengths and weaknesses of the Canary Islands as a destination have been examined by Rodriguez-Diaz and Espino-Rodriguez (2008) and their main findings are summarised in Box 6.2.

Box 6.2: Strengths and weaknesses of the Canary Islands as a destination

Main strengths:

- Climate
- Beaches
- Winter season
- Airlines
- Four- and five-star hotels
- Foreign tour operators
- Golf courses
- Senior, gay and golf tourism
- Tourist security

Key weaknesses:

- Summer season
- Low-cost airlines
- The spanish market
- Alternative leisure offer
- Strategic planning
- Loyalty strategies
- Market research
- Promotions

Source: Rodriguez-Diaz & Espino-Rodriguez.

Yu and Huimin (2005) applied a SWOT analysis to the hotel industry in China. They found that the notable strengths included a growing market, the government's push to upgrade all hotel standards, China's place as a leading world destination and growing international hotel brands. Weaknesses included an overleveraged industry that has long been operated inefficiently by government entities. Opportunities were identified as hotel brand development, mixed-use projects and education and training. The most significant threats were seen as an economic slowdown, other events that interfere with tourist growth, regional political tensions and intensified competition (both international and domestic).

Ahmed *et al.* (2006) used SWOT analysis to perform a situational analysis on Air China, the largest air carrier in China measured by volume of traffic and company assets. Strengths found included ownership of a mostly updated fleet and expertise in repairs and maintenance. Additionally service quality is good, its reputation is high in international and domestic markets and it has attracted increasing loyalty through frequent flyers. A potential weakness is that its international business has been a lesser priority with resources and management time diverted to domestic operations. Opportunities include the fact that the growth of the Chinese airline industry exceeds that of GDP. Key threats are those of competition from world leading airlines and price wars as the Civil Aviation Administration of China deregulates the industry in fulfilment of WTO agreements.

Once the key SWOT elements have been identified, it can be productive to prepare a grid with strengths and weaknesses along the vertical axis, and opportunities and threats along the horizontal axis. This helps to indicate the extent to which an organisation has the capability to take advantage of opportunities or whether its weaknesses will prevent these opportunities from being realised.

Identification of an organisation's situational position by means of a SWOT analysis is an important phase prior to consideration of strategic options which is the subject of the next chapter. Appropriate strategies are likely to:

- ◊ Align opportunities and strengths
- ◊ Transform weaknesses
- ◊ Overcome threats.

Review of key terms

- Resources: physical resources, human resources, financial resources, and intangibles
- Appraisal: setting employee objectives and instigating a periodic system of review.
- Profit: revenue minus cost
- Earnings per share: total earnings divided by the number of shares in issue
- Price/earnings ratio: price per share divided by annual earnings per share
- ROCE: earnings before interest and tax divided by capital employed
- Profit margin: earnings before interest and tax divided by total sales
- RevPAR: rooms revenue divided by rooms available
- Efficiency: the ratio of outputs to inputs
- Liquidity: the amount of cash in hand, or near at hand available to a company
- Value chain: set of connected activities that make up the total service provision
- Balanced scorecard: performance data from a range of an organisation's activities.
- Longitudinal analysis: uses an organisation's historical record to compare data on performance over time.
- Best practice: uses data from other organisations in an industry to provide information on the highest performance standards attainable
- Effectiveness: a measure of how well a particular objective is achieved
- SERVQUAL: measures the gap between customer expectations and customer experience
- Portfolio analysis: evaluates an organisation's range of products in terms of their market share and market growth
- Product life cycle: depicts the four main stages of development as introduction, growth, maturity and decline
- Tourism area life cycle: exploration, involvement, development, consolidation and stagnation
- SWOT analysis: stands for Strengths, Weaknesses, Opportunities and Threats.

Multiple choice questions

1 Which of the following is an intangible resource?
   A Corporate image
   B Human resources
   C Transport
   D Machinery

2 Which of the following is true?
   A Profit = Revenue + Costs
   B Earnings per share = The number of shares in issue/total earnings
   C Price/earnings ratio = Price per share/annual earnings per share
   D Return on capital employed = Rooms revenue/rooms available

3 Which of the following is not part of a balanced scorecard?
   A Financial perspective
   B Customer perspective
   C Historic costing perspective
   D Innovation and learning perspective

4 Which of the following is true for BCG analysis?
   A Dogs have high market share
   B Cash cows have low market growth
   C Question marks have high market growth
   D Stars have high low market growth.

5 Which of the following is not a phase in the tourism area life cycle theory?
   A Exploration
   B Involvement
   C Exploitation
   D Stagnation

Discussion questions

1 Use the RATER (Buttle, 1996) elements of: Reliability, Assurance, Tangibles, Empathy and Responsiveness to carry out a quality audit on a named tourism service. Identify any service gaps and make recommendations.

2 What is value chain analysis? Conduct a value chain analysis for a hotel which focuses on ways of either:
   reducing costs or
   improving service.

3 Identify the position on a Boston Box of the main products of a named tourism organisation. What conclusions can you reach about the balance of the portfolio of products and what points for future planning emerge from this exercise?

4 To what extent can the concept of product life cycles be used to analyse destinations (Butler, 1980)?

5 What is the purpose of a SWOT analysis? Conduct a SWOT analysis for a tourism entity.

References

Agarwal, S. (1997) The resort cycle and seaside tourism: an assessment of its applicability and validity. *Tourism Management*, **18**, 65-73.

Ahmed, A.M., Zairi, M. and Almarri, K.S. (2006) SWOT analysis for Air China performance and its experience with quality. *Benchmarking: An International Journal*, **13**, 160-172.

Butler, R. (1980) Concept of a tourism area cycle evolution: implications for management of resources. *Canadian Geographer*, **24**, 5-12.

Buttle, F. (1996) SERVQUAL: review, critique, research agenda. *European Journal of Marketing*, **30**, 8-32.

Collins-Kreiner, N. and Wall, G. (2007) Evaluating tourism potential: a SWOT analysis of the Western Negev, Israel. *Tourism (Zagreb)*, **55**, 51-63.

Cooper, C.P. (1995) Tourist product life cycle. In S.F. Witt and L. Moutinho (eds), *Tourism Marketing and Management Handbook*, Hemel Hempstead: Prentice Hall, pp. 577-585.

Fick, G.R. and Ritchie, B. (1991) Measuring service quality in the travel and tourism industry. *Journal of Travel Research*, **30**, 2.

Hayllar, B., Crilley, G., Bell, B., and Archer, D. (2006) Benchmarking caravan and tourist park operations. *Tourism Today*, 112-133.

Kaplan, R.S. and Norton, D.P. (1996) Using the balanced scorecard as a strategic management system. *Harvard Business Review*, **74**, 75-87.

Min, H., Min, H., Joo, S.J. and Kim, J. (2008) A data envelopment analysis for establishing the financial benchmark of Korean hotels. *International Journal of Services and Operations Management*, **4**, 201-217.

Moriarty, J. and Simmons, D.G. (2007) Enhancing financial and economic yield in tourism: business interviews: financial yield benchmarks, Christchurch, NZ: Lincoln University. Tourism Recreation Research and Education Centre.

Narayan, B., Rajendran, C. and Sai, L.P. (2008) Scales to measure and benchmark service quality in tourism industry. *Benchmarking: An International Journal*, **15**, 469-493.

Parasuraman, A., Zeithaml, V. and Berry, L. (1988) SERVQUAL: a multiple-item scale for measuring consumer perceptions of service quality. *Journal of Retailing*, **64**, 12-40.

Phillips, P. and Louvieris, P. (2005) Performance measurement systems in tourism, hospitality, and leisure small medium-sized enterprises: a balanced scorecard perspective. *Journal of Travel Research*, **44**, 201-211.

Porter, M.E. (1990) The competitive advantage of nations. *Harvard Business Review*, March and April, 74-91.

Ramsaran-Fowdar, R.R. (2007) Developing a service quality questionnaire for the hotel industry in Mauritius. *Journal of Vacation Marketing*, **13**, 19.

Rodriguez-Diaz, M. and Espino-Rodriguez, T.F. (2008) A model of strategic evaluation of a tourism destination based on internal and relational capabilities. *Journal of Travel Research*, **46**, 368-380.

Tribe, J. and Snaith, T. (1998) From SERVQUAL to HOLSAT: holiday satisfaction in Varadero, Cuba. *Tourism Management*, **19**, 25-34.

Truong, T.H. and Foster, D. (2006) Using HOLSAT to evaluate tourist satisfaction at destinations: the case of Australian holidaymakers in Vietnam. *Tourism Management*, **27**, 842-855.

Vernon, R. (1979) The product life cycle hypothesis in a new industrial environment. *Oxford Bulletin of Economics and Statistics*, **41**, 255-267.

Wang, Y., Vela, M.R. and Tyler, K. (2008) Cultural perspectives: Chinese perceptions of UK hotel service quality. *Tourism and Hospitality Research*, **2**, 312-329.

Witt, S.F., Brooke, M.Z. and Buckley, P.J. (1995) *The Management of International Tourism*. London: Routledge.

Yilmaz, Y. and Bititci, U. (2006) Performance measurement in the value chain: manufacturing v. tourism. *International Journal of Productivity and Performance Management*, **55**, 371-389.

Yu, L. and Huimin, G. (2005) Hotel reform in China: a SWOT analysis. *Cornell Hotel and Restaurant Administration Quarterly*, **46**, 153.

Zhang, X., Song, H. and Huang, G.Q. (2009) Tourism supply chain management: a new research agenda. *Tourism Management*, **30**, 345-358.

Zhong, L., Deng, J. and Xiang, B. (2008) Tourism development and the tourism area life-cycle model: a case study of Zhangjiajie National Forest Park, China. *Tourism Management*, **29**, 841-856.

Part III
Strategic Choice

The next stage of strategy for tourism is strategic choice and by the end of Part III it should be possible to propose and justify a particular strategy for a tourism entity. Strategic choice follows logically from the previous two stages. Strategic analysis resulted in a summary of the opportunities and threats evident in the tourism organisation's external environment and of its internal strengths and weaknesses and it is in the light of this analysis that strategy can be formulated, guided by the organisation's mission. A framework for strategic choice is developed to assist tourism entities in the development of an appropriate strategy.

Chapter 7 introduces the main types of strategy, using Porter's (1998) generic strategies as a starting point.

Chapter 8 considers the directions methods by which an organisation can pursue its strategy.

Chapter 9 offers a template that can be used to evaluate competing strategies so that an appropriate strategy can be chosen. The appropriateness of a strategy will clearly depend on its ability to fulfil the organisation's mission by exploiting strengths and opportunities and counteracting weaknesses and threats.

7 Strategic Options

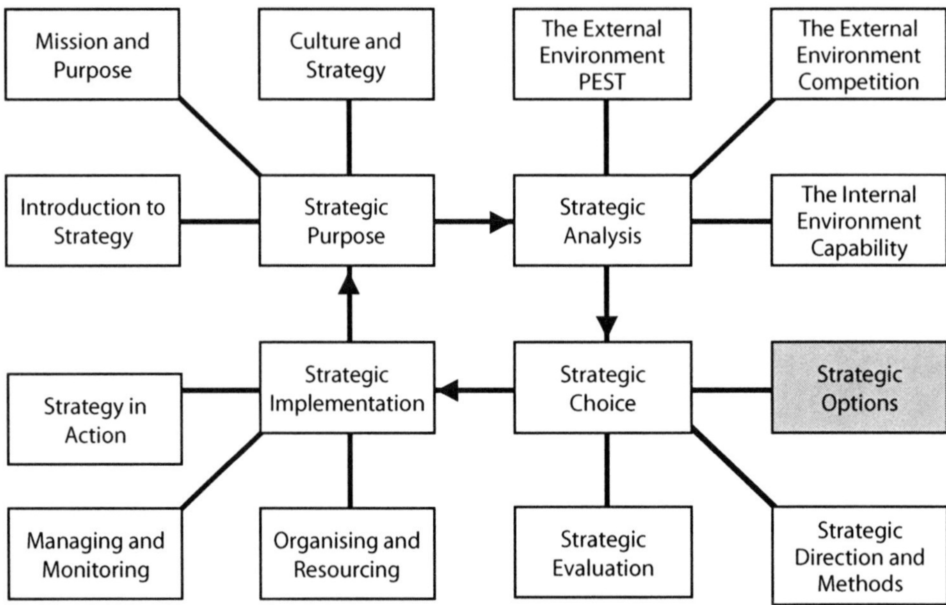

Figure 7.1

Learning outcomes

After studying this chapter and related materials you should be able to understand:

- Porter's generic strategies
- Critiques of Porter
- Price-based strategies
- Differentiation-based strategies
- Hybrid strategies
- Focus strategies
- Elasticity and margins
- Sustaining competitive advantage
- Game theory

and critically evaluate, explain and apply the above concepts.

Introduction

This chapter examines the strategic options available to tourism entities in order to obtain competitive advantage or some alternative mission. As an example Ooi (2002) analysed and contrasted the strategies of Singapore and Copenhagen as tourism destinations. The chapter starts by looking at Porter's (1998) generic strategies. It then considers some of the criticisms made of Porter's framework and introduces a framework that adapts Porter using the work of Bowman (Bowman and Faulkner, 1995). Using this framework, possible strategies are characterised as those which are price-based, differentiation-based or a hybrid combination of these. Additionally, the option of a focused strategy is discussed. Elasticity of demand is then introduced to understand the logic of the two basic strategies. Finally, pursuing a strategy will cause reaction from competitors. Here game theory can help the understanding of possible outcomes and ways of sustaining competitive advantage are discussed.

Case study 7 illustrates how Accor Hospitality pursues price-based, differentiation-based and hybrid strategies through its different groups of brands.

Case Study 7: Accor Hospitality Worldwide

Accor Hospitality is a global player with more than 40 years of expertise in its two core businesses of hotels and services. Accor operates in 100 countries with more than 150,000 employees and its brands represent around 4000 hotels and provide 500,000 rooms. Accor occupies a unique position as the world's only hotel operator that covers all the main market segments. The five segments and the associated hotel brands are:

- Luxury: Sofitel
- Upscale: Pullman, MGallery
- Midscale: Novotel, Mercure, Suitehotel, Adagio
- Economy: Ibis, All seasons
- Budget: Etap, Hotel, Formule 1, hotelF1 and Motel 6

Its luxury and upscale brands represent 9 per cent of its available rooms with midscale and economy rooms representing 36 per cent and the final 55 per cent accounted for by budget brands. It also owns Accor Thalassa (a spa operator) and other strategically related businesses, Lenôtre (a restaurant business) and Compagnie des Wagonlits (a travel logistics company).

In common with many global hotel corporations Accor has moved from a business model based mainly on hotel ownership to a model with a focus on management and franchise contracts. Accor has therefore become a services supplier rather than a property owner. It owns 22 per cent of its properties, leases 36 per cent with 44 per cent franchised or managed. Its key core competences include its broad portfolio of brands, strong brand recognition good repeat business, its investment in innovation to develop its brands and its expertise in revenue development, cost optimisation and room development and management.

Luxury and Upscale

The Sofitel network, comprising 126 luxury hotels, is Accor's luxury brand with the slogan 'Life is Magnifique'. The aim of Sofitel is to deepen its positioning in the luxury market and one key to this is its emphasis on unique, non-standardized luxury hotels. These are decorated by well-known designers and aim to echo the history and environments of their locations, mixing authenticity and tradition. Other features of this brand are a commitment to exceptional service, high specification multimedia equipment and state of the art health and fitness amenities. Sofitel also puts a strong emphasis on the comfort of its beds and its gastronomy where it has forged links with Michelin star chefs. A development priority for Sofitel is to have a presence all major destinations and international capital cities. Sofitel has partnerships with airline companies, American Express and Visa International. Alongside Sofitel is Pullman, a new network of standardised upscale hotels, that was launched in 2007 with a particular aim to appeal to the business and convention segment of the market. Its slogan is 'Check In. Chill Out'.

Midscale and economy

At the heart of the midscale and economy segment are Novotel and Mercure. Novotels are located in main international destinations and focus on business and leisure travellers. Mercure is one of the largest hotel networks in the world with an expansion strategy aimed at creating a strong network in each country where it operates with a particular emphasis on expansion in Europe and new markets in Asia. Ibis is the economy hotel brand of the Accor group offering quality accommodation at competitive local value. It underlines its commitment to quality with its '15 minute satisfaction guarantee' where the hotel team gives itself 15 minutes to find a solution to any room malfunction failing which the guest stays for free. The Ibis growth strategy is to concentrate on emerging markets, particularly in Asia and Latin America. Additionally All Seasons is a chain of non-standardised economy hotels launched in 2007 to strengthen Accor's global leadership in the economy segment mainly using franchising. Its unique selling points are simplicity, an all-inclusive offer, conviviality, interactivity and quality. Each of these midscale and economy brands offers quality standards and value for money.

Budget

The emphasis of Accor's budget brands is affordable no-frills accommodation. Here Motel 6 is the brand leader in the budget hotel market in the United States having been established in 1962. Its guarantee is to offer best price value at all of its locations. Formule1 was established in France in 1984 and introduced the low-cost hotel model to Europe. Since then it has had many imitators. It hotels are functional and cheap, the low price coming from a standardised offering in clean but basic accommodation in sub-prime locations. Its referents would be Ryanair in air travel and McDonald's restaurants. Accor has a development plan that includes expansion in Western Europe in the economy and budget segments, increasing market share through franchising in mature markets, strengthening its position in emerging (esp. BRIC) countries and expanding its upscale and luxury network through management agreements.

Source: http://www.accor.com/en/group.html

Porter's generic strategies

Generic strategy: a strategy of a particular type or form designed to promote a lasting competitive advantage.

A generic strategy is a strategy of a particular type or form designed to promote a lasting competitive advantage for an organisation. According to Porter (1998), organisations are able to secure a competitive advantage by choosing a generic strategy that fits best with its situational position in terms of its external environment and resource capabilities. It should then organise its capability to best deliver and support the chosen strategy.

Porter (1998) identified three generic strategies that organisations could use to achieve competitive advantage. He argued that it was important for organisations to be clear about which strategy was being followed and that lack of a clear strategy could result in muddle and confusion. Porter's generic strategies are:

- ◊ Cost leadership
- ◊ Differentiation
- ◊ Focus.

Cost leadership: becoming the lowest cost provider in an industry.

Cost leadership involves an organisation becoming the lowest cost provider in an industry and Porter's logic for this strategy was that if a firm can charge industry-average prices, but sustains below industry-average costs it will be an above average performer.

Differentiation: seeking product or service uniqueness.

A differentiation strategy is where an organisation seeks product or service uniqueness. It will attempt to establish real (by product design) or perceived (by advertising) differences between its products and those of its competitors so that a premium price can be charged without loss of customers. Porter's logic for a differentiation strategy is that an organisation can be an above industry-average performer if the price premium exceeds the extra costs of providing differentiation.

Focus strategy: a strategy tailored towards a particular market segment.

A focused strategy occurs where a strategy is tailored towards a particular market segment rather than to the whole market and may take the form of cost focus or differentiation focus. A successful focus strategy needs to identify and serve a group of customers that form a distinct market segment. Geographic location can form the basis for focus. Dubai for example offers differentiation focus with its emphasis on ultra quality hotels. Club 18–30 is focused on a specific age group.

Problems with Porter

Problems with Porter's generic strategies arise first from their application to tourism and second from their internal logic. For example, some commentators have noted that Porter's typology is more applicable to manufacturing and that problems arise with their direct application to tourism. Poon (2003) concludes that Porter's generic strategies have little value in today's tourism industry and identified four principles that she viewed as essential for an effective tourism strategy:

- ◊ Put customers first
- ◊ Be a leader in quality
- ◊ Develop radical innovations
- ◊ Strengthen the firm's strategic position within the value chain.

However these principles can be accommodated in an adapted version of Porter, and price remains an important part of strategy which Poon does not sufficiently highlight.

Next, the problems of the internal logic of Porter's typology are addressed. Cost leadership is a problematic concept for several reasons. First, many of the routes to lower costs are easily followed by competitors and therefore cost leadership may be elusive. It is perhaps only where a firm can achieve economies of scale by market leadership that costs may be reduced without compromising the quality of output. Second, where cost leadership is achieved by stripped-down products, consumers are unlikely to pay industry-average price. In this case, price may well follow costs down and in doing so reduce any extra margins. Third there is a tendency for Porter to use the terms 'cost' and 'price' interchangeably. But they are very different – the first measuring input costs (paid by firms) and the second measuring market prices (paid by consumers).

Differentiation may be misinterpreted by managers as being merely a matter of improved technique of production. What is more important in terms of selling a product or service is the notion of consumer perception – does a particular product offer improved quality or value added over the competition in the eyes of the consumer?

Additionally Porter's typology polarises cost leadership and differentiation. Porter drew attention to organisations who were 'stuck in the middle' between cost leadership and differentiation. But there is evidence that many organisations seek to operate in a hybrid region which encompasses both low costs whilst attempting to market a distinctive product. Finally it is argued that it is the development of core competences that give an organisation competitive advantage rather than following generic strategies and therefore competence strategies have superseded generic strategies.

Figure 7.2: Price/Quality matrix

Porter adapted

Bowman and Faulkner (Bowman and Faulkner, 1995) and Johnson *et al.* (2008) have sought to rework Porter's typology of generic strategies to take into account some of the issues raised above. In particular their typology is adapted to reflect the consumer view of things and make it market facing. This takes account of the fact that consumers are more sensitive to prices than costs, and consider perceived quality or value added rather than differentiation. Both Bowman and Faulkner and Johnson *et al.* make use of a 'Strategy Clock' to illustrate strategy options. However these can also be understood using a simple matrix and Figure 7.2 illustrates a price/quality strategy matrix incorporating these ideas.

Price-based strategies

Price-based strategy: reducing costs and prices.

Price-based strategy is similar to cost leadership, but emphasises the fact that low costs need to be passed on to the customer in the form of lower prices. One of the key ways to achieve price leadership is by offering a basic, no-frills product or service with inessential aspects stripped out. A price-focused organisation will be engaged in a perpetual struggle to minimise the costs of its inputs – mainly labour and raw materials. Mass production techniques can also be an important element in price-based strategies. This is because mass production enables economies of scale to be achieved including the reduction of costs by bulk purchasing and the discounts associated with this. To sustain economies of scale, market share may be fought for to achieve the size that brings lower average production costs. Location of production or services under price-based strategies will avoid high cost areas and opt for locations where labour costs and land costs are cheap. The provision of simplified and standardised outputs and systems can also contribute to price reductions. Value chain analysis (see Chapter 6) can help tourism entities identify cost savings throughout the whole value chain.

Low cost carriers such as Ryanair, SouthWest Airlines, Kingfisher and Air Asia have based much of their success on price-based strategies and Box 7.1 lists some of the methods they adopt to attain price competiveness.

Box 7.1 Methods used by low-cost carriers to attain price competiveness

- Operate simple point-to-point services: avoids the complexities and costs of interconnecting flights
- Operate a fleet from a single manufacturer: simplifies training and maintenance, cuts costs and offers scale economies in purchasing aircraft.
- Use of agencies to supply a proportion of pilots and crew: avoids high fixed costs.
- Turn around aircraft in 25 minutes: maximises deployment of major assets.
- No seat allocation: achieves faster turnaround.
- No seat pockets: less rubbish, faster turnaround.

- Operate from secondary airports: cheaper landing fees, less air traffic control delays.
- Charge for checked baggage: reduces baggage handling costs.
- Use dynamic pricing to ensure high load factors: reduces average costs.
- Does not allow staff to charge mobile phones on company premises: underlines a culture of cost savings.
- Encourage on-line check-in: reduces check in staff and costs.
- No free in-flight catering: reduces costs.
- Cross-sell services via website: subsidises low fares.
- Invest in IT: efficient web sales reduce distribution costs.
- Adopt ticket-less e-travel: reduces administration costs.
- Use free publicity and PR: reduces advertising costs.

Price-based strategies also drive the business models of other parts of the tourism industry. For example:

◊ **McDonald's restaurants**: its use of standardised products and processes, self-service, self-clearing up and huge economies of scale are key factors enabling low prices.

◊ **Hotel Première Classe** (France): hotels are located where land prices are cheap but demand strong (e.g. industrial estates near motorway junctions). Fittings are standardised and with no frills. Use of automation reduces labour costs.

◊ **Cheap package holidays**: these cut costs all along the value chain. Internet sales reduce distribution costs. The use of charter flights with high load factors, night flights and secondary airports, together with coach transfers reduce transport costs. High density, no-frills hotels in mass tourism destinations and bulk buying power reduce accommodation costs. Vertical integration along the supply chain reduces 'middleman' costs.

Differentiation-based strategies

This is similar to Porter's differentiation strategy, but with an emphasis on providing extra qualities w hich are valued by the consumer. This value added may be provided by:

◊ Design
◊ Exploitation of the value chain
◊ Advertising.

Differentiation needs to be sustained by innovation, research and development and market intelligence. Investment in research and development is a route to providing products which are different from those of competitors in terms of better design or quality and durability. Another key to product differentiation is thorough market research to discover and deliver product differences which are important to the consumer.

The most obvious differentiation technique is to enhance product or service quality. This may be through design, or quality of materials and workmanship, performance or inclusion of luxury features and extras. Quality of service can also offer a point of differentiation. This can include knowledge and expertise of sales staff, high provision of service staff, personalised service, selection and training of service staff and quality of after-sales care. Branding and promotion can also contribute strongly to differentiating a product or service from those provided by competitors. The value chain (see Chapter 6) can be used to indicate the range of activities associated with the delivery of a service or product where distinctive extras can be built in.

Legacy carriers such as British Airways, Emirates and Singapore Airlines as well as newer carriers such as Virgin Atlantic all emphasise the differentiated characteristics of their first class services and examples of these are presented in Box 7.2.

Box 7.2 Examples of differentiated characteristics of first class services of legacy carriers

- Fully refundable/changeable tickets
- Valet parking or limousine/helicopter transfers
- Express check-in, fast-track security clearance and priority boarding and disembarking
- VIP lounges with office facilities, free drinks, restaurants, entertainment, showers and massage
- Pre-flight drinks, limitless champagne, walk-up bar area
- Quiet cabin, spacious seating, that converts into a full length bed, personal cabins
- Flexible meal times, gourmet food, vintage wines, fine china
- State of the art entertainment systems
- Personalised service
- Generous loyalty and reward schemes

Differentiation-based strategies also drive the business models of other parts of the tourism industry. For example:

◊ **7* hotels:** in 2010 two hotels attempted to differentiate themselves as self-rated 'seven star' hotels. These are the Burj Al Arab in Dubai, United Arab Emirates and the Town House Galleria in Milan, Italy. The Burj Al Arab Hotel offers guests a chauffeur driven Rolls Royce, discreet in-suite check-in, a private reception desk on every floor and a private butler service. It is located in the exclusive Jumeirah Beach area of Dubai and its Royal Suite offers private elevator access, a private cinema and a rotating four-poster canopy bed.

◊ **St Moritz, Switzerland**: this is a destination that has managed to cultivate an up-market exclusive image and appeal to the luxury end of the market.

Its very expense differentiates it from other destinations and its popularity amongst celebrities helps to differentiate it from competing destinations and sustain its elite and glamorous image.

- ◊ **Hong Kong, China**: Okumus *et al.* (2007) used content analysis of booklets, websites and brochures to demonstrate how Hong Kong makes extensive use of food and its unique cuisine as part of its destination marketing. The authors point to this as an important point of differentiation in relation to other destinations.
- ◊ **The Michelin Star** rating of restaurants can provide a distinctive marker of differentiation. Restaurants are assessed over the following criteria:
  - The quality of the products
  - The mastery of flavour and cooking
  - The 'personality' of the cuisine
  - The value for the money
  - The consistency between visits.

  Three stars is the highest rating which means 'Exceptional cuisine and worth the journey'. In 2010 there were less than one hundred 3* rated restaurants including El Bulli (Roses, Spain), The Fat Duck (Bray, UK), Lung King Heen (Hong Kong, China) and L'Osier (Tokyo, Japan).

Gu (2006) examines the importance of product differentiation in revenue management strategies for destinations. This research, based on Macau, offers recommendations on how to maintain gaming revenue growth in the face of strong competition from emerging gaming destinations in Asia using product differentiation. The article notes that Macau has developed its gaming market by bringing in Las Vegas operators. It is noted that this should help modernise its gaming industry but the continued proliferation of destinations using the same Las Vegas-style in the region threatens to remove Macau's market advantage. The author proposes a revenue management strategy whereby Macau should provide a differentiated gaming experience to distinguish itself from competing destinations. The article recommends the enhancement of traditional VIP room operations as an effective way to achieve this goal.

Croes (2006) carried out research on appropriate strategies for the Caribbean. The article notes that the small island states which typify the destinations of the region lack the size to bring economies of scale to their tourism offering and therefore find it difficult to compete on costs and prices. It is concluded that strategies should concentrate on the demand side and a strategy based on four key areas is proposed to consolidate and add to value in the Caribbean. The four factors are first bringing the Caribbean closer to customers; second, the need for the region to identify price elasticities of its various products; third, better understanding of and action in the market to develop unique products; and fourth, strengthening resource planning to encourage refurbishment, regeneration and upgrading with a view to generating quality enhancement.

Miller *et al.* (2008) note the considerable potential that Cuba offers for competitiveness within the Caribbean regional tourism industry and address the question as to whether Cuba can to realise this potential. The authors analyse the position of the Cuban tourism industry using models of competitive advantage. They find that Cuba has implemented ambitious competitive strategies but that execution of these has been less-focused and this has diminished their potential. The article suggests that a careful analysis of Cuba's competitive positioning could provide the basis for greater success and enhanced regional cooperation.

Hybrid strategies

Hybrid strategy: providing high quality products and services at low prices.

A hybrid strategy is an attempt to provide high quality products and services at low prices. It seems contradictory because adding quality adds to costs which should preclude low prices. The key to a successful hybrid strategy is therefore to reduce average costs.

The first route to this is achieving of economies of scale where average costs fall as output increases. Mass production, bulk buying, labour specialisation and economies of increased dimensions become significant as output increases. Economies of scale are therefore open to firms which can achieve high market share, and a virtuous circle as illustrated in Figure 7.3 may become established.

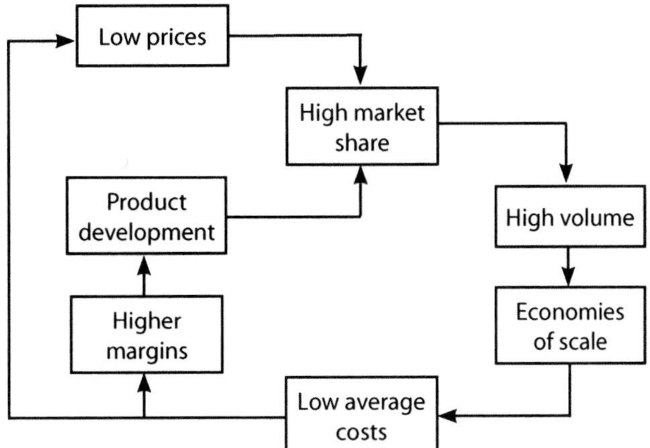

Figure 7.3: Route to hybrid strategy

The second route, important to service providers such as tourism organisations, is to ensure high load factors. Hotels, airlines and attractions all face high fixed costs and a perishable product. An unfilled room is revenue lost forever. Computerised reservation systems can help achieve high load factors, and thus dissipate fixed costs, bringing average costs down.

Virgin Blue is an example of an airline following a hybrid strategy. Virgin Blue operates in Australia and describes how it has:

> *evolved into a new type of network carrier, a New World Carrier, an airline that provides high value and exceptional service at low cost. As a New World Carrier, Virgin Blue offers a product and service distinctly different to that of traditional 'no frills' low-cost carriers and different again to traditional legacy carriers. (Virgin Blue, 2008)*

Virgin explains how it offers innovative products, services and features that extend to the needs of corporate and government travellers but maintains the significant cost advantage of a low-cost carrier. It states that:

> *Unlike traditional 'no frills' low-cost carriers, Virgin Blue's approach is to offer consistently affordable fares, outstanding service and a host of other options available on a pay for use basis.(Virgin Blue, 2008)*

As well as low prices it offers national network coverage, high quality airport facilities, through-checked baggage, greater seat pitch than its competitors, interlining and code-sharing options and a free award winning frequent flier programme. Additionally it offers in-flight meals, premium seating, fully flexible fares and airport lounge facilities as optional extras.

Virgin Blue –
A New World Carrier

Focused strategies

Price-based and differentiation strategies may each be focused on a particular market segment and it is increasingly common for organisations to seek to serve a number of different market segments. Focused strategies are evident in the tourism industry.

- ◊ In the hotels sectors IHG operates both InterContinental and Formule 1 hotels.
- ◊ In the airline industry Qantas offers four different classes of travel – Economy, Premium Economy, Business Class and First Class.
- ◊ At the destination level, the island of Mallorca, Spain offers holidays to both mass budget tourists (e.g. the resorts of Magaluf and Palma Nova) as well as to the upscale segment of the market (e.g. Deja).

There are potential difficulties where organisations offer a range of focused strategies. First it is possible that knowledge of a price-based segment may spoil the image of an overall brand. For example Mallorca finds it difficult to overcome its image of a cheap mass tourism resort and this image may put off potential tourists from its upscale provision. Second it is important to identify distinct products or services so that there is minimum leakage between low price and high quality services. For example transport operators keep their focused strategies separate from each other by imposing conditions to stop a mass movement from high-priced services to low-price offers. The latter may include conditions such as:

◊ No refunds or changes
◊ Minimum / maximum periods of stay
◊ Advance booking
◊ Availability on limited services.

Zone X

Zone X: a combination of high prices and low quality.

Zone X (Tribe, 1997) in Figure 7.2 represents a combination of high prices and low quality and will generally therefore lead to failure. However there are exceptions to this. First, where an organisation has a monopoly it can operate in Zone X without fear of losing customers since they have no choice. Local transportation may operate under conditions of monopoly in some areas.

Second, where consumers have lack of information about quality, or competitive prices, Zone X strategies may persist. Generally Zone X strategies will result in customers not returning and thus Zone X organisations will exist only in the short term. But tourist areas represent a potential site within which organisations may operate such strategies since new and naive tourists are continually arriving. Restaurants, hotels and taxis may be able to operate Zone X strategies under such conditions.

Elasticity and margins

Elasticity of demand: the responsiveness of demand to a change in price.

Understanding elasticity of demand can be helpful to organisations when looking at strategic options. Elasticity of demand measures the responsiveness of demand to a change in price. Its definition is:

$$\text{Elasticity of demand} = \frac{\text{percentage change in quantity demanded}}{\text{percentage change in price}}$$

Where demand is sensitive to changes in price, demand is said to be elastic and where a change in price has less of an effect on demand it is inelastic.

A price leadership strategy will therefore be appropriate in a market or market segment where demand is elastic. This is because for any percentage reduction in price, demand will rise by a greater percentage. Since revenue earned is price × quantity sold then a reduction in price should lead to a rise in total revenue. On the other hand, increasing price to cover the extra costs of differentiation has the danger that demand will fall reducing total revenue earned. Elasticity theory helps us to understand that effective differentiation strategies will result in demand becoming more inelastic. So the aim of differentiation in quality, design and branding should be to create uniqueness and brand loyalty and thereby reduce direct competition. This will cause demand to become more inelastic so that a given percentage increase in price leads to a smaller percentage fall in demand so that total revenue will increase.

It is also essential that organisations keep an eye on their profit margins when choosing a strategy. Actions which only consider low prices or high quality will fail unless associated costs are also considered. Above all, a sustainable level of margin is necessary to provide funds for investment for future cycles of competitive positioning.

Sustaining competitive advantage

The degree of competition within an industry will influence the position adopted by an organisation in Figure 7.2. The greater the competition, the more an organisation will be forced to deliver greater value added and or lower price (away from Zone X). Less competition means more of a likelihood of strategy drifting towards Zone X.

One of the key challenges faced by organisations in more competitive markets is that their strategy can be readily imitated by other organisations. Cost reductions by one airline are often soon followed by others. All this does is reduce margins and profits since any initial competitive advantage is lost. Similarly airlines who offer first-class travel find themselves in quality wars. Flat beds are overtaken by private cabins and free transfers are overtaken by chauffeur-driven limousine services. Again any initial competitive advantage can be lost and rising costs will reduce margins and profits.

The following may help organisations to maintain their competitive advantage:

- ◊ Becoming the industry leader. Being known for the cheapest or the best can become self-reinforcing and produce a virtuous circle of success.
- ◊ Protecting invention and innovation through patents.
- ◊ Maintaining leadership through innovation and organisational responsiveness.
- ◊ Cross-subsidisation from elsewhere in an organisation's business portfolio where competition is less.
- ◊ Exploiting 'deep pockets' that is substantial surplus financial resources.
- ◊ Concentrating on a set of organisational capabilities that are difficult to replicate. Whilst competitors can often imitate single initiatives (e.g. price) it may be possible to sustain competitive advantage by creating a unique organisational culture or team or expertise generated out of group dynamics.
- ◊ Collaboration to obtain competitive advantage.
- ◊ Seeking the benefits of clustering. Clustering is a geographic concentration of suppliers, similar businesses and associated entities that serve an interconnected field of activity.

- ◊ Revolutionising the business model. Low-cost carriers invented a model that was so different from that of legacy carriers that the latter struggle to replicate its advantages.

Poon (2003) emphasises the importance of innovation in maintaining competitive advantage in tourism. She discusses the importance of the formation and sustenance of continuous clusters of innovation (p. 139). She illustrates this point by reference to:

> *A detailed comparative analysis of the Jamaican SuperClub hotel in Jamaica and the Benetton clothing concern in Italy [which] revealed unambiguously that the ability of these organisations to evolve continuous clusters of innovation were vital ingredients in the success of both enterprises.*

Clusters can bring external economies of scale to organisations (i.e. economies which result from concentrations of similar entities). These can include labour force skills, a localised pool of specialised knowledge and expertise, supplier economies and regional reputation.

Hassan (2000) draws attention to the importance of environmental sustainability when evaluating models of competitiveness for travel destinations. The article notes the number, range and diversity of industries involved in planning and development in destinations. Because of this, it is argued that any model of competitiveness needs to take account of the relationships among all stakeholders involved in creating and integrating value-added in products and services. A key challenge is to sustain a destination's resources at the same time as competing for market position with rival destinations. The author stresses the need to systematically exploit unique comparative advantages that can provide long-term appeal to the target travel customer segments. It is concluded that sustaining the competitive advantage of a destination requires both responsiveness to market demand and competitive challenges and preservation of the integrity of the environment.

Game theory

Game theory: used to model competitor reactions in situations of interdependence.

Game theory can be used to model behaviour in strategic situations. The problem is that any move made by one party in a competitive situation will cause subsequent moves in others and each of those moves will cause further moves. So a strategy which might appear successful based upon current configurations of competitor actions may well turn out to have different consequences once competitor actions and reactions have taken place. The five key components common to models derived from game theory are:

- ◊ The player
- ◊ The action
- ◊ The sequence
- ◊ Information
- ◊ Utility.

There are a number of ways of expressing moves in game theory. One common way is using the extensive form. Here games and moves are represented by tree diagrams as illustrated in Figure 7.4. So if we were to assume two organisations we could represent the following moves as branches of that tree. Firm 1 (Player) starts and chooses to raise price or lower price (Action). Firm 2 responds to Firm 1's move (Information) and then chooses to raise price or lower price and so on. A commentary to the side of the diagram will track the likely pay-offs (Utility) of these moves to each firm.

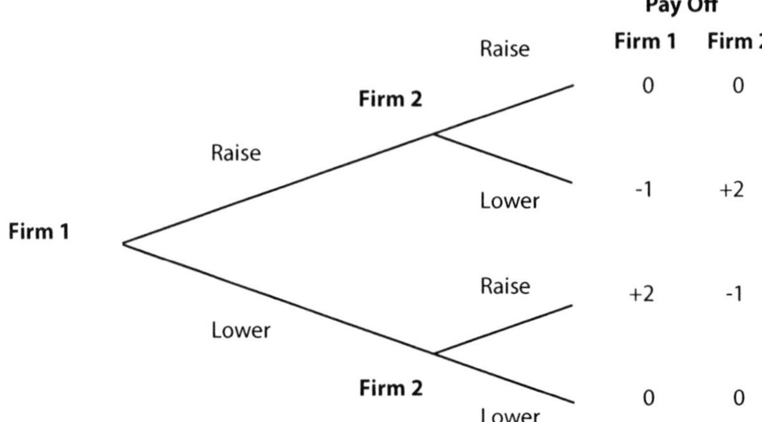

Figure 7.4: Sequential game moves

The use of game theory can be extended to investigate inter-organisational dynamics in a number of tourism contexts and using different choice variables. Huybers and Bennett (2003) investigated inter-firm cooperation at nature-based tourism destinations. The problem they investigated was one of competition or co-operation over environmental resources between firms and destinations. The authors found that inter-firm cooperation at a nature-based tourism destination could be expected to occur with regard to the sustainable use of the region's natural environment. They added that this suggests that the environmental resources shared by businesses at nature-based tourism destinations can be used without the potential for 'tragedies' (i.e. competitive over-use).

Zhang *et al.* (2009) used game theory to analyse the mechanism of zero-commission Chinese outbound tours. The zero-commission tour has been adopted by some local tour operators at destinations that receive Chinese package tourists. In these tours local operators make no up-front charges and try to recoup their outlay by getting tourists to spend on additional items during the tour. The authors concluded that zero-commission tours create a strong negative impact on all of the stakeholders.

Taylor *et al.* (2007) also used game theory to understand determinants of cluster activities in the Australian wine and tourism industries. The authors specifically looked at concept of micro-clusters which in contrast to outright competition rely on trust, networking and collaboration between organisations. They argue that game theory and the presence of sunk costs are drivers of cluster activity. Their study found members of the wine tourism industry participate more in these activities than members of the tourism or hospitality industries and that sunk costs are important in the determination of cluster activities.

Finally Oliveira and Huse (2009) undertook an empirical investigation into the price reactions to the entry of Gol Airlines, a low-cost carrier, on the Brazilian domestic air travel market in 2001. The study emerged with two key findings. First, it was noted that both airport and route presence are relevant at explaining the pricing behaviour of competitors. Second, the authors found that flight distance and the quantity of seats supplied by the new entrant were important. More specifically they noted that price reactions from the existing operators were significantly stronger where routes were shorter and where the new entrant airline was offering more seats. The authors estimated that price reactions would lead to 22–26 per cent yield reductions on routes as short as 350 km.

Review of key terms

- Generic strategy: a strategy of a particular type or form designed to promote a lasting competitive advantage.
- Cost leadership: becoming the lowest cost provider in an industry.
- Differentiation: seeking product or service uniqueness.
- Focus strategy: a strategy tailored towards a particular market segment.
- Price-based strategy: reducing costs and prices.
- Hybrid strategy: providing high quality products and services at low prices.
- Zone X: a combination of high prices and low quality.
- Elasticity of demand: the responsiveness of demand to a change in price.
- Game theory: used to model competitor reactions in situations of interdependence.

Multiple choice questions

1 Which of the following is not one of Porter's generic strategies?
   A Competitive positioning
   B Cost leadership
   C Differentiation
   D Focus

2 Which of the following is true?
   A SouthWest Airlines follows a differentiation strategy
   B Ryanair attempts price leadership
   C The Sofitel brand exemplifies price leadership
   D McDonald's demonstrates a hybrid strategy

3 Which of the following best explains a hybrid strategy?
   A Providing high quality products and services at low prices
   B Providing high quality products and services at high prices
   C Providing low quality products and services at low prices
   D Providing low quality products and services at high prices

4 Which of the following best explains Zone X?
   A Providing high quality products and services at low prices
   B Providing high quality products and services at high prices
   C Providing low quality products and services at low prices
   D Providing low quality products and services at high prices

5 Which of the following is least likely to maintain competitive advantage?
   A Exploiting 'deep pockets'
   B Innovation and organisational responsiveness
   C Creating unique organisational capabilities
   D Follow my leader strategies

Discussion questions

1. 'Market share is crucial for a hybrid strategy.' Explain, using examples from tourism, what is meant by this statement.
2. Explain how a hotel brand could achieve price leadership.
3. Explain how a no-frills airline could maintain competitive advantage.
4. Explain how the concept of elasticity of demand helps to understand the logic of price and differentiation strategies.
5. Under what circumstances is it possible for a tourism organisation to survive by charging high prices for low quality services?

References

Bowman, C. and Faulkner, D. (1995) *The Essence of Competitive Strategy*. Harlow: Prentice Hall.

Croes, R.R. (2006) A paradigm shift to a new strategy for small island economies: embracing demand side economics for value enhancement and long term economic stability. *Tourism Management*, **27**, 453-465.

Gu, Z. (2006) Product differentiation: key to Macau's gaming revenue growth. *Journal of Revenue and Pricing Management*, **4**, 382-388.

Hassan, S. S. (2000) Determinants of market competitiveness in an environmentally sustainable tourism industry. *Journal of Travel Research*, **38**, 239-245.

Huybers, T. and Bennett, J. (2003) Inter-firm cooperation at nature-based tourism destinations. *Journal of Socio-Economics*, **32** 571-587.

Johnson, G., Scholes, K. and Whittington, R. (2008) *Exploring Corporate Strategy*. Harlow: Prentice Hall.

Miller, M.M., Henthorne, T.L. and George, B.P. (2008). The competitiveness of the Cuban tourism industry in the twenty-first century: a strategic re-evaluation. *Journal of Travel Research*, **46**, 268-278.

Okumus, B., Okumus, F. and McKercher, B. (2007) Incorporating local and international cuisines in the marketing of tourism destinations: the cases of Hong Kong and Turkey. *Tourism Management*, **28**, 253-261.

Oliveira, A.V.M. and Huse, C. (2009) Localized competitive advantage and price reactions to entry: full-service vs. low-cost airlines in recently liberalized emerging markets. *Transportation Research Part E: Logistics and Transportation Review*, **45**, 307-320.

Ooi, C.S. (2002) Contrasting strategies: tourism in Denmark and Singapore. *Annals of Tourism Research*, **29**, 689-706.

Poon, A. (2003) Competitive strategies for a new tourism. In C. Cooper (ed.), *Classic Reviews in Tourism*, Clevedon: Channel View, pp. 130-142.

Porter, M.E. (1998) *Competitive Strategy: Techniques for Analyzing Industries and Competitors: with a New Introduction*. Glencoe, IL: Free Press.

Taylor, P., Rae-Williams, P. and Lowe, J. (2007) The determinants of cluster activities in the Australian wine and tourism industries. *Tourism Economics*, **13**, 639-656.

Tribe, J. (1997) *Corporate Strategy for Tourism*. London: International Thomson Business Press.

Virgin Blue (2008) *Annual Report*. Brisbane: Virgin Blue.

Zhang, H.Q., Heung, V.C.S. and Yan, Y.Q. (2009) Play or not to play – an analysis of the mechanism of the zero-commission Chinese outbound tours through a game theory approach. *Tourism Management*, **30**, 366-371.

8 Strategic Directions and Methods

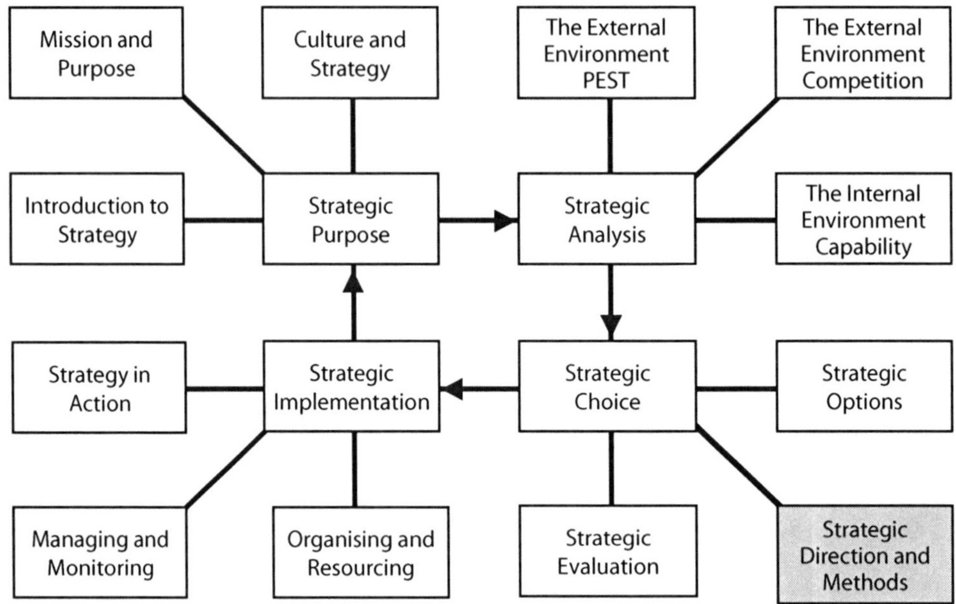

Figure 8.1

Learning outcomes

After studying this chapter and related materials you should be able to understand:

- Strategic directions such as consolidation, market penetration, market development, product development, diversification and withdrawal.
- Strategic methods of growth including internal growth, mergers and takeovers, and joint ventures and alliances.
- Strategic methods of development such as innovation and entrepreneurship.

and critically evaluate, explain and apply the above concepts.

Introduction

Chapter 7 examined the types of strategy a tourism entity could adopt, distinguishing between price competitiveness, value added and hybrid strategies. This chapter follows this up by looking at two key areas that would support these strategies. The first area of analysis here is strategic directions. This examines the products or services and markets that an entity should participate in and how these should be developed. The second area of analysis is strategic methods. This in turn divides into three further subheadings. The first of these is strategic growth which analyses how entities themselves can grow, develop and extend their reach. The second subheading under strategic methods is development via innovation and the third is development via entrepreneurship. This underlines the fact that the highly competitive environment that most tourism entities operate in both stimulates and demands successful innovation for entities to maintain their competitive environment.

Case study 8 uses Merlin Entertainment to show how a tourism organisation delivers its strategy through directions and methods that include product development, rolling out its brands internationally and acquisition of other operators in the attractions industry.

Case Study 8: Merlin Entertainment

Merlin Entertainment is an international attractions-based organisation incorporating the well known international brands of Legoland, Madame Tussauds, Sea Life and Dungeons as well as owning the London Eye, and UK theme parks such as Alton Towers, Chessington World of Adventures and Thorpe Park. In 2010, Merlin comprised 57 attractions and operated in 12 countries employing 13,500 people at peak season with over 35 million visitors a year.

The Merlin Entertainments London Eye

Merlin's vision

'To become the world wide leader in branded, location based entertainment.'

Merlin's strategy

'To build on our position as a high growth, international, family entertainment Group with strong brands and a portfolio that is naturally hedged against external factors such as weather or localised market conditions.'

Strategic directions and methods

Merlin plans to deliver its strategy through directions and methods that include:

- Product development
- Rolling out its proven chainable brands internationally.
- Acquisitions of other operators in the attractions industry

Product development

Merlin plans capital expenditure programmes appropriate to each estate. This can include product development such as the launch of the SAW, the ride at Thorpe Park, development of Land of the Pharaohs at Legoland Windsor, and the installation of Sharkbait Reef by Sea Life at Alton Towers. A £12.5m upgrade for the London Eye has also been commenced to ensure it is ready for the 2012 London Olympics. The upgrade included adding ceiling-mounted screens and enhanced multi-media and wi-fi capabilities so that music and on-screen visuals can be offered in the capsule. A more efficient and environmentally-friendly heating and ventilation system has also been added.

The Merlin Annual Pass has been introduced in the UK and Germany which offers unlimited entry to all Merlin attractions for 12 months. A focused advertising campaign led to a growth in market share in both countries. Merlin is also developing hotels and/or holiday villages at its major attractions. It already owns and operates hotels across Europe including the Alton Towers Hotel, Alton Towers, England and the Gardaland Resort Hotel, Lake Garda, Italy. Further hotel developments are underway at Thorpe Park and Legoland Windsor.

Roll out

Merlin's roll out strategy is illustrated by the following:

- The Madame Tussauds waxworks museums which are famous around the globe have been opened in London, New York, Amsterdam, Las Vegas, Shanghai, Hong Kong, Washington DC, Berlin and Hollywood.
- Sea Life is the world's biggest aquarium brand with over 30 centres in more than 11 countries including UK, Spain, the USA, Germany and Portugal.
- Dungeons use a combination of actors, rides and special effects to bring the dark and gory side of local history to life. There are now five Dungeon sites in London, Hamburg, Amsterdam, Edinburgh and York.

Merlin claims to have the development skills to identify, secure and build up to five new attractions every year. In 2008, Merlin rolled out two new Sea Life centres and two new Legoland Discovery Centres as well as a new Madame Tussauds. In 2009 it opened Sea Life Porto, in Portugal and Madame Tussauds Hollywood. The year 2010 witnessed the opening of the Legoland Discovery Centre and the Pepsi Globe in New Jersey, USA. It also plans to open new Legoland theme parks starting with Malaysia in 2012 using partnership funding.

Acquisitions

Merlin makes full use of acquisition opportunities where they enhance its strategic aims. Its previous acquisitions include Legoland Parks (2005), Gardaland (The biggest theme park in Italy) (2006) and Tussauds Group (2007) which increased the scale of Merlin by over 10 times in three years. The London Aquarium which was acquired in 2008.

Directions

Strategic directions: how an entity should develop its products and services as well as the markets.

This section considers the strategic directions an organisation might take in pursuit of its overall strategy. The specific directions referred to relate to how an entity should develop its products and services as well as the markets for these in order to maximise its strategic benefit. The main directions are:

- ◊ Consolidation
- ◊ Market penetration
- ◊ Market development
- ◊ Product development
- ◊ Diversification
- ◊ Withdrawal.

In many cases a combination of these directions will be appropriate.

These directions are summarised and located in Figure 8.2 on the matrix developed by Ansoff (1988). The Ansoff matrix offers a range of alternative strategic directions based on an analysis of markets and products or services. These form the axes of the matrix which also distinguishes between existing and new situations giving rise to four distinct quadrants. However the quadrants should not be viewed as having rigid boundaries – for example current products are generally under a state of perpetual review. Each of the four quadrants is now examined in more detail.

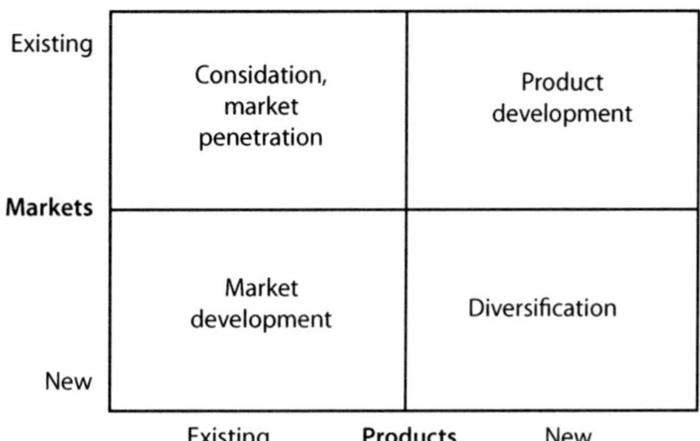

Figure 8.2: Mapping strategic directions
Source: adapted from Ansoff (1988)

Consolidation

Consolidation: concentrating an organisation's efforts on existing products and existing markets.

Consolidation implies a period of concentrating an organisation's efforts on existing products and existing markets. It may follow a period of rapid change to enable an organisation to settle down or may result from a lack of resources to pursue a more active policy. This can be caused by lack of profits in the private sector or lack of government grants to a public sector organisation such as a national tourism organisation. In cases where the external environment is unfavourable, consolidation may be a sensible defensive position and this is illustrated by the position taken by Emirates in Box 8.1. Consolidation may also be chosen by smaller organisations who do not wish to grow any further.

Box 8.1 2009 A year of consolidation for Emirates

Despite record passenger numbers, the continuing global economic slump in 2009 has meant falling passenger revenues for Emirates Airlines and this has caused it to review its ambitious growth plans. Rather it entered a period of consolidation of its position and this has had an impact on both recruitment and plane orders.

Emirates stopped recruiting in February/March 2009, although by September 2009 it recommenced recruitment of both cabin crew and flight crew. It was also forced to consider delays to delivery of its new planes. Emirates president Tim Clark, speaking at a meeting of the International Air Transport Association meeting in Kuala Lumpur, said that it was likely that the airline would cut aircraft deliveries over the period 2009 to 2011 depending on market conditions but that he did not expect the slowdown in deliveries to last for longer than this. The airline has a long-term expansion plan to increase its fleet to 196 passenger planes by 2018 compared to 126 as of 2009.

Sheikh Ahmed bin Saeed Al-Maktoum, Chairman, of Emirates Airline also underlined the fact that 2009 would be one of consolidation and the airline would launch fewer new routes previously. He was also quoted as saying that:

> Instead, we will concentrate on strengthening our presence on routes where there is a greater demand from our customers. All of our new capacity will be deployed in markets where we see growth potential, particularly Africa and the West Asia.

Market penetration

Market penetration: increasing market share in existing markets using existing products or services.

Market penetration involves increasing market share in existing markets using existing products or services and is an important aim of generic strategies previously discussed. It generally involves building on existing strategic capabilities and avoids undue risk in terms of either market or product development. In the short term, market penetration may be won by reducing margins and prices, but sustainable market penetration can only be achieved by price-based strategies that are coupled with cost reductions, or by differentiation or hybrid strategies.

The exception to this is if a price war is successful in forcing a weaker competitor out of business. Box 8.2 shows changes in market share in the Australian international air travel industry in 2009 with both Emirates and Pacific Blue increasing their market share.

Box 8.2 Changes in market share for Australia's international scheduled passenger traffic

Data released by the Bureau of Infrastructure, Transport and Regional Economics shows the following trends in market share for international scheduled passenger traffic operating in Australia between July 2008 and July 2009:

Qantas Airways' market share decreased by 3.6 per cent down to 20.6 per cent. This was the biggest drop of all the airlines although Qantas remains the carrier with the largest market share.

- Singapore Airlines' share decreased by 1.8 per cent to 9.8 per cent
- Air New Zealand decreased by 1.3 per cent to 8.4 per cent
- Emirates increased market share by 1 per cent to 8.1 per cent of the market share
- Pacific Blue's market share doubled from 3.1 per cent to 6.2 per cent

Source: Travel Blackboard (http://www.etravelblackboard.com)

Market penetration may also be limited by legal constraints designed to curb any one organisation gaining excessive market share and therefore too much market power. Most countries have monopolies or anti-trust legislation which can investigate situations where an organisation's market share exceeds a given threshold and in some cases require steps to be taken to reduce market share.

Market development

Market development: taking an existing product range into new market areas.

Market development generally involves an attempt to take the existing product range into new market areas which can include new geographical areas, new market segments and new users. It may be that some product development is required to adapt the product range to the new market areas. Case study 7 has shown how IHG an has a growth strategy for its Mercure hotels based on expansion in Europe and new markets in Asia whilst the growth strategy of its Ibis hotel brand is to concentrate on emerging markets, particularly in Asia and Latin America.

Product development

Product development encompasses the development of existing products and the development of completely new products for existing markets.

The continuing development of existing products is almost an essential strategy in the dynamic environment which organisations operate in. For differentiation strategies, product development is necessary to maintain differences

Product development: the development of existing products and the development of completely new products for existing markets.

as competitors imitate previous innovations. Equally, price-based strategies require product development in order to maintain low production costs and even budget products or services must eventually incorporate recent innovations or they will fail to sell even at low prices.

New product development is a more risky strategy since research and development are expensive and only a minority of new products reach the market and succeed. Reference to product life cycle analysis (are current products in the decline phase?) and the BCG matrix (which products will be the cash cows of tomorrow?) (see Chapter 6) can be useful tools in judging the appropriateness and timeliness for product development within an organisation.

Billington *et al.* (2008) investigated tourism product development in the Blackstone Valley. The Blackstone River Valley is famous as being the first industrialised valley in North America. Located in New England it was where the American Industrial Revolution was launched and it has now evolved into a tourism destination. The authors describe how the visitor destination is developed using 'whole place-making techniques' and how the Blackstone Valley Tourism Council has developed a Sustainable Tourism Planning and Development Laboratory (STPDL) to help enhance the product. The laboratory has developed symposiums, conferences, and programmes and some of its key projects include:

- **Riverfront development**: the STPDL is working with communities and private landowners to open up the river to recreation and commerce and helped establish safe, accessible river landings in five communities.
- **Heritage and cultural preservation**: this has included the restoration of the St Anne's Arts and Cultural Center in Woonsocket. The STPDL is also developing funding sources to create a museum to Thomas Wilson Door who was an activist for voting rights.
- **Footsteps in history**: this is an open house weekend for over 100 recreational, environmental, cultural, artistic, and historic sites along the Blackstone River Valley.

Diversification

Diversification: moving into completely new products and markets which are unrelated to an entity's present portfolio.

Diversification involves an organisation moving into completely new products and markets which are unrelated to its present portfolio. The motives for this may be first to take advantage of a new growing market – particularly if an existing product has a static or declining market. Second diversification allows an organisation to spread its risks. Third, economies of scope may be achieved. These are reductions in average costs that result from provision of a range of different goods and services. Such economies result from sharing marketing, or brand names, or customers, or outlets. Box 8.3 shows how Malaysia is diversifying its tourism offering using medical tourism.

Box 8.3 Medical tourism in Malaysia

Malaysia is traditionally known as a tourist destination for its natural attractions as well as cultural and historical tourism but there are signs of diversification as medical tourism develops as a new product and in doing so appeals to new markets. Here Malaysia competes regionally with Singapore and Thailand as many of its private hospitals offer medical packages including accommodation and travel to cater to foreign patients. Medical tourism numbers rose by over 300 per cent between 2003 and 2007 when they exceeded a third of a million patients. Research has shown that medical tourists spend more than double the amount of traditional tourists averaging over US$350 per day. Over two-thirds of patients are from Indonesia with much smaller numbers from Singapore, Japan, Europe and India. However Malaysia is also targeting new markets such as Vietnam, Cambodia, the Middle East and North America.

Source: The Star (http://biz.thestar.com.my)

Henderson (2006) describes how international tourism was adopted by the Dubai authorities as a core element in a programme of economic diversification despite apparently unfavourable circumstances. Dubai was part of an area that in the 1960s was largely economically undeveloped. Henderson shows by her study of Dubai:

> *how a small and comparatively remote state with an imperfect supply of conventional natural and cultural attractions can become an internationally known tourist destination. Possible weaknesses have been turned into selling points of consistently hot weather and awesome desert landscape and elaborate attractions have been constructed to satisfy modern tastes, with technology allowing them to function irrespective of climatic and other geographical impediments. Economic wealth has meant funds to support expansion in all sectors of the industry, including the fostering of a global air transport system and stock of lavish accommodation. (Henderson, 2006, p. 97)*

Withdrawal

Withdrawal: removal of product or service or pulling out from a market.

This does not appear in Figure 8.2 since it involves neither new nor current markets or products, but is rather, a position of retreat. There are some cases in which an organisation may withdraw from a particular market. These might include:

- De-cluttering
- Contracting out
- Raising money
- Legal compliance
- Competition, market decline and economic prospects
- Liquidation
- Privatisation.

De-cluttering

This occurs where an organisation has grown into a range of diversified areas and now seeks to concentrate its efforts in its core business. The case study of the International Hotel Group (IHG) in Chapter 6 shows how in the year 2000, Bass, the former owners of IHG, sold off its brewing arm in order to concentrate on its core businesses. More recently after a period of rapid transformation, the travel company TUI has emerged from the German industrial conglomerate Preussag AG as a focused tourism and shipping company.

Contracting out

Organisations may cease to provide a service related to their business, preferring to buy in the services from a contractor. This enables the service to be more flexibly provided. Contracting out is common amongst airlines which often contract third-party organisations to provide ground handling services (such as check-in, boarding and baggage handling), in-flight catering and sometimes aircraft maintenance.

Raising money

Withdrawal may be used to raise money for expansion elsewhere or to fight off a take-over bid. For example, in 2008, the Queensland government in Australia announced that it would sell off two regional airports that it owns in Cairns and Mackay as well as its 12 per cent stake in the Brisbane Airport Corporation with a target of raising AUS$1 billion and use the funds to pay for three new hospitals.

Legal compliance

Monopoly or anti-trust legislation may require an organisation to divest its holdings if it is acting against the public interest. For example in the UK the British Airports Authority (BAA) had a 40-year near monopoly control of London's three main airports through its ownership of Heathrow, Gatwick and Stansted. A government Competition Commission inquiry reported that this situation resulted in a lack of competition and initially ordered BAA to sell one of its airports. In 2009, BAA took action selling Gatwick airport to Global Infrastructure Partners for £1.51 billion.

Competition, market decline and economic prospects

Poor prospects for a particular market may cause an organisation to make a partial or wholesale tactical withdrawal. For example competition in an area may be so strong as to force an organisation out of this particular market. For example the airline Virgin Nigeria made a decision to withdraw from long-haul operations because of an influx of foreign carriers following the Nigerian government's granting of licences to new operators. This led to a softening of fares on the Lagos–London market and meant that the airline has reallocated its provision to its short-haul network in Africa.

Liquidation

An organisation may withdraw because of untenable losses. Philippine Airlines collapsed in 1998 only two years after privatisation as it was unable to cover its operating costs without government support.

Privatisation

The government may wish to sell assets as part of a privatisation programmes. Examples of this in the tourism sector are particularly common in airlines and include British Airways (UK), and Qantas (Australia).

Methods: growth

Strategic methods: how a strategy may be developed by growth, development, innovation and entrepreneurship.

This part of the chapter examines the main methods by which a particular strategy may be developed. This section considers strategies for growth whilst the following section analyses strategies for innovation and entrepreneurship. Strategies for growth include:

- ◊ Internal growth
- ◊ Mergers and take-overs, and
- ◊ Franchises, joint ventures and alliances.

Internal growth

Internal growth: development of markets and products without recourse to mergers with other organisations.

Internal growth means that markets and products are developed without recourse to mergers with other organisations. This route may be chosen because:

- ◊ Owners and managers wish to retain control of an organisation
- ◊ Organic growth is less disruptive and can be more readily accommodated
- ◊ Finance may be limited
- ◊ There may be no suitable targets for mergers
- ◊ Problems of cultural fit between merging organisations can be avoided.

However, internal growth may dictate a pace of adaptation which is too slow to keep up with environmental changes, and does not preclude the possibility of a takeover bid. Also opportunities to benefit from already developed products and markets will be lost as will the positive aspects of cultural change which can result from mergers.

Mergers and takeovers

Merger: integration between organisations.

Whilst mergers represent voluntary integration between organisations, takeovers may occur without the agreement of the target company. Integration can be divided into three main types:

- ◊ Horizontal integration
- ◊ Vertical integration, and
- ◊ Diversification or conglomerate integration.

The package holiday industry can be used to understand the basic differences between vertical and horizontal integration. The vertical dimension of the industry represents a series of stages of production from raw materials or suppliers through to the consumer. There are three basic vertical stages in the package holiday industry – the supply of services (for example air transport and hotels), the packaging of the elements of the trip and the retailing or distribution of the package. The horizontal dimension of the industry represents a series of separate firms engaged in the industry at similar stages. So a horizontal view of the industry would be along an air transport axis, or a packaging axis or along a retail distribution axis.

Horizontal integration

Horizontal integration: merger between firms operating at the same stage of production in the same industry.

Horizontal integration occurs between firms operating at the same stage of production in the same industry. For example, in 1990, the Accor Hotels group acquired the Motel6 chain in the United States as reported in the case study in Chapter 7. Market development is an important motive for horizontal integration. The Accor Hotel Group's acquisition of Motel6 represents an attempt to broaden its market base and extend its operations into the US market. Second market penetration can result from horizontal integration. In 1975 Accor acquired the 3-star chain, Mercure and in 1980 it acquired Sofitel, the French 4-star hotel operator. Both of these moves mean that the customer databases of the acquired hotels are obtained, expanding Accor's customer base and market at a stroke.

Third, there are economies of scale to be achieved by horizontal integration. The German airline Lufthansa has grown to be one of the world's largest aviation groups through a policy of horizontal integration. This it has achieved through acquiring large or majority shareholdings of competing airlines to its portfolio including Swiss, Brussels Airlines, Jet Blue, Eurowings, British Midland, LuxAir, Air Dolomiti, Condor and Austrian Airlines. Integrated firms can share the same management overheads and advertising and marketing campaigns may be merged. As Lufthansa grows larger, so its bulk purchasing opportunities grow, especially for aircraft and fuel. Larger turnover also justifies the use of more sophisticated specialised support (both in terms of staffing and technology). State of the art computerisation for reservations and yield management becomes more feasible. Financial economies in terms of access to cheaper capital are also open to larger firms. Rationalisation can occur as firms merge and unnecessary duplication of services can be avoided. The result of such economies may be substantial reductions in average costs.

Horizontal integration can also be a short cut to product development as competitors' products and support systems are acquired as part of the business. For example: in 2006, First Choice (now part of TUI) entered the Asia Pacific market through the acquisition of Pacific World and in 2007, First Choice made further strategic acquisitions in niche segments including Quark Expeditions and iExplore as well as purchasing LateRooms.com which expanded the company's portfolio into late availability online accommodation provision. In these ways, First Choice was able to broaden its product base (and by implication its market base) without developing new products from scratch and bring its considerable marketing and promotional strengths to its expanded portfolio.

Finally horizontal integration is a way of reducing competition. Less competition means that an organisation needs to make less effort in terms of low prices or improved products. The merger of TUI and First Choice Holidays to form TUI Travel in 2007 (see case study 9) along with the merger of MyTravel Group and Thomas Cook to form the Thomas Cook Group reduced the competition in the market for package holidays at a stroke.

Vertical integration

Vertical integration: where two organisations at different stages of production in the same industry merge.

Vertical integration occurs where two organisations at different stages of production in the same industry merge. The holiday industry provides another good example of this in each of the two leading European organisations of TUI Travel and the Thomas Cook Group.

In 2010, the Thomas Cook Group demonstrated strong vertical integration through its ownership of a fleet of 93 aircraft, a network of over 3400 owned and franchised travel stores and interests in 86 hotels and resort properties. Similarly TUI UK & Ireland owns the UK's third largest airline through the merger of Thomsonfly and First Choice Airways. It has several of the largest travel brands including First Choice and Thomson and retails its products through over 1000 shops across the UK.

Market penetration has been an important motive for forward (towards the consumer) vertical integration in the package tour industry. Ownership of retail travel agents means that a tour operator can allocate its own brochures best rack space and offer its staff incentives to sell in-house holidays. Equally, forward integration ensures a ready market for airline seats, ensuring high load factors.

Product development is another important motive for vertical integration. Control of airlines means that tour operators can influence a key element in the value chain of the holiday package. Departure times and quality of service can all be directly controlled and this part of the service can help to support the overall corporate image and help add value to a product. Vertical integration also means that tour operators have close contact with their customers which can ensure that product development is customer-driven.

Diversification

Diversification: taking over a firm in a different line of business.

Diversification means taking over a firm in a different line of business. It is also a strategy that many destinations have embarked upon especially those which had an over-reliance on sun and sea package tours. Diversification of the tourism product in destinations includes wellness and spa holidays and rural tourism. For example, Turkey includes a diversification strategy in its Tourism 2023 strategy document noting that the goal of spreading the tourism season over the entire year is dependent upon diversification. Its specific objectives for diversification are:

> *To develop means for alternative tourism types led particularly by health, thermal, winter, golf, sea tourism, ecotourism and plateau tourism, conference and expo tourism activities.* (Ministry of Tourism, 2009)

Problems with mergers

Some of the potential problems of mergers can also be noted. First there is the potential problem of lack of fit in terms of products, or processes (information technology system incompatibility can be a problem here), or the culture of merging organisations. Second, diseconomies of scale may arise. This may occur particularly if an organisation becomes too big for effective management. Poor communications and ineffective control and co-ordination may arise causing costs to rise.

Finally there is monopolies and mergers and anti-trust legislation. Most countries have legislation to control mergers where anti-competitive practices result in the interests of consumers being adversely affected. In this respect vertical integration in the UK package tour industry has been criticised by the Consumers Association who allege that customers do not get unbiased advice when using vertically integrated travel agents.

Franchises, joint ventures and alliances

These methods of strategic development represent a desire for the benefits of collaboration without complete merging of ownership and resources. It can take the following forms:

- ◊ Franchising and licensing
- ◊ Joint ventures
- ◊ Alliances.

Franchising and licensing

Franchise: new owners and businesses are recruited to replicate a successful business model under licence.

Franchising occurs where new owners and businesses are recruited to replicate a successful business model. The central franchising business licenses new operators the right to replicate its products or services, techniques, and trademarks in return for a fee. This can be appropriate when a successful product would benefit from rapid market development but funds for expansion are insufficient to cope with the product's development potential. The franchising concept has been successfully applied to hotels and restaurants. The owner of a successful brand undertakes marketing, and is responsible for ensuring quality control, but outlets are franchised out in return for an initial fee and royalties. Thus the product can be expanded quickly as new capital is available and the brand owner can extend profits, whilst the franchise holder enjoys the marketing benefits of a well-known brand.

The IHG case study in Chapter 6 referred to franchising as a key driver of growth to the group with over 3700 franchised hotels operating under IHG brands. The benefits of franchising include the incentives that arise from ownership of a business and local knowledge coupled with the advantages of operating under a globally recognised brand and access to global marketing and reservation systems.

Joint ventures

Joint venture: where two or more parties agree to cooperate in business activities.

A joint venture is where two or more parties agree to cooperate in business activities. It requires an agreement between the parties on contribution of resources and sharing of profits. Joint ventures have typified tourism developments with governments of the ex-Soviet bloc of countries, and the governments of China and Cuba. Experienced companies provide expertise and finance with land and some labour being supplied locally. For example, in 2008, a joint investment company for developing a chain of four and five-star hotels in Russia was formed between International Hotel Investments Plc (IHI) under the Corinthia brand and the Russian public limited company Intourist. The initiative aims to develop accommodation capacity in Russia where a lack of quality hotels remains a significant obstacle for the development of tourism. The joint venture will seek to develop hotels in outlying cities, such as Sochi, N. Novgorod and Rostov-na-Donu, as well as in Moscow and St Petersburg.

Alliances

Strategic alliance: an agreement between two or more parties to co-operate on some aspects of mutual interest while remaining independent organisations.

A strategic alliance is an agreement between two or more parties to co-operate on some aspects of mutual interest while remaining independent organisations. Strategic alliances are a way of capturing some of the benefits of globalisation by producing and marketing a product to a world-wide market. Alliances can therefore help to win global coverage for marketing a product and use the expertise that alliance partners have developed in different parts of the world. They can also reduce competitive pressures as former rivals seek to co-operate. Research and development costs may be shared.

Alliances may take many forms, from partial share holdings, collaboration on specific projects to loose networks for marketing. They avoid the problems of full mergers such as expense and re-organisation. They are easier to withdraw from and are more flexible in that they can be used to focus on particular aspects of an organisation's strategy.

Strategic alliances have proliferated in the airline industry and Box 8.4 examines the issues involved.

Box 8.4: Airline alliances

An airline alliance is an agreement between two or more airlines to cooperate in some way. Co-operation ranges from co-ordination of timetables through code-sharing agreements to equity links. The three main airline alliances are the Star Alliance, Sky-Team and Oneworld. Star Alliance is the biggest serving 1071 destinations and covering about 30 per cent of the market. Its members include Air China, Air New Zealand, Continental, Lufthansa, Singapore Airlines and United.

Alliances offer airlines both product and market development. The product is developed in that it becomes more comprehensive. British Airways' continued ambition is to become the leading global airline so that passengers can pick up its flights from any one point to any other in the world. This is what code-sharing is all about. Whilst BA does not fly from Melbourne to London, through code-sharing with Qantas, it appears to do so on reservation systems. Also Alliance airlines share their frequent flier programmes – increasing their attractiveness. Cost-savings arise from higher load factors and a single advertisement for a world audience can offer considerable economies.

Alliances offer a point of entry into distant markets with reciprocal benefits to the partners – so just as United finds a new market in Europe through Lufthansa, Lufthansa is able to develop its US market. An effective airline alliance offers good coverage across all the continents. Not all alliances have been successful and reasons for failure may include procrastination, differing objectives, mistrust, failure to integrate timetables and differing product standards – in summary, incompatibility.

One important reason for the favouring of alliances over full mergers is the political regulation and state ownership of many airlines. There are widespread restrictions of foreign ownership of flag-carrying airlines.

Methods: innovation

Innovation: bringing newness or positive change to products, processes, thinking, or organisations.

Innovation refers to bringing newness or positive change to products, processes, thinking, or organisations. It generally thought of as the practical application of invention. There are many notable examples of innovation affecting tourism, ranging from the invention of the jet engine, to traveller's cheques and ATMs, immunisation, South West Airlines, boutique hotels, computerised reservation systems, trip advisor, scuba equipment and skiing. In a sense innovation is an extension of the discussion about generic strategies since much innovation is designed to achieve cost reductions or differentiation. But sometimes it is about specific problem solving such as metal and explosive detection security systems at airports and increasingly about how to combat CO_2 emissions. Hjalager (2010) offers a comprehensive review of the literature on tourism innovation and an agenda for future research in this area.

Hall and Williams (2008) identify a number of key drivers of tourism innovation that include:

- ◊ Competition and protection
- ◊ Knowledge and creativity
- ◊ Innovation policies
- ◊ Firm-led strategies
- ◊ Entrepreneurship.

Competition and protection

It is not difficult to understand the role played by competition and entrepreneurship in stimulating innovation. Here reference to the era of central planning in Russia and its satellite states demonstrates the deadening effects of the absence of competition and entrepreneurship and the over-presence of the state on innovation in airlines, hotels and the hospitality industry. Equally globalisation and the increasing power and extent of Internet-based knowledge intensify competition between tourism entities and thus further stimulate innovation. The fact tourism entities operate in a highly competitive environment both stimulates innovation and demands successful innovation for entities to maintain their competitive environment.

An important consideration in innovation is the extent to which an organisation is able to protect its investment. Most tourism products are highly visible and because of this it is often relatively easy for competitors to replicate innovative features. Where imitation is easy, incentives to invest in innovation will be reduced. It may be preferable to be an early follower adopter of innovation rather than a leader. However there are ways in which innovation can be protected through regulation and other means. Regulatory protection of rights of invention can be sought through patents and copyrights which offer legal protection against infringement. Regulation may also occur through the obtaining of concessions and licences. Other means of protecting innovation include entry costs and branding. Some innovations are associated with significant investments costs and this may provide entry barriers that make it difficult for others to imitate. Alternatively creating a strong link between a particular innovation and an organisation's brand can be strengthened through advertising. This too can offer some ownership benefits of innovation.

Knowledge and creativity

Innovation depends on knowledge acquisition, transfer and management (Cooper, 2006). Tribe (1997) distinguished between mode 1 knowledge generated by academic institutions and mode 2 knowledge generated by organisations involved in tourism. This is a useful distinction as it portrays one of the challenges for innovation in tourism as elsewhere. That is the challenge to improve co-operation and knowledge transfer between industry and academia. It also raises the question of how to stimulate innovation in knowledge creation in both sectors and this will be considered in the next section.

An important distinction can also be made between codified knowledge and tacit knowledge (Polanyi and Sen, 2009). Codified knowledge is that which is readily communicable and recorded. Tacit knowledge is 'know-how' and describes the ability of individuals to do things without necessarily being able to describe how or why. Since tacit knowledge is by definition difficult to decode, it can be difficult for competitors to access and therefore can be a source of competitive advantage through innovation.

Creativity is also closely connected to innovation. Creativity is a broader, less task-orientated term than innovation. For creativity is about imagination and thinking and seeing in new ways. It is often associated with lateral thinking or thinking outside the box. Fusion cuisine exemplifies this where, for example, Asian and English cooking are imaginative combined. Other extreme examples of this are exemplified by creations from the chef Heston Blumenthal which include snail porridge, parsnip cereal and bacon-and-egg ice cream.

Creativity can be understood at the individual and group level. Creative individuals tend to combine expertise, creative thinking skills (which are in turn related to personality and working styles) with a strong passion (Amabile, 1998). They are often non-conformists. Creative groups need a stimulating physical working environment and a diversity of ideas and skills and can be extended to the concept of creative cities (Leslie, 2005) which thrive on their diversity of racial, ethnic and lifestyle groups and a strong presence of arts and cultural industries.

Innovation policies

Despite the fact that competition in free markets is undoubtedly a key stimulus for innovation, there is much interest in devising policies to cultivate and sustain innovation. These policies can include elements such as taxation and incentive schemes to stimulate research and development, partnership initiatives and regional co-ordination and planning.

An example of an incentive schemes is the R&D Law in Turkey. This offers special incentives for R&D investment projects in Turkey where a minimum of 50 personnel are employed in a R&D centre. The incentives include tax reductions and exemptions.

An example of a partnership initiative funded by national government was Australia's Sustainable Tourism Cooperative Research Centre (STCRC) which was set up in 1997 to improve co-operation and knowledge transfer between industry and universities. It was a partnership between tourism companies, industry bodies, government, universities and technical education institutes. Its vision was:

> *To deliver innovation to destinations, businesses, communities and governments; ultimately enhancing the environmental, economic and social sustainability of tourism in Australia. (www.crctourism.com.au)*

Hall and Williams (2008) note that tourism can be an important (though rarely leading) element in regional innovation systems. They distinguish between innovative knowledge-based 'high road' and imitative 'low road' policies concluding that tourism has often been associated with the latter category citing the 'serial replication of the waterfront marketplace, heritage precinct, art gallery, museum, casino, marina and shopping centre' (p. 166).

Firm-led strategies

Hall and Williams (2008) identify a number of value creation points in tourism entities that have innovation potential. They note that:

> *maintaining and innovating along the various points of the service business will potentially bring greater returns to the firm and therefore enhance the likelihood that the firm will survive and/or expand. (p.196)*

The value creation points have similarities with value chain analysis and are:

- ◊ Business models
- ◊ Networks and alliances
- ◊ Enabling processes
- ◊ Service design and development
- ◊ Service value
- ◊ Distribution
- ◊ Brand
- ◊ Servicescape
- ◊ Customer service experiences
- ◊ Customer satisfaction
- ◊ Customer loyalty.

(Hall and Williams, p.188)

Entrepreneurship

Entrepreneur: the factor of production that brings together the other three basic factors of land, labour and capital in order to obtain profit.

In economic terms, the entrepreneur is the fourth factor of production, the one that brings together the other three basic factors of land, labour and capital in order to obtain profit. Entrepreneurship is associated with risk taking, the exploitation of new ideas and the pursuit of financial reward. Classic entrepreneurs in tourism have included Thomas Cook (the package tour), Vladimr Raitz (the air-package tour) and Stelios Haji-Ioannou (easyJet). Indeed Stelios Haji-Ioannou might be termed a serial entrepreneur as he followed the introduction of low-cost air travel with easyCar, offering low-cost car rental: easyCruise, offering cruising to younger age groups: easyBus, which offers low-cost bus transportation between city centres and airports and easyHotel, which offers low-cost city-centre accommodation.

Ateljevic and Doorne (2000, p. 380) defined the key descriptors of entrepreneurs as 'risk-taking, innovation, creativity, alertness and insight'. There is little doubt that entrepreneurial success is characterised by aspects of nurture, nature and opportunity. Nature conditions may include ethnicity, temperament, quick wittedness and risk tolerance. Nurture might include frustrated educational and/or career development, marginalisation and upbringing in a business-focused sub-culture. Finally, opportunity may be the catalyst that enables a latent entrepreneur to seize the moment and turn an innovative vision into a highly profitable future.

Review of key terms

- Strategic Directions: how an entity should develop its products and services as well as the markets.
- Consolidation: concentrating an organisation's efforts on existing products and existing markets.
- Market penetration: increasing market share in existing markets using existing products or services.
- Market development: taking an existing product range into new market areas.
- Product development: the development of existing products and the development of completely new products for existing markets.
- Diversification: moving into completely new products and markets which are unrelated to an entity's present portfolio.
- Withdrawal: removal of product or service or pulling out from a market.
- Strategic methods: how a strategy may be developed by growth, development, innovation and entrepreneurship.
- Internal growth: development of markets and products without recourse to mergers with other organisations.
- Merger: integration between organisations.
- Horizontal integration: merger between firms operating at the same stage of production in the same industry.
- Vertical integration: where two organisations at different stages of production in the same industry merge.
- Diversification: taking over a firm in a different line of business.
- Franchise: new owners and businesses are recruited to replicate a successful business model under licence.
- Joint venture: where two or more parties agree to cooperate in business activities.
- Strategic alliance: an agreement between two or more parties to co-operate on some aspects of mutual interest while remaining independent organisations.

- Innovation: bringing newness or positive change to products, processes, thinking, or organisations.
- Entrepreneur: the factor of production that brings together the other three basic factors of land, labour and capital in order to obtain profit.

Multiple choice questions

1 Market penetration means …
   A Increasing market share in existing markets using existing products or services
   B Increasing market share in new markets using existing products or services
   C Increasing market share in existing markets using new products or services
   D Increasing market share in new markets using new products or services

2 The situation where new business recruits are used to roll out a successful business model is best described as:
   A A joint venture
   B An alliance
   C A franchise
   D Innovation

3 Which of the following is a reason why an organisation would choose internal growth in preference to mergers and acquisitions?
   A To obtain synergies
   B To retain control of an organisation
   C To obtain more capital
   D To encourage diversification

4 The acquisition of British Midland by Lufthansa is an example of:
   A Horizontal integration
   B Vertical integration
   C Diversification
   D Decluttering

5 The reward for entrepreneurship is:
   A Profit
   B Rent
   C Interest payments
   D Wages

Discussion questions

1 Examine the advantages and disadvantages to producers and consumers of the strong vertical integration that is evident in the package holiday industry.

2 Locate two recent examples of horizontal integration in the tourism industry and critically evaluate the success of each.

3 Discuss the relative merits of mergers versus alliances for airlines.

4 With reference to a tourism organisation of your choice explain which of the following methods would be most appropriate for a programme of international expansion:

Internal growth

Mergers

Franchising

Joint ventures

Alliances.

5 How can successful innovation be encouraged in tourism destinations or business organisations?

References

Amabile, T.M. (1998) Keep doing what you're doing. Or, if you want to spark innovation, rethink how you motivate, reward, and assign work to people. *Harvard Business Review*, **76**, 77-87.

Ansoff, H.I. (1988) *Corporate Strategy*. Harmondsworth: Penguin.

Ateljevic, I. and Doorne, S. (2000) Staying within the fence: lifestyle entrepreneurship in tourism. *Journal of Sustainable Tourism*, **8**, 378-392.

Billington, R.D., Carter, N. and Kayamba, L. (2008) The practical application of sustainable tourism development principles: a case study of creating innovative place-making tourism strategies. *Tourism & Hospitality Research*, **8**, 37-43.

Cooper, C. (2006) Knowledge management and tourism. *Annals of Tourism Research*, **33**, 47-64.

Hall, C.M. and Williams, A.M. (2008) *Tourism and Innovation*. London: Routledge.

Henderson, J.C. (2006) Tourism in Dubai: overcoming barriers to destination development. *International Journal of Tourism Research*, **8**, 87-99.

Hjalager, A.M. (2010) A review of innovation research in tourism. *Tourism Management*, **31**, 1-12.

Leslie, D. (2005) Creative cities? *Geoforum*, **36**, 403-405.

Ministry of Tourism (2009) *Tourism Strategy of Turkey – 2023*. Ankara: Ministry of Tourism.

Polanyi, M. and Sen, A. (2009) *The Tacit Dimension*. Chicago: University of Chicago Press.

Tribe, J. (1997) The indiscipline of tourism. *Annals of Tourism Research*, **24**, 638-657.

9 Strategic Evaluation

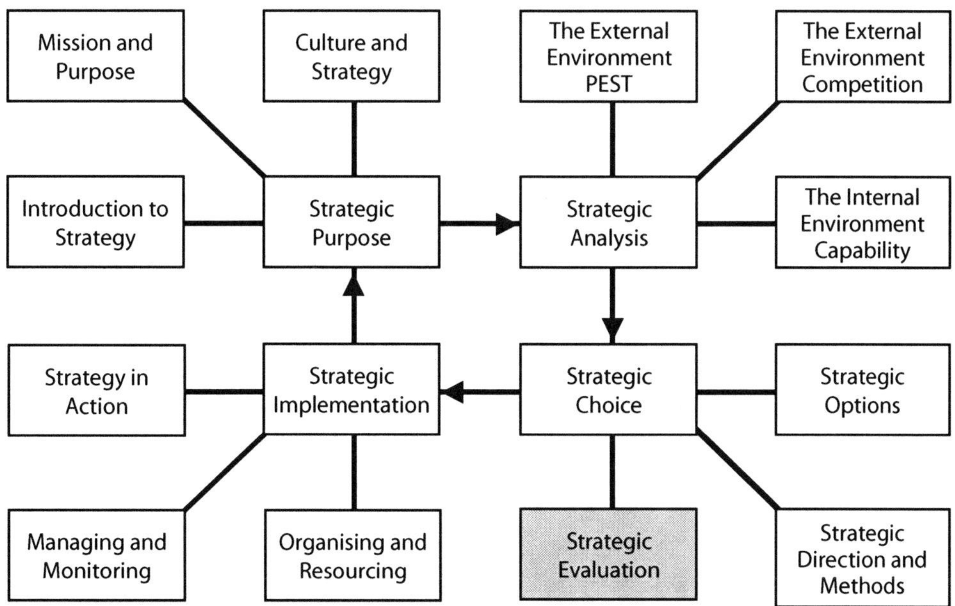

Figure 9.1

Learning outcomes

After studying this chapter and related materials you should be able to understand:

- Suitability analysis
- Acceptability analysis
- Feasibility analysis
- Ranking.

and critically evaluate, explain and apply the above concepts.

Introduction

This chapter introduces a framework for evaluating strategic options. There are three essential questions used to evaluate a strategy or competing strategies:

- ◊ Does it fit our situation?
- ◊ Do we want to do it?
- ◊ Can it be done?

These questions are examined using:

- ◊ Suitability analysis
- ◊ Acceptability analysis
- ◊ Feasibility analysis.

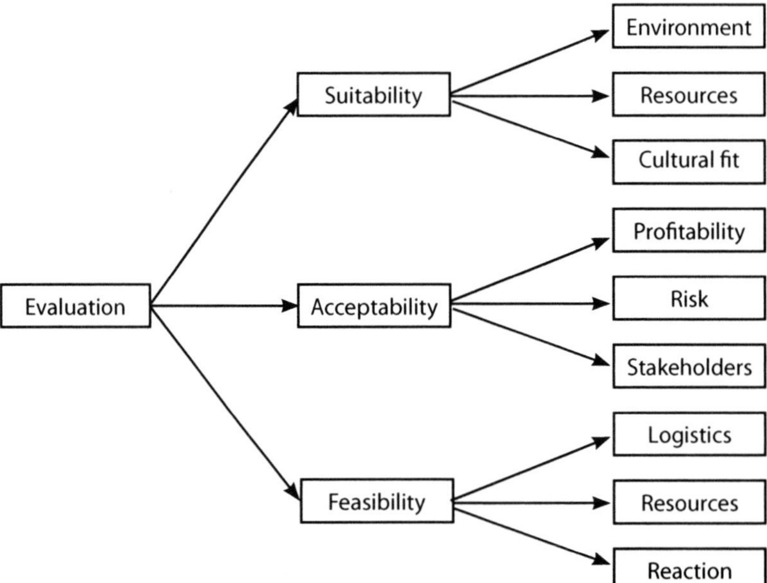

Figure 9.2: Evaluation framework

Suitability analysis: tests whether a strategy fits the situation facing an organisation.

Suitability analysis considers the fit of a strategy in terms of C-PEST factors in the external environment, as well as considering an organisation's resource capability and culture. Acceptability analysis reviews strategy in relation to the aims and missions of an organisation. Feasibility examines whether an organisation is able to muster the necessary resources to follow a particular strategy, and scrutinises plans in terms of their logistics and likely competitor reaction. Of course not all of these aspects will necessarily apply to every strategic option. A ranking matrix can help in strategic decision making particularly where strategic impacts are mixed. Here, competing strategies are awarded scores according to how well they meet particular criteria.

Case study 9 presents the strategy of merging TUI Tourism and First Choice to form TUI Travel and covers aspects of suitability, acceptability and feasibility.

Case Study 9: The merger of TUI Tourism and First Choice to form TUI Travel

The TUI logo and the Thomson brand

The deal

In 2007 the boards of TUI AG and First Choice recommended a merger between TUI Tourism and First Choice to form the £12 billion travel group TUI Travel plc. The move followed soon after their key rivals Thomas Cook and MyTravel had agreed to join in a £3 billion merger. The new company was created by the acquisition by TUI Travel of First Choice and the newly formed TUI Travel is owned 51 per cent by TUI AG and 49 per cent by First Choice Shareholders. This all-share agreement was achieved by a share exchange where First Choice Shareholders received one TUI Travel share for each First Choice share held. TUI's shares closed up 10 per cent in Frankfurt, while First Choice's rose by more than 8 per cent in London after the merger plans were announced. The main conditions of the merger include approval by a majority of First Choice shareholders and clearance by the European Commission under its Merger Regulations. Clearance by the Commission was subsequently given subject to TUI divesting its ownership of Budget Travel in Ireland, where First Choice's ownership of Falcon had led to concerns over monopoly power in the market.

The suitors

The portfolio of TUI Tourism comprised around 3200 travel agencies, 70 brands, 120 aircraft, 40 inbound agencies and access to over 165,000 hotel beds. It has extended its products from package holidays to component parts offered on the Internet. First Choice had a portfolio of 80 brands, 33 aircraft and 420 travel agencies. Its strength has been its development of differentiated and exclusive products and a successful acquisition strategy. Profits of each company prior to the merger are shown.

Profit for the year (€m)	2006	2005	2004
TUI Tourism	(563.9)	72.0	115.0
First Choice	72.3	80.3	45.8

Competitive strengths

The competitive strengths from the merged Group were forecast to include:

- The breadth of operations including flights and accommodation, package tours and niche travel products, organised into the four sectors of Mainstream, Specialist, Activity and Online Destination Services.
- A strong portfolio of over 170 brands, including leading brands such as TUI, Thomson, First Choice, JetAir and Sunsail.
- A variety of distribution channels in all major source markets.
- The opportunity to cross-sell differentiated travel products into the combined markets of the merged Group.
- A leading position in the attractive long-haul market segment.

- Enhanced economies of scale.
- Sophisticated Internet travel offerings.
- Experience in making acquisitions.

Synergies

A merged group would combine the resources of each of the companies to create a comprehensive business that would satisfy most needs of the travel consumer including the independent traveller, the traditional package holidaymaker and more specialist requirements focusing on a variety of controlled distribution channels.

The merger prospectus estimated that the merged group would result in cost benefits of around £100 million per year offset by restructuring costs of about £130 million in total. Cost synergies would arise from economies of scale resulting from consolidation of the First Choice and TUI Tourism operations. Specifically these were forecast to stem from improvements in the operational efficiency of the combined charter airline operations and the rationalising of duplicate central functions, overheads and retail distribution capability.

Strategy and objectives and of the merged group

TUI Travel's primary strategic objectives are:

- To be one of the world's leading leisure travel groups by providing customers with a wide choice of products with the flexibility to meet their changing needs.
- To deliver earnings growth and margin expansion through the combination of organic development and selected acquisitions.
- To deliver cost synergies and maintain a lean and efficient business model.
- To maximise shareholder value.

(Merrill Corporation, 2007, p.19)

TUI Travel plans to operationalise this strategy through the following objectives:

- Offering a comprehensive range of travel products
- Increasing its share of controlled distribution
- Developing the brand portfolio
- Improving yield management
- Maintaining an efficient and flexible business model
- Making quality acquisitions.

Suitability

Suitability analysis aims to test whether a strategy fits the situation facing a tourism organisation or destination as identified by strategic analysis. Therefore suitability can be initially divided into:

- ◊ Environmental fit
- ◊ Resource fit, and
- ◊ Cultural fit.

Environmental fit

The key questions relating to a strategy's fit with external environmental factors are whether the strategy exploits opportunities and whether it effectively counters threats. Therefore strategic options need to be evaluated against the factors which emerged from the C-PEST analysis, i.e.:

- ◊ The competitive environment
- ◊ The political environment
- ◊ The economic environment
- ◊ The socio-cultural environment
- ◊ The technological environment.

The competitive environment

Chapter 5 provided a number of approaches that may be used to understand the competitive environment. These may be turned into questions for evaluation of a strategy in terms of its competitive environment:

- ◊ **Strategic group analysis**: does the strategy enhance competitive advantage against firms who compete on a similar territory?
- ◊ **Porter's five forces:**
  1. Does the strategy diminish the threat of new entrants?
  2. Does the strategy reduce the bargaining power of buyers?
  3. Does the strategy reduce the bargaining power of suppliers?
  4. Does the strategy reduce the threat of substitutes?
  5. Does the strategy reduce the degree of competitive rivalry and reduce the intensity of competition in the industry?
- ◊ **Competitor analysis:** is the strategy formulated in the light of an assessment of the capabilities of key industry rivals?

In case study 9 the TUI/First Choice merger appears suitable in terms of the competitive environment. It represents a good move in terms of the key strategic groupings in the industry – especially as a response to the merger of Thomas Cook and MyTravel which otherwise would have been a dominant player in this strategic grouping. The size of the merged TUI Travel also has potential to reduce the bargaining power both of buyers and suppliers. Less firms in the industry inevitably means less competitive rivalry and the merged group offers a broad range of capabilities to match or exceed those of existing competitors.

The political environment

Chapter 4 identified pertinent issues for strategy in the political environment and these prompt the following questions for evaluation of strategies:

- ◊ Does the strategy identify possible political change in the future and the likely effects of this on the business?

- ◊ Does the strategy identify different political environments in the destination countries where it operates?
- ◊ Does the strategy take account of influential pressure group activity?
- ◊ Does the strategy take account of possible policy changes in the areas of:
    - ♦ Competition policy
    - ♦ Health and safety
    - ♦ Transport and infrastructure
    - ♦ Global carbon agreements and targets
    - ♦ Taxation and spending plans
    - ♦ Disability and access legislation
    - ♦ Foreign policy
    - ♦ Visa policy and home security
    - ♦ Regulation and deregulation
    - ♦ Regeneration plans
    - ♦ Employment and training policy
    - ♦ Travel advisories
    - ♦ Minimum wages?

The economic environment

Chapter 4 also identified economic issues related to strategy and these are reflected in the following questions:

- ◊ Does the strategy take account of the economic environments that affect the expenditure patterns of the business's clients?
- ◊ Does the strategy take account of economic environments in which their tourism product is located and which may affect the supply of tourism services?
- ◊ Does the strategy take account of changing conditions of destination competitiveness?
- ◊ Does the strategy take account of possible changes in the specifics of
    - ♦ Consumers' expenditure
    - ♦ Investment expenditure
    - ♦ Government expenditure
    - ♦ Taxation
    - ♦ Exchange rates
    - ♦ Interest rates
    - ♦ Inflation
    - ♦ Employment
    - ♦ Expectations?

Box 9.1 presents data from the TUI Travel Annual Report for 2008 which demonstrates its strategy of diversification of source markets and entry into growth markets as a means of overcoming economic downturns in its traditional markets of Northern Europe.

Box 9.1 TUI Travel strategies for a turbulent economic environment

TUI Travel has a unique combination of differentiated content and specialist product offerings, catering to a wide range of customers across 25 source markets which means we are not overly reliant on any one source market or customer segment.

As global travel and tourism continues to expand, certain destinations are set to grow faster than others. For instance the first eight months of 2008 saw the Middle East (+17.3%), Central America (+9.4%), South America (+7.2%), South Asia (+7.5%) and North Africa (+6.9%) significantly outperform the total market, which was up 3.7% over the same period (Source: United Nations World Tourism Organisation). Our Online Destination Services Sector already has a considerable presence in these emerging destinations and is consequently well placed to benefit from their continued expansion.

Source: TUI Travel annual report 2008

The socio-cultural environment

Chapter 4 also provides the basis for questions to evaluate the suitability of a strategy in terms of its socio-cultural fit:

- ◊ Does the strategy take account of forecast changes in
  - ♦ Population size
  - ♦ Age distribution
  - ♦ Sex distribution
  - ♦ Geographical distribution
  - ♦ Income distribution?
- ◊ Is the strategy sensitive to changes in attitudes and values about travel?
- ◊ Is the strategy informed about the availability of paid leave?

The technological environment

Finally Chapter 4 also provides the basis for questions to evaluate the suitability of a strategy in terms of technological issues. These include:

- ◊ Will the strategy take advantage of changes in information communication technology?
- ◊ Will the strategy take advantage of changes in other technology such as:
  - ♦ Construction techniques
  - ♦ Materials technologies
  - ♦ Energy technology – especially alternative sources of energy such as wind and solar power and biofuels?

Box 9.2 describes some of the ways in which TUI travel's strategy takes advantage of opportunities in the technological environment.

Box 9.2: TUI travel and technology

First Choice moved onto the Thomson in-house reservation platform (TRACS) in 2009, two years after the merger of TUI/First Choice. It moved from the Gemini platform that it had been previously using joining most of TUI Travel's other UK brands. This is part of a wider programme of other IT standardisation and integration designed to cut costs and develop innovative systems.

The merged Group was an early adopter in Europe for the new Boeing 787 Dreamliner. The Boeing 787 is technologically advanced with extensive use of lightweight carbon fibre components which help it achieve fuel savings of 20 per cent over previous generations of similarly sized airplanes. The Dreamliner also has a greater range capacity allowing TUI Travel to offer more long-range destinations.

Resource fit

Consideration of strategies in terms of an organisation's internal strengths and weaknesses enables the degree of resource fit to be evaluated. This fit between strategy and reality can be analysed using:

- ◊ Resource audit
- ◊ Portfolio analysis
- ◊ Product life cycle analysis, and
- ◊ Value chain analysis:

Resource audit

An initial audit of an organisation's resources may answer a key question here:

- ◊ Is a strategy suitable in terms of current resources?

Strategic options do not always find such a ready fit in terms of existing resources and in many cases the acquisition of new resources will be necessary. Such issues are addressed later in this chapter under feasibility. In the case of the TUI Travel merger, the strategy itself by joining resources across two previously separate companies created a wealth of resources and indeed some duplication of resources that could subsequently be rationalised.

Portfolio analysis

Chapter 6 used the BCG Matrix to analyse the balance within an organisation's product portfolio (refer to Figure 6.2) and this prompts the question:

- ◊ Does a proposed strategy offer a well-balanced portfolio?

TUI Tourism's portfolio of products prior to its merger had a historic emphasis on package holidays. Market growth for some of these key products (particularly in Spain) was low, positioning them as deteriorating cash cows.

Thus TUI Tourism's portfolio was in need of refreshing. The merger strategy represented the opportunity to acquire question mark products available from First Choice (low market share/high market growth) with good prospects for transformation into a star (high market share/high market growth) and develop a more balanced portfolio.

The General Electric Business Screen (Hofer and Schendel, 1978) can also be a useful tool in assessing the suitability of a strategy. It analyses current and future products in terms of:

◊ The business unit's competitive position (strong/weak)

◊ Long-term market attractiveness (high/low).

Figure 9.3 places highlights of the combined portfolio of TUI tourism (TT) and First Choice (FC) on a General Electric Screen, and illustrates the suitability of the First Choice Merger in terms of refreshing TUI Tourism's portfolio. For example, the strength of First Choice in specialist, adventure and long-haul markets are all areas of long-term market attractiveness. In particular it should be noted that the merging of the two company's airline operations under TUI Airline Management (TAM) brings significant competitive strength to the new combined group (CG).

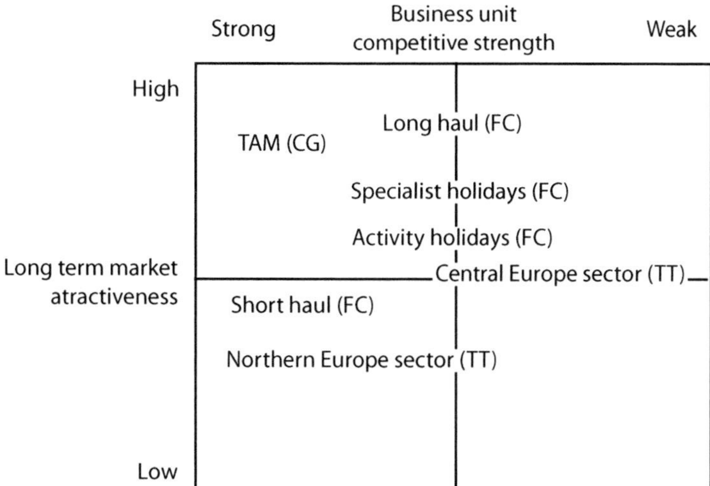

Figure 9.3: General Electric screen

Product life cycle

The question about suitability here is:

◊ Does a strategy ensure a balanced portfolio in terms of the life cycles of its products or services?

Where do the activities of the enlarged TUI Travel group figure on a product life cycle curve (see Figure 6.3)? The basic product of package holidays is long established and is thus probably at the maturity/decline phase. But the product is undergoing constant development which enables new aspects to be repositioned in a growth phase. Here we might include activity holidays and specialist holidays. The acquisition policy of TUI Travel (and First Choice) means that growth products (e.g. Exodus) are strategically added to the portfolio once they have passed the risky introduction phase of the product life cycle.

Value chain analysis

Here the suitability question is:

◊ Does a strategy offer clear enhancements to an organisation's value chain?

The main benefit of the TUI/First Choice merger is that it fills in gaps in the value chain that existed in the previously separate companies and offers a comprehensive portfolio covering the whole spectrum of tourism products. By adding TUI Tourism's large volume consumer tour operating brands, flight and accommodation offer and web presence to First Choice's specialist brands and differentiated products a business is created that is able to satisfy nearly all the tourism needs of the consumer including independent travellers, package holidaymakers and those with specialist needs. In summary, these benefits may be termed as synergies. Synergies arise where the benefits of the merged group of TUI Tourism and First Choice exceed those attributable to the separate activities of those organisations – i.e. something extra is added in the process.

Cultural fit

Test of cultural fit: how well a strategy can be accommodated by an organisation.

Suitability in terms of cultural fit requires the following clarification:

◊ Are there any insurmountable difficulties of integration of work practices presented by a strategy?

Cultural fit considers how well a proposed strategy can be accommodated by an organisation. Chapter 3 considered how an organisation's culture gave rise to a particular paradigm – a way of seeing things and way of doing things.

Mergers such as TUI Tourism/First Choice can result in difficulties of cultural integration if firms have markedly different paradigms. In this case, however, the dangers of a serious cultural clash are likely to be low. This is because both TUI Tourism and First Choice operate in the broadly similar business cultural setting of Western Europe and the similarities between the organisations are sufficient to ensure similar operational practices. However lack of cultural fit of a proposed strategy should not necessarily rule it out. It may be that an organisation's existing culture is in need of change. The feasibility of effecting cultural change will need to be examined and this is addressed later in this book.

Acceptability

Acceptability analysis: scrutinises strategic options in terms of whether organisational objectives are fulfilled.

Acceptability scrutinises strategic options in terms of whether organisational objectives are fulfilled and investigates factors such as:

◊ Profitability (in the private sector)

◊ Social profitability (in the public sector)

◊ Risk

◊ Stakeholder satisfaction.

Profitability

Test of profitability: return on capital employed and payback period.

Since profit is a key element of the mission of most private sector organisations, profitability will be one of the most important ways of assessing the merits of the acceptability of a strategic option and the simple question to be addressed is:

◊ Will the proposed strategy enhance profitability?

Strategies with highest projected profitability will tend to be favoured. In the TUI Tourism/First Choice case study, First Choice had a particularly good track record at generating profits, hence its attraction to TUI Tourism. The main tests for profitability include return on capital employed, and payback period.

Return on capital employed

The formula for calculating return on capital employed (ROCE) is:

$$\text{ROCE} = \frac{\text{Profit before interest and tax}}{\text{Capital employed}} \times 100$$

It is likely that a date will be specified for a particular ROCE to be achieved.

Payback period

This method compares strategies by measuring the length of time it takes to repay the original investment from the revenues earned. Table 9.1 shows an example of the payback method.

Table 9.1: Payback period

Year	0	1	2	3	4
Costs	100				
Revenue	0	20	40	60	80
Cash flow	(100)	20	40	60	80
Cumulative cash flow	(100)	(80)	(40)	20	100

In this example, the project generates a positive cumulative cash flow in year 3. This method may favour projects with the quickest payback irrespective of overall profitability. On the other hand, the sooner the payback, the less a project will be subject to uncertainties, and some organisations may see speed of return as a priority over total return. In the TUI Tourism/First Choice case it was predicted that there would be restructuring costs of about £130 million in total and cost benefits of around £100 million per year suggesting a very short payback period for the merger.

A key problem with the simple payback method is that revenues are not discounted so earnings within the payback period are given equal weight irrespective of the year they appear in. This means that future earnings are overvalued. Discounted cash flow techniques are used to address this problem.

Payback method using discounted cash flow

Discounted cash flow takes into account the fact that future earnings have a lower value than current earnings. For example, if £100 today could be invested at a rate of interest of 10 per cent, it would be worth £110 in a year's time. Working this backwards, £110 in a year's time is only worth £100 today at a rate of interest of 10 per cent. In other words it has been discounted at a rate of 10 per cent to find its present discounted value. Discount tables exist to assist such calculations but there is also a formula for calculating present discounted value:

$$PDV = R_t / (1 + i)^t$$

R = return
t = year
i = rate of interest or discount rate (expressed as decimal)

Table 9.2: Payback period using DCF

Year	0	1	2	3	4
Costs	100				
Revenue (actual)	0	20	40	60	80
Revenue (discounted)		18.2	33.1	45.1	54.6
Cash flow (discounted)	(100)	18.2	33.1	45.1	54.6
Cumulative cash flow (discounted)	(100)	(81.8)	(48.7)	(3.6)	51

Table 9.2 applies this formula to recalculate the payback data from Table 9.1 to present discounted values using a discount rate of 10 per cent. Notice that this method pushes back the payback by one year.

Problems in using profitability analysis

Problems of using profitability analysis for strategy evaluation include first the fact that it may be difficult to isolate the costs and revenues that come from a particular strategy if it is not a clearly discrete project. Its costs and revenues may be inextricably mixed with other projects. Second, it is difficult to quantify the benefits of some strategy elements (e.g. investment in corporate image may lead to intangible benefits). Third, there are the inherent dangers of uncertainty in forecasting.

Social profitability

Test of social profitability: cost–benefit analysis.

Profitability analysis only includes expenditures and revenues which are internal to an organisation (i.e. directly received or paid). Whilst such a narrow view of profitability (i.e. private profitability) may be appropriate to many private sector organisations it is not always appropriate to the public sector or for evaluation of strategies of tourism destinations. In such cases, social profitability will often be a more useful indicator of acceptability. The technique used to determine social profitability is cost–benefit analysis and the evaluation question for strategies using this method is:

◊ Does the strategy enhance net social benefit?

Social profitability attempts to measure the total costs and benefits of a strategic option beyond those that just affect the entities sponsoring the project. These external costs and benefits are not visible in an entity's profit and loss account but may have strong impacts on the wider community affected by an entity's activities. Thus an acceptable project in terms of private profitability would be one where:

$$\Sigma Bp - \Sigma Cp$$

is maximised, whilst an acceptable project in terms of social profitability would be one where:

$$(\Sigma Bp + \Sigma Bs) - (\Sigma Cp + \Sigma Cs)$$

is maximised, where,

Σ = the sum of
Bp = private (internal) benefits
Bs = social (external) benefits
Cp = private (internal) costs
Cs = social (external) costs.

Table 9.3 considers the development of Suvarnabhumi, Bangkok's new airport. The airport has two runways and 120 aircraft parking slots, five of which are capable of accommodating the Airbus A380 aircraft. It has a handling capacity of 76 flights per hour with 45 million passengers and 3 million tonnes of cargo per year. Its development and operations generates potential private profitability (net revenue generated for private sector firms who contribute to its development and operation), and its social profitability (net benefit to everyone affected by the airport).

Table 9.3: Suvarnabhumi Airport, Bangkok: private and social profitability

	Costs	Benefits
Private	Construction costs Finance costs Running costs	Revenue from airlines Revenue from leases
Social	Noise pollution More traffic generated Air / CO_2 pollution Loss of land to other uses	Employment provision Reduction in waiting time More tourism to Thailand

Whilst calculating private costs and benefits is relatively straightforward, it is more difficult to attribute monetary values for public costs and benefits and some of these issues are discussed by Dwyer *et al.* (2007) where the authors attempts to develop financial, social, and environmental measures of tourism yield.

Risk

The pursuance of a new strategy inevitably exposes an organisation to some risk and an evaluation of the risk factors will help to determine the acceptability of a particular strategy. Jang and Chen (2008) applied a financial portfolio theory to understand risk and offer tourism authorities and policy-makers explicit guide-

Tests of risk: financial risk and sensitivity analysis.

lines for risk management in the destination planning process. They note that if the Taiwanese government is to achieve its Doubling Tourist Arrivals Strategy, introduced in 2002, the tourism authorities should take the high-return/high-risk option and shift available resources to the Japan market. For the low-return/low-risk option, tourism policy-makers of Taiwan should, according to Jang and Chen, allocate fewer resources for Japan and instead should use more resources for other markets, especially the USA, to increase the number of tourists. In particular, the risk of a strategy may be evaluated in terms of financial risk and sensitivity.

Financial risk

The financial risk inherent in a strategy will depend upon the capital cost of the project in comparison to the current capitalisation and turnover of an organisation. It is also important to consider the sources of funds to finance the project, its effects on the organisation's overall liquidity position and the likely period of negative cash flow before a project breaks even. Thus a strategy which requires a large investment relative to current operations, which involves finance from banks, and which has a distant break-even point is likely to be of high risk. In short, failure of the strategy could jeopardise the whole organisation. The question to be posed here is:

◊ Are the financial risks of a strategy reasonable and acceptable?

Sensitivity analysis

The question raised by sensitivity analysis is:

◊ Is the sensitivity of a strategy to changes in its underlying assumptions acceptable?

Taylor and Sparkes (1977) discuss the importance of sensitivity analysis in strategic evaluation. Sensitivity analysis considers how sensitive a project is to changes in the assumptions that underlie profitability forecasts. This is sometimes called risk analysis. In particular changes in the economic environment, competitor reaction and legislative changes may be important factors in causing actual prices and sales deviating from predictions. Box 9.3 illustrates the risk factors that were inherent in the TUI Tourism/First Choice merger and identified in the prospectus that was published to present the merger to interested parties.

A number of different scenarios may be considered and computer simulations can plot the predicted effects of changes revealed in these scenarios. Large projects, or projects whose profits are sensitive to small changes, or for which the key assumptions are subject to a large degree of uncertainty will carry a high risk. Table 9.4 illustrates a sensitivity analysis conducted by Eurotunnel in 1994. Eurotunnel was a huge project linking England and France which required substantial borrowings to finance the construction and initial running phases. Figure 9.7 shows the sensitivity of the date of the first declaration of a dividend, to a number of different scenarios. X represents the parameters known in 1994 and the various scenarios show deviations from this in relation to revenues, costs and interest rates. It can be seen that under scenario 5, where Eurotunnel is unable to secure its desired level of refinancing, the declaration of first dividend is delayed considerably.

Box 9.3 Examples of risk factors associated with the TUI Tourism/First Choice merger to form TUI Travel

- Changes economic conditions
- Concerns over the environmental impact of airline travel
- Competition could lead to reduced prices or a loss of customers
- Political instability, terrorism or natural disasters
- Fluctuations in exchange rates
- Fuel costs
- Changes to regulations
- Loss of key personnel
- Industrial relations
- Inability to develop information technology
- Dependent on third party service and facility providers
- Liabilities in connection with under-funded pension schemes
- Failure to satisfy conditions to completion of the merger
- Inability to achieve the anticipated synergies and cost savings
- Fall in the price of TUI Travel Shares.

Source: Based on the TUI Travel plc Prospectus (Merrill Corporation Ltd, 2007)

Table 9.4: Sensitivity analysis for Eurotunnel (1994)

Scenario	First dividend declared in the year...
Current projections (x)	2003
Revenue at x + 10%, costs at x – 3%	2000
Revenue at x – 10%, costs at x + 3%	2006
Real interest rates at x – 1%	2001
Only limited refinancing obtained in 1994	2014

Source: Eurotunnel

Stakeholder satisfaction

Stakeholder analysis, covered in Chapter 2, enables the key stakeholders who will be affected by a particular strategy to be identified. It may be recalled (see Figure 2.4) that it is important to identify stakeholder influence (as measured by stakeholder power) as well as stakeholder interest when assessing acceptability. Once again, those stakehol ders with high power/interest will be the key players to whom stakeholder satisfaction analysis needs to be primarily addressed. In the TUI Tourism/First Choice case, stakeholders that need to be considered and questions asked include:

- ◊ Shareholders (How will share prices/dividends be affected?)
- ◊ Bankers (Will the strategy affect credit worthiness?)
- ◊ Unions (What impact will the strategy have on employment?)
- ◊ Government (Will the strategy infringe monopoly laws?)
- ◊ Local people (How will local environment be affected?)

Key stakeholders for acceptability analysis: shareholders, bankers, unions, government, local people.

In the immediate aftermath of the announcement of the merger, TUI's shares closed up 10 per cent in Frankfurt, while First Choice's rose by more than 8 per cent suggesting that the merger would add value to shareholdings. However Figure 9.4 shows the progress of TUI Travel's share prices between mid-2007 and the end of 2009 and it can be seen that the share price at the end of this period was less than that at the time of the merger. The merger would be not be acceptable to some union members as cost reductions are an important logic of the merger strategy and these would be achieved by consolidation and rationalisation of retail outlets and office support activities and the inevitable loss of jobs. In terms of acceptability to government, the EC only gave approval to the merger on the condition that TUI Travel divested its ownership of Budget Travel in Ireland.

Figure 9.4: TUI Travel share price (p) mid 2007 to end 2009

Soliva *et al.* (2008) put stakeholders at the centre of their quest to understand the acceptability of alternative strategies for land use in the uplands of Europe where agriculture is in decline. They note the need for involvement of stakeholders if land use and social and cultural conflicts are to be avoided. They argue that involving stakeholders in upland areas can be facilitated by using scenario techniques and by discussing alternative futures in local stakeholder panels. Their article presents four scenarios of land-use change for the year 2030, and their assessments by stakeholder panels in Scotland, France, Norway, Switzerland, Slovakia and Greece. It also explores how stakeholders in different countries weight the visual landscape impacts and the livelihood and biodiversity aspects of the scenarios and discusses the reasons for their different weightings.

Feasibility

Feasibility: test whether a strategy can be realistically achieved.

Feasibility seeks to test whether a strategy can be realistically achieved, and asks whether an organisation already possesses or has access to the necessary resources. It therefore subjects strategic options to scrutiny in terms of:

- ◊ Funding
- ◊ Human resourcing
- ◊ Timing/logistics
- ◊ Competitive reaction.

Funding

Main sources of funding: retained profits, disposals, loans, new share capital.

Whilst profitability analysis tests whether a strategy yields an acceptable rate of return, funding analysis asks the question:

- ◊ Is the organisation able to obtain finance for a particular strategy?

Funding will generally be funded from:

- ◊ Retained profits
- ◊ Disposals
- ◊ Loans
- ◊ New share capital.

An organisation may already have the necessary cash in hand to fund a particular strategy. Such assets may arise from profits retained from current and past activities or from cash generated by the disposal of companies, business units or brands. Where strategies can be financed from cash in hand, feasibility is clearly not a problem. In the absence of sufficient funds at hand, organisations will need to seek new finance. Bank loans are a possible option. Here funding feasibility can be broken into two components. First, can funds be obtained? This will depend upon the bank's evaluation of the strategy to be financed as well as its assessment of the borrowing organisation's overall credit rating. Second, how much will bank funding cost? A key issue here is how much the cost of loans (the rate of interest) adds to the costs of the project.

The other main source of new funds for public limited companies is by a rights issue. This is where new shares are sold to existing shareholders, thus raising new capital. The feasibility of a rights issue depends upon whether shareholders agree to a rights issue, the costs of the issue, and whether shareholders are prepared to buy the new shares (i.e. shareholder evaluation of a project's profitability, and thus its potential to contribute to increased share prices and healthy share dividends into the future).

In the case of the TUI Tourism/First Choice, the merger was arranged by an all-share agreement with First Choice shareholders receiving one TUI Travel share for each First Choice share held. There were therefore no large capital funding requirements for the strategy.

Human resourcing

The feasibility of a strategy may also be reviewed in terms of the question:

◊ Does the organisation's workforce have sufficient skills to execute the proposed strategy?

An audit can be useful in determining whether the skills necessary for the success of a particular strategy are available or accessible. Such audits need to consider several dimensions. First, are skills available in the relevant functional area – e.g. marketing, operations management, financial management, purchasing? Second, it may be important to have personnel with knowledge of a particular market, e.g. hotels, airlines, theme parks, or geographical area. Third, the dynamics of a team assigned to a particular strategy are important. Here considerations include skills in project management as well as a range of team attributes. For example, is the project team balanced in terms of innovators, team workers, finishers, and sceptics?

The new board of TUI Travel included directors from the boards of First Choice and TUI Tourism to provide adequate representation from each of the merging companies and a balance of skills necessary for the newly merged company.

Timing/logistics

Logistics: the order in which aspects of a strategy should be carried out.

Timing and logistics (the order in which aspects of a strategy should be carried out) are crucial to some projects, and timing has a knock-on effect on profitability. Therefore the question that needs to be asked here is:

◊ How feasible are the logistics, scheduling and completion date for a strategy?

Here break-even analysis can be a useful device. The question that needs to be asked is whether the assumptions underlying the initial analysis are realistic ones, and what would be the effects on the break-even point of a failure of a project to complete to its original timetable. Figure 9.5 illustrates a break-even analysis for the Channel Tunnel and shows how its break-even point was profoundly affected by delay in its opening.

For the Channel Tunnel project, the initial projections were that the tunnel would open in 1993, and that total revenues would then increase sharply (C) to achieve break-even (E) by 1997, with costs B. However construction and fitting delays meant that a full service did not occur until 1995. Thus the revenue curve shifts outwards to D and the cost curve shifts upwards from B to A as new borrowing is needed to finance the delay. Break-even (F) moves to around the year 2003. However, under some scenarios, break even is not achieved at all.

Competitive reaction

Competitive reaction is an important consideration for the feasibility of any new strategy. The question to be asked here is:

◊ Does the proposed strategy take account of likely competitor reaction?

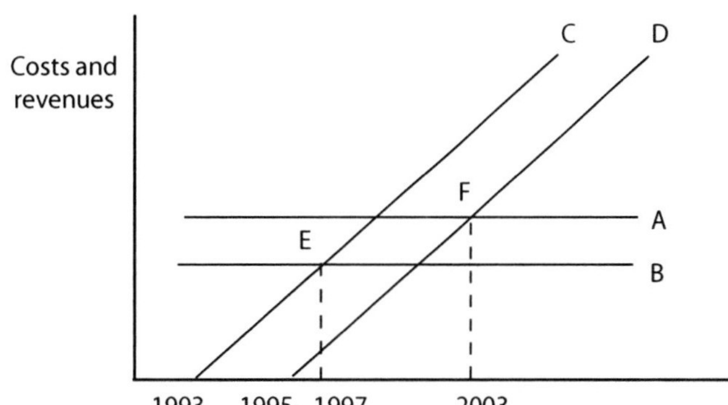

Figure 9.5: Break even analysis
Key: A, B = Total costs
C, D = Total revenues

Competitive reaction: how competitors respond to a strategic move

Competitor reaction is likely to be fierce when there is a high degree of competitive rivalry (see Porter's (1998) five forces analysis, Chapter 5). It may take the form of imitation of a strategy thereby reducing any competitive advantage, price reduction or advertising strategies. The case of the TUI Tourism/First Choice merger itself demonstrates an imitative competitor reaction to the earlier merger between Thomas Cook and My Travel. In this case any competitive cost reductions achieved by the Thomas Cook/My Travel merger would be lost as similar or greater savings are achieved by the TUI Tourism/First Choice merger.

Padilla and McElroy (2007) argue that Cuba has become a major destination in Caribbean tourism and that any lifting of US travel restrictions would enable it to become the dominant player luring American tourists from competitors. The authors present possible strategies for the development of tourism in post-Castro Cuba including tourism products it might introduce into the Caribbean market. Their study uses historical trends and interviews to predict tourism growth in Cuba after a five-year transition period and predicts the diversion of US tourists from competing destinations. However they also note that:

> *Once the transition is complete, one would expect a 'sales' profile that rises sharply in the early stages of product introduction, then peaks, and falls off to some equilibrium level determined, among other things, by the ability of other destinations to lure back repeat tourists, as well as by the competitive reactions and countermoves of their key rivals. (p. 657)*

Choosing between options

The preceding analysis has surveyed some of the analytical tools available to assist in evaluating strategic options. However it is likely that evaluation of options will generate a series of mixed results with each strategic option having a conflicting list of good and bad points. Under such a situation, no clear winning strategy may emerge and resolution of this kind of stalemate requires clarification and prioritisation of evaluation criteria.

Screening of options: ruling out options according to specific criteria.

This may involve listing objectives that must be achieved (e.g. minimum ROCE) and effects that must be avoided (e.g. loss of ownership and overall control of the organisation). These may be classed as essential criteria. It is then possible to attach weightings to other criteria to reflect their relative importance. Thus an initial screening of options can rule out those which fail the essential tests, and options may then be ranked according to their performance against the other, weighted criteria.

Ranking: putting strategic options in order of preference.

Table 9.5 illustrates the situation facing a destination where the current strategy is mainly concentration on exclusive markets rather than mass tourism. This is achieved by a ban on charter flights. It shows a possible system of screening and ranking of four strategic options available for tourism development:

1 Do nothing
2 Concentrate on an exclusive image (sell to existing markets)
3 Concentrate on exclusive image (sell to new markets)
4 Mass tourism (lift ban on charter flights/allow more hotel development).

Most of the options are a mixture of pluses and minuses and evaluation is not clear. However if protection of the environment is made an essential criterion, then options 1 and 4 are screened out as not acceptable. Options 2 and 3 remain, each with a score of +8. If responsiveness of strategy to a changing environment is thought to be a particularly important criterion of evaluation it could be double-weighted. This changes the overall scores to +9 for option 2 and +11 for option 3 which emerges as the most appropriate strategy.

Table 9.5: Screening and ranking of options

	Minimise resource costs of new investment	Generate extra employment	Protect environment	Achieve high economic growth	Responsive to changing external environment
Do nothing	+5	0	-2	0	0
Concentrate on exclusive image (sell to existing markets)	+5	0	+1	+1	+1
Concentrate on exclusive image (sell to new markets)	+3	0	+1	+1	+3
Lift ban on charter flights/ allow hotel development	-3	+4	-5	+2	0

Key: More unfavourable — More favourable

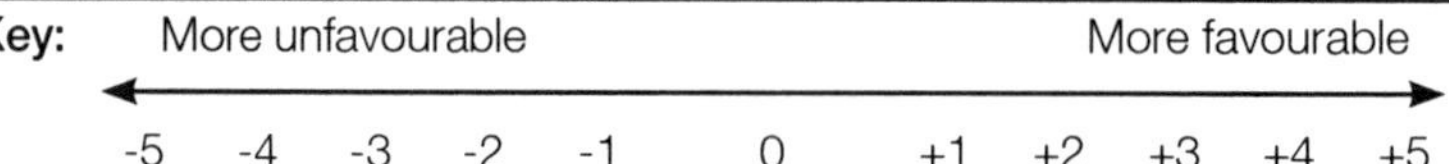

Review of key terms

- Suitability analysis: tests whether a strategy fits the situation facing an organisation.
- Tests of suitability: environmental fit, resource fit and cultural fit.
- Tests of environmental fit: compatibility with the competitive, political, economic, socio-cultural and technological environments.
- Test of resource fit: resource audit, portfolio analysis, product life cycle analysis and value chain analysis.
- Test of cultural fit: how well a strategy can be accommodated by an organisation.
- Acceptability analysis: scrutinises strategic options in terms of whether organisational objectives are fulfilled.
- Test of acceptability: profitability (in the private sector), social profitability (in the public sector), risk and stakeholder satisfaction.
- Test of profitability: return on capital employed and payback period.
- Test of social profitability: cost–benefit analysis.
- Tests of risk: financial risk and sensitivity analysis.
- Key stakeholders for acceptability analysis: shareholders, bankers, unions, government, local people.
- Feasibility: test whether a strategy can be realistically achieved.
- Tests of feasibility: funding, human resourcing and timing/logistics.
- Main sources of funding: retained profits, disposals, loans, new share capital.
- Feasibility constraints caused by human resources: does the organisation's workforce have sufficient skills to execute the proposed strategy?
- Logistics: the order in which aspects of a strategy should be carried out.
- Competitive reaction: how will competitors respond to a strategic move?
- Screening of options: ruling out options according to specific criteria.
- Ranking: putting strategic options in order of preference.

Multiple choice questions

1 Which of the following is true?
   A Suitability analysis tests whether a strategy can be put into action
   B Suitability analysis tests whether a strategy fits the given situation
   C Suitability analysis tests whether a strategy is beneficial to stakeholders
   D Suitability analysis tests whether there is sufficient capital to fund to a strategy

2 Which of the following is not one of the three key tests for evaluating strategy?
   A Suitability analysis
   B Acceptability analysis
   C Historical analysis
   D Feasibility analysis

3 Which of the following is a part of acceptability analysis?
   A Stakeholder analysis
   B Economic analysis
   C Political analysis
   D Competitor analysis
4 Which of the following demonstrates social profitability?
   A Social benefits exceed private benefits
   B Social and private benefits exceed social and private costs
   C Private benefits exceed private costs
   D Social and private costs exceed social and private benefits
5 Which of the following statements is true?
   A Cost–benefit analysis is a test of feasibility
   B Logistics is putting strategic options in order of preference
   C Cost–benefit analysis is a test of private profitability
   D Sensitivity analysis is a tests of risk

Discussion questions

1. What is meant by cultural fit? Which factors suggest a good cultural fit, and which suggest a poor one, between TUI Tourism and First Choice?
2. Under what circumstances will cost–benefit analysis rather than profitability be used to determine the acceptability of a strategy?
3. What factors would make a strategy a high-risk one?
4. Evaluate a recent or proposed merger or takeover between tourism organisations.
5. What is sensitivity analysis? What variables would the merger between TUI Tourism and First Choice be sensitive to and with what effects?

References

Dwyer, L., Jago, L., Deery, M. and Fredline, L. (2007) Corporate responsibility as essential to sustainable tourism yield. *Tourism Review International*, **11**, 155-166.

Hofer, C. and Schendel, D. (1978) *Strategy Formulation: Analytical Concepts*. St Paul: West.

Jang, S. and Chen, M.H. (2008) Financial portfolio approach to optimal tourist market mixes. *Tourism Management*, **29**, 761-770.

Merrill Corporation Ltd (2007) *TUI Travel plc Prospectus*. London: Merrill Corporation.

Padilla, A. and McElroy, J.L. (2007) Cuba and Caribbean tourism after Castro. *Annals of Tourism Research*, **34**, 649-672.

Porter, M.E. (1998) *Competitive Strategy: Techniques for Analyzing Industries and Competitors: with a New Introduction*. Glencoe, IL: Free Press.

Soliva, R., Rønningen, K., Bella, I., Bezak, P., Cooper, T., Bjørn Egil Flø (2008) Envisioning upland futures: stakeholder responses to scenarios for Europe's mountain landscapes. *Journal of Rural Studies*, **24**, 56-71.

Taylor, B. and Sparkes, J.R. (1977) *Corporate Strategy and Planning*. London: Heinemann.

Part IV Strategic Implementation

The final stage of tourism corporate strategy is strategic implementation. By the end of Part IV it should be possible to construct a plan to operationalise a strategy for a tourism organisation, systematically monitor that strategy and create a comprehensive strategy document.

Strategic implementation follows logically from the previous three stages where an appropriate strategy has been selected from a number of options after a comprehensive situational analysis of the tourism organisation.

Chapter 10 discusses the detail of implementation in terms of financial, physical and human resources. Chapter 11 examines the management of change and reviews methods of control and evaluation of strategy. Chapter 12 concludes the book. At its centre is a guide on how to write and present a strategy document and this is followed by a look at turnaround and crisis strategies and some final concluding remarks.

10 Organising and Resourcing

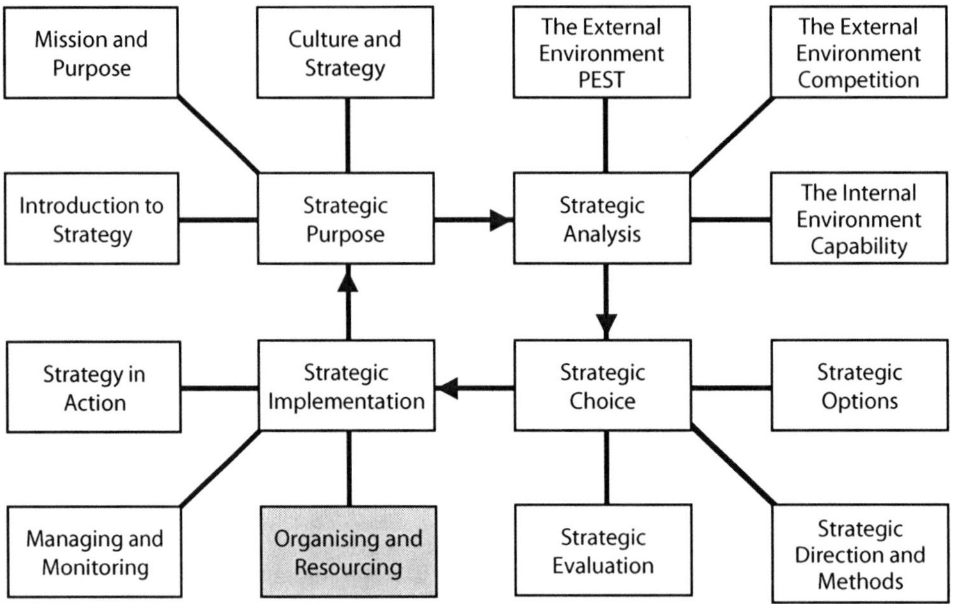

Figure 10.1

Learning outcomes

After studying this chapter and related materials you should be able to understand:

- Resource planning
- Formulation of a coordinating plan
- Design of an organisational structure
- Issues in organisational design

and critically evaluate, explain and apply the above concepts.

Introduction

This book has previously addressed the issues that enable an entity to make a reasoned choice of a strategy that is appropriate to its mission. In this chapter, issues of how to put a strategy into practice are covered and two important aspects of strategic implementation are addressed. The first is resource planning where emphasis is on identification of resources needed to support a strategy, issues of resource fit, and formulation of a co-ordinating plan. The second aspect of strategic implementation involves designing an organisational structure that can best support a particular strategy. This in turn prompts a discussion of structural types, structural elements and issues in organisational design.

The following case study on the London Olympics illustrates some of these issues. Crucial matters for implementing the strategy for the 2012 Games included choosing an organisational structure for the games, questions of funding and the co-ordination and logistics challenges posed in delivering such a highly complex project.

Case Study 10: The London Olympics 2012

In 2005 the Games of the XXXth Olympiad for 2012 were officially awarded to London against strong competition from Madrid, Moscow, New York and Paris. The main site of the Games and the Olympic village is situated in Stratford in East London and the Games bring substantial regeneration benefits to a previously run-down area of London as well as the promise of a lasting legacy. Each of the bidders had to submit a strategy in the form of a candidate file covering the following aspects:

- Olympic Games concept and legacy
- Political and economic structure
- Legal
- Customs
- Environment and meteorology
- Sports and venues
- Paralympic Games
- Olympic Village
- Medical services
- Security
- Accommodation
- Transport
- Technology
- Media operations
- Olympism and culture

Building logistics of the London 2012 Olympic stadium.
Picture: Graham Miller

Organisation

Execution of the Games project is a highly complex task and the main organisational structure is divided into two key organisations:

- The London 2012 Organising Committee
- The Olympic Delivery Authority

The Olympic Delivery Authority is responsible for providing the venues and infrastructure, and the London 2012 Organising Committee is responsible for staging the Games. These two organisations are in turn supported by:

- The Mayor of London who leads the Greater London Authority group to ensure Londoners benefit from the Games.
- The Department for Culture, Media and Sport which is the department responsible to the Government for the Games.
- The Nations and Regions Group which ensures that all parts of the UK benefit from the Games.
- International and UK commercial partners which provide sponsorship to fund the Games.

Funding

The London 2012 Organising Committee has budgeted about £2bn for the staging of the Games. It receives most its funding from the International Olympics Committee and by its own revenue generation through sponsorship, ticket sales and merchandising. On the other hand the budget needed by the Olympic Delivery Authority to provide the infrastructure is around £9.5bn (2009 data). This represents a substantial increase from the original estimate of around £3.4bn. The Olympic Delivery Authority relies upon public funding and the sources of this (and the increase over the original estimates) are as follows:

- Central Government £5975 million (increase of £4931 million)
- National Lottery £2175 million (increase of £675 million)
- Greater London Authority £925 million (increase of £300 million)

- London Development Agency £250 million (no change)
- Total £9325 million (increase of £5906 million)

The Government has also underwritten the overall cost of the Games in the form of a guarantee as required by the International Olympics Committee.

Co-ordination and logistics

An Olympic Board, made up of representatives of the above organisations and other key stakeholders, provides overall strategic coordination and monitoring of the 2012 Games project and is responsible for ensuring the delivery of the commitments made to the International Olympic Committee.

The first meeting of the Olympic Board in 2005 determined that common objectives should be agreed, mechanisms for reporting and monitoring the delivery of the objectives should be set up and progress reported to the Board. So, for example, the Olympic Delivery Authority had in place various milestones with target completion dates for different parts of the project. These included:

- 2009: 'The big build: foundations' milestone goal to ensure building had started on all permanent venues in the Olympic Park.
- 2010: Completion of the structure and roof of the Olympic Stadium, the Aquatics Centre, Velodrome, the new Energy Centre and the majority of homes in the Olympic Village.

The complex Olympic Delivery Authority programme includes burying of power lines, site preparation, relocation of unwanted existing infrastructure, upgrades to transport infrastructure and building of facilities. The management of the complex logistics is supported by a GANT schedule and a Games time masterplan showing the timing of procurement activities, design, construction and test events.

Resource planning

Resource planning: identification of resources, ensuring resource fit, and formulation of a co-ordinating plan.

The evaluation stage of the strategy process involved analysis of the feasibility of an option in terms of finance and availability of resources. At the implementation stage, resource planning is concerned with:

- ◊ Identification of resources
- ◊ Resource fit
- ◊ Formulation of a co-ordinating plan.

Identification of resources

The identification of resources can be divided into the four categories of:

- ◊ Financial resources
- ◊ Physical resources
- ◊ Human resources
- ◊ Information and technology resources.

Financial resources

At the financial level it is essential to have budgets prepared which show how an entity's strategy is to be financed. In particular, plans need to show sources of finance and the logistics of finance (to ensure co-ordination between income and expenditure). As discussed in Chapter 9, the main sources of financial resources are accumulated profits (cash at hand), external loans, share capital and government assistance.

For destinations in developing countries, external aid agencies can be an important source of funding. For example Hawkins and Mann (2007) describe the role of the World Bank in funding tourism-related development strategies. In the period 2000–2006 the authors note World Bank participation in 94 tourism-related projects with a total active portfolio of over $3.5 billion. These and previous projects have included a Wildlife and Tourism Project in Kenya, a Wastewater Disposal for Tourism Centres Project in the Dominican Republic and Jordan's Second Tourism Development Project.

The article also underlines the importance of other agencies in providing financial assistance such as the European Union, the United Nations World Tourism Organization and the United Nations Development Program and demonstrates that the strategic objectives of these institutions are partially achieved through their distribution of funds. For example Hawkins and Mann (2007) note that there is renewed interest within the World Bank in the role of tourism in the fulfilment of the United Nations Millennium Development Goals.

Physical resources

A change in strategic direction will generally require adjustments in physical resources at the level of plant and machinery or consumables. A tourism organisation may have a dedicated purchasing department to co-ordinate the buying of physical resources. Important considerations in physical resources planning include:

Fitness for purpose: the match between a given resource and the specifications required.

- **Specification**: this may involve a careful audit of the uses to which physical resources are to be put. The result will be a list of required specifications.
- **Fitness for purpos**e: this will examine the match between the specifications offered and the specifications required.
- **Cost**: prices between suppliers need to be compared, taking into account running and maintenance costs.
- **Terms**: is it more appropriate to lease or buy capital goods?

For airlines, purchasing decisions range from the ordering of in-flight catering, through computer systems, to the ordering of aircraft and requirements will vary according to different strategic aims. For example, in-flight meals will be differently specified for the different strategies of low price, hybrid or high value added. Large airlines will have a powerful influence on suppliers and the specific requirements of the biggest carriers such as Singapore Airlines, American

Airlines and British Airways will generally liaise with aircraft manufacturers at the design stage for incorporation of required features into the finished product. Box 10.1 illustrates this in the case of the Airbus A380.

Box 10.1 A380 Passenger cabin specifications

The seat configurations for the Airbus A380 range from 450 to 840 passengers. For example, Singapore Airlines operates three classes of seat. Suite class comprising of 12 suites, business class comprising of 60 flat beds and an economy class of 399 seats. At the other extreme, Air Austral has operated a service with the entire configuration in economy class allowing 840 seats.

Precise specifications for different airlines particularly reflect competition to differentiate in first and business class. Virgin Atlantic announced plans to include casinos and gymnasiums on its A380s. Emirates offers private suites for fourteen first-class passengers who also have access to shower spas. Four of the suites offered by Singapore Airlines can be configured into double suites with double beds.

Tour operators will similarly choose hotels to fit particular marketing strategies. Thus while price-based packages may well tolerate thin walls, high rise and Spartan service, high value-added packages would have more exacting specifications.

Human resources

Strategic implementation will have consequences for human resources, and manpower planning will need to address:

- ◊ Manpower numbers
- ◊ Skills
- ◊ Recruitment and selection
- ◊ Training and development
- ◊ Grading and remuneration.

Strategic plans will need to determine both the quantity and the quality of the future workforce and often the size of the workforce is a key issue. Productivity gains and 'downsizing' are central to many strategic plans in order to achieve reductions in costs. Careful consideration to the design of a redundancy programmes and industrial relations is therefore central in these cases. On the other hand, some strategies involve expansion and therefore particular attention needs to be given to recruitment and selection of new personnel.

In both cases, a programme of manpower training and development needs to be thought out. Often new strategies demand cultural change and here staff development should include programmes which communicate new strategic thinking with the workforce. Worker re-education is more difficult in situations of downsizing than expansion as in the latter, new appointees may be more easily inducted into company practices and culture.

Two key tourism strategies have been published by Fáilte Ireland (2005a, b). These are a human resource development strategy for Irish tourism and a strategy and implementation plan for competing through cultural diversity. They devote a section to the human resource needs in implementing these strategies and they stress the importance of the following:

- Flexibility (mutual between employee and employer)
- Participation (encouraging staff to be involved in decision-making)
- Performance management (regular systems of performance review to ensure service delivery)
- Recognition (attribution of credit to high-achievers)
- Reward (linked to performance)
- Communication (routine dialogue with staff)
- Learning and development (access and support for learning progression)
- Empowerment (enabling active participation in the workplace).

Performance management: regular systems of performance review to ensure service delivery.

Empowerment: enabling active participation in the workplace.

Burns (1995, p. 61) identified the particular problems of training which face the hotel industry in Romania in its transition from communism and central planning to capitalism and market forces. He noted that:

> *existing business culture has historically been focused on maintaining existing structures...[leading] to an operational culture unable to cope with the notion of customer-focused business activities.*

Human resource skills are particularly critical for new venture businesses. For example Haber and Reichel (2005) conducted a study on the contribution of human capital, planning and environment resources to small venture success in the tourism industry. Their findings showed that the human capital of the entrepreneur, particularly managerial skills, were the greatest contributing factor to successful performance.

Information and technology resources

The tourism industry has widely deployed information and technology resources to improve products and services, reduce costs, improve competitive positioning and create barriers against competitors' imitation of selling points. Information and technology resources need to be carefully planned during strategic implementation. Information and technology competence may be obtained by:

- In-house development
- Purchase from external providers for internal use
- Contracting out of services
- Alliances
- Acquisition of organisations that possess the desired technology.

Law *et al.* (2009, p. 614) conclude that:

> *Managers can, and should, deal with future IT-related issues by integrating IT into the company's strategic management and business mission. A way to achieve this goal is to constantly upgrade the IT knowledge and skills of staff, as in this way overall technical proficiency can be assured. Additionally, managers should maintain close contact with the IT industry so that they will be able to appreciate technological trends and developments. After careful analysis, the right IT can then be incorporated into the business and be part of a business process re-engineering exercise that can support the business to maximize its full potential.*

Resource fit

There are two potential problems of resource fit. First there is the technical issue of how new resources will fit with existing ones. This is a particular problem for areas such as computer resources, where new software may just not technically operate on old systems, or the computer systems of two merging organisations may be incompatible.

The second problem of resource fit concerns fit between resources and organisational skills. An airline may be tempted for example to purchase planes from a different manufacturer offering better specifications and lower prices. However the problem of integration of new planes into the existing fleet may be problematic in areas such as crew competence and maintenance expertise. Thus there are some clear manpower planning considerations in physical resource planning.

Formulation of a coordinating plan

Co-ordinating plan:
a plan covering project logistics and objectives.

A co-ordinating plan is a key to strategic implementation. It comprises the following elements:

- ◊ Project logistics (planning)
- ◊ Project objectives (operations).

Project logistics (planning)

Logistics:
the organisation and management of the flow of goods, information, human and other resources in order to achieve a particular goal.

In planning, logistics is the organisation and management of the flow of goods, information, human and other resources in order to achieve a particular goal. The problem of logistics arises because in complex plans there is a necessary order in which things have to be carried out. A failure to anticipate logistics can lead to costly delays as one part of a project waits for an essential prerequisite to be completed.

Minis *et al.* (2006) investigated the organisation, processes, and systems of Olympic logistics. They developed a methodology to review the strategy and tactics of logistics operations for the Athens 2004 Olympic Games. Their analysis took account of Olympic-specific characteristics, host country characteristics and lessons learned from previous games. They found that successful principles included model venue planning, standardisation of materials, the establishment of a Logistics Command Center (LCC) and the establishment of an independent administration function. They also discussed the role of outsourcing, warehousing and just-in-time deliveries.

Some of the key logistics considerations for the London 2012 Olympics are illustrated in Box 10.2. The Olympics are a large scale and complex project and Box 10.2 illustrates some of the key deliverables as well as stages of development. In the Games time masterplan each stage is assigned an estimated time slot so that an overall schedule for completion may be planned and a critical path can be formulated. A critical path demonstrates the order in which the deliverables for project must be executed as well as showing those deliverables which may be programmed at the same time. The Games time masterplan enables the project to be organised in the most efficient way. The importance of such analysis is first, to enable materials ordering and subcontracting to be co-ordinated and second, to highlight the impact of delays that may arise in any deliverable on other deliverables.

Box 10.2 London Olympics: Logistics

Deliverables

- Land acquisition
- Planning consent
- Undergrounding of power lines
- Provision of utilities
- Structures, bridges and highways
- Landscape and public realm
- Enabling works
- Olympic stadium
- Aquatics centre
- Velodrome
- Olympic village
- Thornton field railway sidings relocation
- Stratford regional station upgrade

Stages

- Procurement
- Design
- Construction
- Organising committee overlay
- Infrastructure
- Enabling works
- Games preparation/commissioning
- Decommissioning

It may be that the outcomes associated with some strategies could potentially be achieved at the same time. For example there is no logistical obstacle to retraining managers in Romanian hotels (Burns 1995) in service delivery, personnel management, and computer literacy. However an attempt to achieve all the desired outcomes immediately will tend to lead to overload and superficial change. Here priorities need to be set to enable each objective to be properly met and monitored.

Project objectives (operations)

Management by objectives: a system whereby strategy is translated into a number of clearly stated outcomes or objectives.

Management by objectives (MBO) is a system whereby strategy is translated into a number of clearly stated outcomes or objectives. The achievement of these objectives is assigned to specific personnel. MBO has been defined as:

a system that integrates the company goals of profit and growth with the manager's needs to contribute and develop himself personally.

(Humble, 1970, p.21)

directing each job towards the objectives of the whole business

(Drucker, 1968, p.150)

Thus MBO can be an important contributor to strategic implementation. First MBO helps to clarify the strategy – what does the strategy mean in terms of measurable performance targets? Second, MBO, assists implementation since this now becomes attributable to personnel who have been assigned specific tasks. The key stages to effective MBO are:

- **Introduction of MBO**: here, the purposes, and the workings of MBO need to be explained to those who will be part of it.
- **Setting of objectives**: objectives should be generated from the strategic plan in consultation with relevant personnel. They should be prioritised, allocated, quantifiable and subject to time constraints.
- **Performance review**: participants require feedback about performance. Review, which may take the form of appraisal, should consider both past performance and future goal setting. There may be some form of performance related pay included.
- **Monitoring**: there should be periodic checking that objectives are being fulfilled and that strategic goals are being met and an adjustment of future objectives in the light of the findings.

Farrell and Marion (2002) discuss the role of management by objectives (MBO) in the management of visitor impacts in protected areas. They explain how MBO frameworks provide a:

formal process for specifying prescriptive management objectives that define desired resource and social conditions, and selecting appropriate indicators and standards that reflect those objectives. (p. 35)

They further explain that if standards are violated, an evaluation of causes and influential factors is conducted so that effective management responses can be identified and selected. Monitoring is also used to evaluate the success of actions that are implemented.

Design of organisational structure

Organisational structure: the framework which describes how an organisation's activities are arranged.

An organisational structure is the framework which describes how an organisation's activities are arranged. It shows how its personnel are grouped together and the purposes of the groupings (e.g. marketing, human resource management). It shows lines of communications between groupings, organisational hierarchy and control. Mintzberg (1979, p. 2) defines an organisation's structure as:

> *the ways in which its labour is divided into distinct tasks and then its co-ordination achieved amongst those tasks.*

Organisational structure is a key consideration in determining how successful an organisation is in achieving its aims. For this reason it has been said that 'structure follows strategy' (Chandler, 1962; Child, 1977; Sloan, 1990). In other words, if a change in strategic direction has been decided, organisational structure will need to change to implement that strategy. However Mintzberg *et al.* (1998, p. 335) observe that:

> *Structure...no more follows strategy than the left foot follows the right in walking. The two exist interdependently, each influencing the other.*

The point here is that any emerging strategy will itself be strongly influenced by the existing organisational structure.

Structural types

The main types of organisational structure include:

- ◊ Simple
- ◊ Functional
- ◊ Multidivisional
- ◊ Matrix structure
- ◊ Holding company
- ◊ Experimental/organic.

However it should be remembered that as well as the formalised organisational structure, informal structures generally also establish themselves. Whilst the formal structure is found in company manuals and handbooks, individuals within organisations frequently establish informal networks and ways of circumventing the formal structure. Burns and Stalker (1961) argue that employees' private purposes form the basis of an 'informal organization' in contrast to the 'formal organization' which is depicted in its official structure diagram.

Simple structure

Simple structure: absence of formal structure.

This is typically found in small businesses, and is often characterised by the absence of structure. There is little in the way of formalised division of responsibilities or clear lines of reporting. Such structures clearly can only operate when personnel are in close contact and therefore as an organisation grows in size, formal structures inevitably arise.

Functional structure

Functional structure: groupings arranged according to functional areas.

The basic groupings within this form are those of functional areas, typically finance, production, marketing, personnel and research. and development. This structure is often used in a single-product, single-market organisation. An example of this structure as used by the Belize Tourism Board is illustrated in Figure 10.2. Here its 35 staff are housed in simple functional areas of marketing and public relations, hotels, product development and finance and administration.

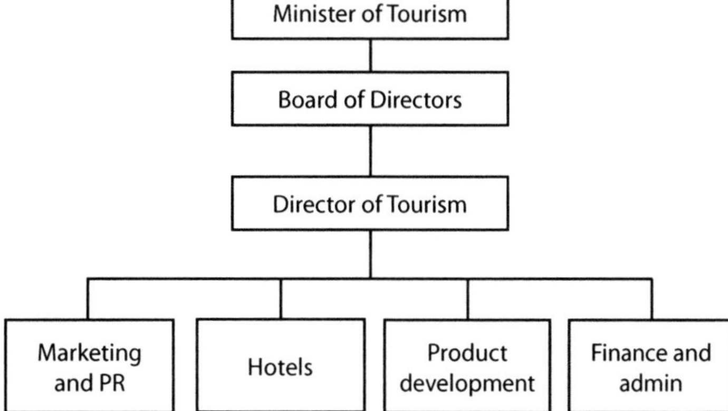

Figure 10.2: Functional structure at the Belize Tourism Board.
Source: http://www.belizetourism.org

The benefits of this structure are that roles and responsibilities are clearly defined and that overall control by the chief executive is simplified. However these are offset by the problem of difficult horizontal communications between functional groups. This often involves the unnecessary referring up of relatively routine decisions. The focus of the organisation on its customers may also be lost as functional groups compete with each other for power and status. Indeed such structures have been seen to generate significant problems such as:

◊ Little co-ordination between activities
◊ A marked inability to adapt
◊ Hierarchical management
◊ Excellence in technical rather than commercial aspects
◊ Preoccupation by staff with their own job rather than service provision.

Multidivisional structure

Divisional structure: groupings arranged according to an organisation's products or services or geographical areas.

A divisional structure groups activities according to an organisation's products or services or geographical areas and is therefore more suitable for organisations with a diversity of products or services and markets. It avoids conflicts which are based on different functions (e.g. disputes between marketing and finance departments) and allows greater concentration on the customer. Also each division can be monitored as a separate unit encouraging a close supervision of costs and sales. However although some functions (such as finance) may be provided centrally, others need to be provided within each division which may lead to duplication of effort. A typical divisional structure is illustrated in Figure 10.3.

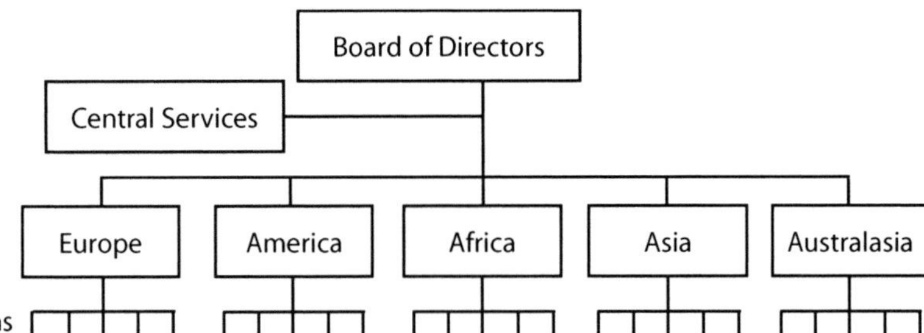

Figure 10.3: Divisional structure

TUI Travel is organised into four major division – mainstream, specialist, activity and online destination services. Mainstream is the largest and so is divided further into Central Europe, Northern Region and Western Europe.

The Taiwan Tourism Bureau is organised into a mainly two-divisional structure around products and services. The product division includes the Planning and Research Division, Hotel, the Travel and Training Division, the Technical Division, the International Affairs Division, the Domestic Tourism Division, the Secretariat, the Personnel and the Accounting Departments. The services division includes domestic Tourism Service Centres and 10 overseas offices to handle international tourism promotion in Tokyo, Osaka, Hong Kong, Seoul, Singapore, Kuala Lumpur, New York, San Francisco, Los Angeles, and Frankfurt.

Matrix structure

Matrix structure: groups workers by both function and product.

A matrix structure groups workers by both function and product and can be used where an organisation wants to encourage collaborative tension between two arms of management. It may be appropriate if an organisation has a number of products or services which are sold in a number of markets (product/market matrix) or to provide balance between the divisional organisation of a firm and its functional operations (functional/divisional matrix). A product/market matrix for a multinational organisation is illustrated in Figure 10.4.

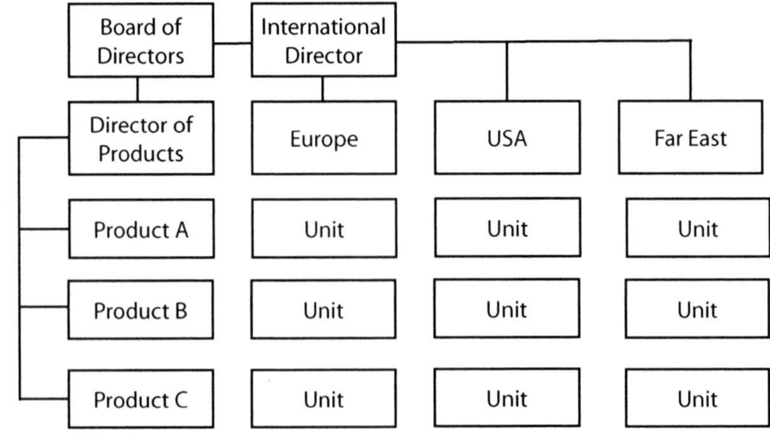

Figure 10.4: Matrix structure

It can be seen that this structure creates a number of units which report to different management arms. Its benefits include a more collaborative approach to decision making. However responsibility for decisions may become less clear. Members of units may prefer to have a single line manager rather than two potentially conflicting managers. Also resolution of disputes between the axes of the matrix may lead to overburdening of senior management, since co-ordination of the two arms only occurs at a senior level. Decision making may therefore involve a better quality of debate but at the expense of increased time taken in reaching decisions.

Holding company

Holding company: an umbrella-type structure for the ownership and co-ordination of a number of clearly separated business units.

A holding company is an umbrella-type structure for the ownership and co-ordination of a number of clearly separated business units which are allowed a high degree of independence in decision-making. Control is exercised at arm's length, with each unit having its own internal organisational structure. The benefits to the holding company are that it can spread its risks through its holdings of a cross-section of businesses. It can also adjust its portfolio, selling subsidiaries which do not meet profit targets and acquiring companies in growth sectors. The size of the overall group can enable cheaper finance to be obtained, and temporary setbacks within individual markets to be weathered. Problems may include difficulties in managing such cumbersome organisations.

Some holding companies are more akin to investment companies and own substantial shares in other companies rather than owning them outright, For example, Kingdom Holding Company (Saudi Arabia) is a diversified investment company with holdings in a large number of Saudi Arabian, Middle Eastern and international companies. It main investments are shown in Box 10.3.

Box 10.3 Investment interests of the Kingdom Holding Company (Saudi Arabia)

Banking and financial services

Citigroup Inc.

Real estate

Songbird Estates plc (Canary Wharf, London)
George V Hotel (Paris)
Plaza Hotel (New York)
Savoy Hotel (London)

Hotel management companies

Fairmont Raffles Hotels International
Four Seasons Hotels and Resorts Inc.
MövenPick Hotels and Resorts AG

Technology, media and telecommunications

News Corporation
Time Warner Inc.

Other interests

Apple Inc
Eastman Kodak Co
eBay Inc.
Euro Disney SCA
Hewlett-Packard Co
Motorola Inc.
PepsiCo Inc
Priceline.com Inc
Procter & Gamble Co
The Walt Disney Co

Experimental and organic structures

Organic structure: a flexible and fluid network of people and communications.

Ricardo Semler, CEO of Semco, adopted an unorthodox organisational structure for his company. His thesis (Semler, 1994) was that rigid, top-down management is inappropriate for contemporary business conditions particularly in view of the difficult, diverse, dangerous and dynamic external environments discussed in Chapter 1. He therefore discarded secretaries, reserved parking spaces, executive dining rooms, dress codes and most rules. In their place he introduced the guiding principles of democracy, and common sense and just two main grades of staff. The two grades are Managers who set their own salaries and Associates who vote on company strategy, decide their own working hours and are responsible for all aspects of production.

Less radical than fully experimental structures is the concept of the organic organisational mode (Burns and Stalker, 1961). In organic structures, employees should have equal status with no rigid job descriptions. The structure would resemble a flexible and fluid network of team members who contribute to a variety of tasks and communicate freely. This is in contrast to the mechanistic mode which describes traditional bureaucratic structures with hierarchical leadership and strong management.

Ögaard et al. (2008) investigated the tension between organic and mechanistic organization forms in the hospitality industry and the relationships of both to individual employees' commitment, job satisfaction and performance. Their findings indicate that managers' and employees' perceptions of their work environments are different and that employees find the organization to be less organic than managers. This leads the authors to point to the importance of both types of structure. They note that:

> *Organic structures are considered important when it comes to employees' and organizations' learning, innovations and development. However, this study strongly indicates the importance of mechanistic organizational forms for the individuals. In addition, both this study and previous research indicate that the hospitality industry might have a general problem with their managers, who are characterized by traditional leadership styles that fail to make the most of the employee's resources. ... the dichotomy of transactional and transformational leadership styles may be an oversimplification of the challenges hospitality managers face, strategically as well when running the daily operations. (p. 670)*

Structural elements

Mintzberg (1979) identified six basic elements common to all organisational structures. These are:

- ◊ The operating core – the employees who produce the goods or provide the services.
- ◊ The strategic apex – the management of the organisation.
- ◊ The middle line – as organisations grow, middle-managers are needed.

◊ The techno-structure – analysts such as accountants and statisticians who perform a monitoring role.

◊ The support staff – who provide internal services such as catering, cleaning and legal services.

◊ Its ideology – which describes the overarching values, beliefs and aims of the organisation.

Mintzberg used this classification of structural elements to analyse how organisations were co-ordinated and how different styles of organisation could develop.

Issues in organisational design

Strategic change will generally require structural change. For example a policy of expansion may require a move towards a divisional structure to co-ordinate the introduction of new products or new markets. A policy of diversification and acquisition of new companies may lead to the establishment of a holding company type structure.

But organisational change may need more than just a change in structural type. For example the emergence of a strong new competitor/service (for example a new low-cost carrier airline startup) may require a fast and adaptable response. In this case organisational responsiveness and flexibility will be a key consideration. Here organisational characteristics are important. Key issues in organisational design include:

◊ Nature of structural groupings

◊ Tall vs. flat structures

◊ Bureaucratic vs. flexible

◊ Centralisation vs. decentralisation

◊ Co-ordination of structural elements.

Nature of structural groupings

Here the issue is the basis on which the cells in an organisational structure should be grouped. Functional structures have departments such as personnel, finance, research and development differentiated according to different types of work. The benefits of this are that specialists work together and support each other. However the danger is that employees focus on their job role rather than on service to the customer.

Product or service departments are organised around single products or services and all the activities in the value chain relating to that product – inputs, processing and marketing, are controlled within that division. Market departments are organised around specific geographical markets or customer types. The particulars of individual markets thus become the focus of organisational activity.

Tall vs. flat structures

Flattened structure: levels of management are stripped out leaving fewer steps between the organisational apex and its base.

A tall structure is one with many levels of management. Benefits derived from tall structures include first that the span of control at each level is narrow. This means that each manager supervises perhaps three or four subordinates on the next level and therefore effective supervision of activities can take place. Communication lines are generally clear, as are lines of authority. Tall structures enable specialisation of effort and concentration on tasks.

However in recent years there has been a movement towards flattened structures. Here levels of management are stripped out leaving fewer steps between the organisational apex and its base. Flat structures are favoured by low-cost carrier airlines such as SouthWest Airlines and easyJet. One of the prime motives for this is the reduction in costs. Communication lines are shorter leading to a more responsive organisation. The management is more in touch with its customers. However the reduction in levels may make delegation of tasks more difficult since there are fewer subordinates.

A flat organisation is not necessarily the same as a lean organisation where the aim is to reduce staffing. This may cause a reduction in specialists and reduce an organisation's capability to continue to add value to its products.

Bureaucratic vs. flexible

Bureaucratic organisation: rigid structure with formal procedures.

Flexible structure: negotiable structure where employees are encouraged to take initiative.

A bureaucratic organisation will relate its operations to its organisational structure fairly rigidly. It will be most suitable in stable environments, and where procedures and end products or services are standardised. There will be clear supervision of activities. This may be contrasted with a flexible structure where employees are encouraged to take initiative. Here the structure is indicative rather than rigid and it is thus open to negotiation and change. Employees are likely to be multi-skilled and their responsibilities may overlap. This type of structure may be necessary for an organisation operating in a turbulent environment.

Scandinavian Airline Systems (SAS) under Jan Carlson in the 1980s moved from a policy of strict adherence to company manuals when Carlson urged staff to 'throw out the manuals and use your heads instead'. A move from the bureaucratic to the flexible was thus heralded and front-line staff were given the decision-making power to do what was reasonably appropriate to please the customer.

Centralisation vs. decentralisation

Centralised organisation: decisions are taken at the apex of the organisation in top-down manner.

In a centralised organisation, decisions are taken at the apex of the organisation in top-down manner. The benefits are that a unified strategy can be more easily directed and a strong corporate identity and image imposed. On the other hand, decentralised organisations encourage decision making to be made at the lowest possible level. This may be more appropriate for large organisations and where flexibility and responsiveness to changing environments are paramount. The focus of many tourism organisations on profit centres reflects the philosophy of decentralisation.

Co-ordination of structural elements

Mintzberg (1979) concluded that there were three basic ways in which the elements of organisational structure could be co-ordinated. First through mutual adjustment where the different elements communicate and adjust their behaviour to reach agreed ends in what is a democratic process. Second through direct supervision. Here co-ordination is achieved through instruction from the strategic apex – essentially an autocratic process. Finally co-ordination is possible through standardisation. Mintzberg showed that there were several possible targets for standardisation. Thus work processes, outputs, skills or norms and beliefs may be standardised in order to co-ordinate the organisation's operations.

Review of key terms

- Resource planning: identification of resources, ensuring resource fit, and formulation of a co-ordinating plan.
- Fitness for purpose: the match between a given resource and the specifications required.
- Performance management: regular systems of performance review to ensure service delivery.
- Empowerment: enabling active participation in the workplace.
- Co-ordinating plan: a plan covering project logistics (planning) and project objectives (operations).
- Logistics: the organisation and management of the flow of goods, information, human and other resources in order to achieve a particular goal.
- Management by objectives (MBO): a system whereby strategy is translated into a number of clearly stated outcomes or objectives.
- Organisational structure: the framework which describes how an organisation's activities are arranged.
- The main types of organisational structure: simple, functional, multidivisional, matrix, holding company, experimental/organic.
- Simple structure: absence of formal structure.
- Functional structure: groupings arranged according to functional areas.
- Divisional structure: groupings arranged according to an organisation's products or services or geographical areas.
- Matrix structure: workers grouped by both function and product.
- Holding company: an umbrella-type structure for the ownership and co-ordination of a number of clearly separated business units.
- Organic structure: a flexible and fluid network of people and communications.
- Structural elements: the operating core, the strategic apex, the middle line, the techno-structure, the support staff and ideology.
- Flattened structure: levels of management are stripped out leaving fewer steps between the organisational apex and its base.

- Bureaucratic organisation: rigid structure with formal procedures.
- Flexible structure: negotiable structure where employees are encouraged to take initiative.
- Centralised organisation: decisions are taken at the apex of the organisation in top-down manner.

Multiple choice questions

1 The system whereby strategy is translated into a number of clearly stated outcomes is known as:
   A Management by logistics
   B Management by statistics
   C Management by heuristics
   D Management by objectives

2 The organisational structure that groups workers by both function and product is termed:
   A Multidivisional structure
   B Matrix structure
   C Flat structure
   D Organic structure

3 Which of the following is not one of Mintzberg's (1979) identified six basic structural elements?
   A The operating core
   B The middle line
   C The bottom line
   D The strategic apex

4 Which of the following is not a recognised choice pair in organisational design?
   A Tall vs. flat structure
   B Centralised vs. decentralised structure
   C Bureaucratic vs. flexible structure
   D Organised vs disorganised structure

5 Which of the following statements is true?
   A The Olympic Delivery Authority is responsible for staging the Olympic Games.
   B Structure always follows strategy.
   C A matrix structure assigns clear roles and responsibilities to individuals.
   D Organic structures are based around flexible and fluid networks.

Discussion questions

1 Discuss the suitability of using an experimental or organic type of organisational structure for a tourism organisation with which you are familiar.

2 Does structure follow strategy or strategy follow structure? Discuss with reference to a named tourism organisation.

3 Identify and explain Mintzberg's six structural elements by reference to a tourism organisation you are familiar with.

4 Prepare a project plan which demonstrates the logistics of a named tourism strategy.

5 Identify the type of organisational structure which exists for a named tourism organisation. Is this structure appropriate for the future?

References

Burns, P.M. (1995) Hotel management training in Eastern Europe: challenges for Romania. Progress in Tourism and Hospitality Research, 1, 53-62.

Burns, T. and Stalker, G.M. (1961) The Management of Innovation. Oxford: Oxford University Press.

Chandler, A. (1962) Strategy and Structure. Cambridge, MA: MIT Press.

Child, J. (1977) Organisation: A Guide to Problems and Practice. London: Harper and Row.

Drucker, P. (1968) The Practice of Management. London: Pan Piper.

Fáilte Ireland (2005a) A Human Resource Development Strategy for Irish Tourism. Competing through People, 2005-2012. Dublin: Fáilte Ireland.

Fáilte Ireland (2005b) Fáilte Ireland, Cultural Diversity Strategy and Implementation Plan. Dublin: Fáilte Ireland.

Farrell, T.A. and Marion, J.L. (2002) The protected area visitor impact management (PAVIM) framework: a simplified process for making management decisions. Journal of Sustainable Tourism, 10, 31-51.

Haber, S. and Reichel, A. (2005) Physical design correlates of small ventures' profitability. Annals of Tourism Research, 32, 269-272.

Hawkins, D.E. and Mann, S. (2007) The World Bank's role in tourism development. Annals of Tourism Research, 34, 348-363.

Humble, J. (1970) MBO in Action. London: McGraw-Hill.

Law, R., Leung, R. and Buhalis, D. (2009) Information technology applications in hospitality and tourism: a review of publications from 2005 to 2007. Journal of Travel and Tourism Marketing, 26, 599-623.

Minis, I., Paraschi, M. and Tzimourtas, A. (2006) The design of logistics operations for the Olympic Games. International Journal of Physical Distribution and Logistics Management, 36, 621-642.

Mintzberg, H. (1979) The Structuring of Organizations. New York: Prentice Hall.

Mintzberg, H., Quinn, J. and Ghosal, S. (1998) The Strategy Process. London: Prentice Hall.

Ögaard, T., Marnburg, E. and Larsen, S. (2008) Perceptions of organizational structure in the hospitality industry: consequences for commitment, job satisfaction and perceived performance. Tourism Management, 29, 661-671.

Semler, R. (1994) Maverick: The Success Story Behind the World's Most Unusual Workplace. London: Arrow Books.

Sloan, A.P. (1990) My Years with General Motors. New York: Doubleday.

11 Managing and Monitoring

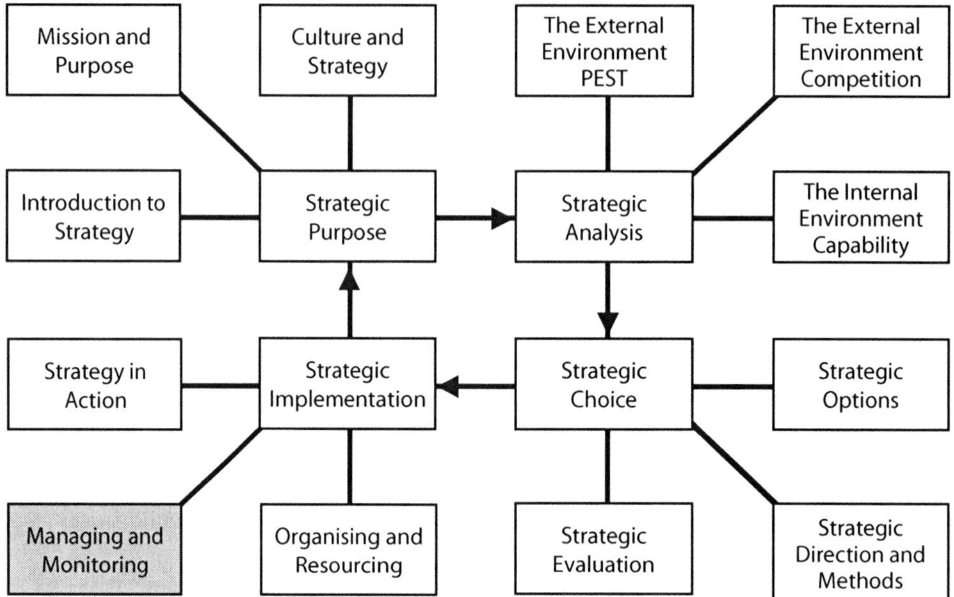

Figure 11.1

Learning outcomes

After studying this chapter and related materials you should be able to understand:

- Management of change
- Methods of monitoring
- Methods of control
- Identification of key factors for effective strategic management

and critically evaluate, explain and apply the above concepts.

Introduction

This chapter analyses issues of managing and monitoring change as well as those of implementation that are required for a new strategy. Management of change may in itself be a challenging task, particularly where a traditional organisation faces the prospect of fundamental change.

Key issues for management of change include:

- ◊ Calculation, and the use of force field analysis to identify drivers and resisting forces of change.
- ◊ Effective communication of the rationale and elements of strategy throughout the organisation.
- ◊ Political and tactical methods of achieving compliance with a strategy.
- ◊ Attention to the issue of organisational culture.

It is also necessary to devise control mechanisms to ensure that a strategy is translated into objectives and key tasks and that the attainment of these objectives is monitored. Strategic performance needs to be monitored to ensure that strategy is being effectively carried out. Any problems that are revealed from the monitoring process then need to be addressed. Finally the chapter considers aspects of effective implementation of strategy.

Case study 11 demonstrates how Australia's strategy for action on tourism and climate change is translated into a number of key objectives or actions, how each of these are assigned resources and timeframes and how implementation is monitored.

Case Study 11: Australia's framework for action on tourism and climate change

A tourism action plan on climate change

The Australian Government identified tourism as a key sector that is vulnerable to climate change concluding that:

> the impact of climate change on infrastructure and the natural environment has the potential to affect the tourism industry. In some cases this could result in social and economic impacts in regions with a high dependency on tourism as a source of income and employment. (Department of Resources Energy and Tourism, 2008, p .2)

In response, the tourism ministers established the Tourism and Climate Change Taskforce to develop a Framework for Action. Its membership included state and territory government tourism officials, officials from the Australian Greenhouse Office and representatives of peak tourism bodies. The plan was predicated on the recognition that:

> a failure to act will leave an industry which currently contributes $38.9 billion to Australia's annual GDP exposed, and undermine industry's capacity to contribute to the economy. (Department of Resources Energy and Tourism, 2008, p.2)

The Framework for Action notes that the Australian government is committed to a reduction of CO_2 emissions by 60 per cent of 2000 levels by 2050 underpinned by an Emissions Trading Scheme planned from 2010. This involves an overall cap on emissions supported by a market-led price scheme for permits to emit greenhouse gases. The resulting costs will have impacts for the tourism industry as well as most other sectors of the economy.

Actions

The are five main actions contained in the framework:

- The need to accurately identify the tourism industry's vulnerabilities.
- The need to develop adaptation strategies to address the tourism industry's vulnerabilities.
- The need to establish a business case for action to reduce emissions and a communications strategy to explain this.
- The need to measure the carbon footprint of the tourism industry and to model the economic impact of the emissions scheme and other climate change policy measures.
- The need for climate change related market research on consumers in key markets and the development of subsequent marketing strategies.

Outcomes

In turn these actions have been translated into a series of outcomes. Each of these identifies who is responsible for resourcing the outcome and in what timescale they should be delivered. Examples of these are:

Outcome 1

Understanding of the vulnerabilities of tourism to climate change and improving the adaptive capacity of the industry:

- Improve the climate change knowledge base for decision-making by tourism operators, destinations and regions.
  Resources: DRET, STOs
  Timing: 3 months, with ongoing updates
- Complete the Destinations Adaptation Research project
  Resources: STCRC, DRET
  Timing: 6 months
- Incorporate the Destinations Adaptation model into tourism planning and decision making tools.
  Resources: DRET, STOs, RTOs, PIBs
  Timing: More than 2 years

Outcome 2

Preparing the tourism industry for a carbon-constrained future.

- Develop best practice guides to emissions management.
  Resources: STOs, PIBs
  Timing: 6 months
- Complete the carbon footprint project and release it publicly.
  Resources: DRET, STCRC
  Timing: 3 months

- Model the impacts of future carbon prices on the Australian tourism industry.
  Resources: DRET, STCRC
  Timing: 12 months

Outcome 3
Repositioning tourism marketing strategies in the light of climate change
- Use climate change consumer market research when developing tourism marketing strategies.
  Resources: DRET, TA, STOs
  Timing: 3–12 months

Outcome 4
Communicating to the tourism industry
- The distribution of fact sheets tailored to tourism enterprises on emissions management through key communications channels.
  Resources: DRET, TA, STOs, PIBs
  Timing: 3 months
- Use the Tourism Australia corporate website to provides information on climate change.
  Resources: DRET, TA, STOs.
  Timing: 3–6 months, with ongoing updates

Outcome 5
An inclusive and cooperative approach to implementation.
- Responsibilities for implementation established and responsible parties report progress to Tourism Ministers' Council.
  Resources: Tourism Ministers' Council Secretariat, and responsible parties
  Timing: ongoing
- Australia and New Zealand to work collaboratively on tourism and climate change issues.
  Resources: DRET and NZ Ministry of Tourism
  Timing: ongoing

Key to stakeholders
DRET: Department of Resources, Energy and Tourism
TA: Tourism Australia
STO: state and territory tourism organisations
STCRC: Sustainable Tourism Cooperative Research Centre
PIB: peak industry bodies

Management of change

Management of change: how strategic change is identified and implemented.

Management of change (Paton and McCalman, 2008; Page, 2007) is the process by which strategic change is identified and implemented as a specific objective. A key challenge for many tourism entities is that their structures were generally designed to solve yesterday's problems. In other words, organisational structure and culture tend to evolve reactively. So an audit of an organisation's capability may well find that it is perfectly structured to deal with the challenges that the organisation faced in the past five years, but inappropriately equipped to deal with the future.

A frozen organisation: one which has become rigidly routinised.

To compound this problem organisations may become 'frozen' in a particular state (Lewin, 1952). A frozen organisation is one which has become rigidly routinised. This tendency may occur because once a particular organisational structure and culture has evolved there is a strong tendency for structural and cultural reproduction. An organisation will tend to recruit, induct and reward its staff in line with its established culture, and the organisation will stay the same.

Lewin's model for creating successful organisational change identified three important stages. First the unfreezing of current organisational behaviour patterns is necessary in order to make the organisation more receptive change. Second, Lewin identified the importance of movement, which involves the carrying out of change or the reconceptualisation of the organisation. Finally, Lewin noted the importance of refreezing the organisation so as to institutionalise the change.

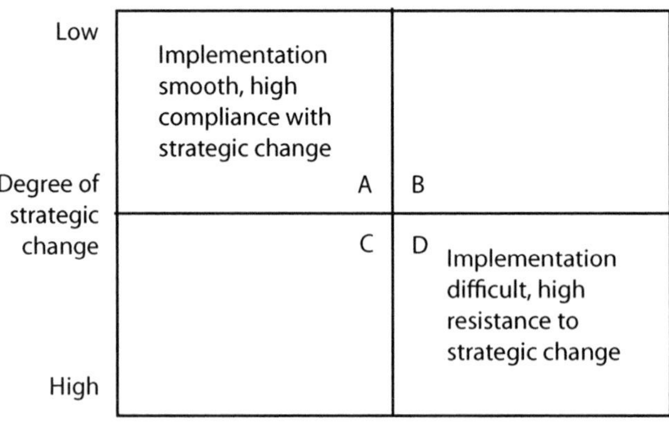

Figure 11.2: Strategic implementation

There is a considerable challenge for management of change particularly where such change is both extensive and to be introduced in the face of a conservative organisation (quadrant D of Figure 11.2). Change in these circumstances is likely to be strongly contested in parts of the organisation. The management of strategic change must therefore pay attention to the four Cs of change (Tribe, 1997) which are:

Four Cs of change: calculation, communication, culture and compliance.

- ◊ Calculation
- ◊ Communication
- ◊ Culture
- ◊ Compliance.

Calculation

Calculation: the identification of the likely impacts of a strategy to identify where critical blockages may occur.

Force field analysis: investigates forces that are either driving movement toward an objective or blocking such movement.

Calculation involves the identification of the likely impacts of a strategy both internally and externally to the organisation with a view to discovering where critical blockages may occur. These may inhibit the implementation of change and are known as resisting forces. At the same time it is important to record those factors (driving forces) which may help promote the desired strategy. Force field analysis (Lewin, 1951; Brager and Holloway, 1992) is a method of examining this. Its aim is to enhance the management of change by generating a tactical approach (Nutt, 1989). It does this by marshalling and encouraging those forces that are driving movement toward an strategic objective whilst reducing the power of resisting forces. The steps in force field analysis are:

- ◊ Identification of planned change
- ◊ Identification of resisting forces
- ◊ Identification of driving forces
- ◊ Formulation of tactics to reduce or eliminate resisting forces
- ◊ Formulation of tactics to encourage driving forces.

Box 11.1 Air France recovery strategy under Christian Blanc

When Christian Blanc became chairman of Air France his major task was to put a rescue-strategy into effect. The strategy involved an attack on costs and a concentration on improvement in service quality in order to generate more revenue – in short, a classic hybrid strategy. Central to the cost-cutting measures was a package which had little obvious attraction to the workforce. The proposals included a pay freeze, productivity gains of 30 per cent to be achieved within 5 years and the loss of 5000 jobs. Needless to say this package was opposed by the majority of Air France's unions and strike action seemed inevitable.

Blanc responded to this impasse in a novel way by going over the heads of the trade unions and putting the package directly to the company's 40,000 workforce by way of a referendum. 30,000 employees participated in the referendum and more than 80 per cent of those who voted were in favour of the plan. This led to the eventual approval by a majority of the trade unions, enabling cost-cutting to be put into effect.

With regard to improving service quality, one key blockage was a dysfunctional culture where cost efficiency was given a low priority. A team of consultants summarised other challenges as follows:

- A marked inability to adapt
- Hierarchical and centralised management with little co-ordination between activities.
- Excellence in technical rather than commercial aspects of airline operations
- Preoccupation by staff with their own job rather than service provision.

The consultants recommended a reorganisation of the company structure that would bring about decentralisation and improved co-ordination. Decision-making was to be encouraged at the lowest possible level and smaller operating units were designed to improve team working and communications. The original management structure which consisted of a few large managerial divisions such as the personnel, transport, airport and commercial divisions was replaced. Eleven profit centres were created to focus on more specific activities. These included distinct geographical markets such as America, France, and the Paris airport services. The new profit centres took responsibility for personnel, transport and airport responsibilities as it affected them.

Two other important agents of change were introduced. First, a share incentive scheme where employees were offered shares in Air France in return for a pay cut. This reduced costs and increased incentives. Second, there was a review of senior management. The executive committee of the company was reduced from 40 to 25 and many of them were new appointments.

Box 11.1 discusses Air France's recovery strategy under Christian Blanc and Table 11.1 identifies key change management issues in a force field analysis.

Table 11.1: Air France recovery strategy – force field analysis

Resisting forces	Driving forces
Trade unions Bureaucratic organisation Job-focused rather than customer-focused workers Defender mentality of senior staff	Survival Competition Self-interest
Tactics for overcoming resistance	**Tactics for enhancing drivers**
Bypass trade union and appeal directly to workforce Reorganisation of company Create profit centres 'Shake up' of senior management	Education programme designed to communicate severity of situation to the workforce Imitation of winning features of successful competitor airlines Instigate profit-related pay schemes

Communication

Effective communication is at the heart of successful strategic implementation. Even organisations which engage in a systematic process of strategic planning may overlook this vital aspect so that the strategy may remain the property of senior management and its circulation may be intentionally or unintentionally restricted. Such organisations may see strategy formulation as an end in itself and overlook the important process of communicating strategy throughout the organisation.

Thatcher (2006) draws attention to four important considerations for effective communication of strategy. First communications should be focused on simple and clear messages and avoid clutter. For example the main communications message to British Airways (BA) staff ahead of their move into Terminal 5 at London Heathrow airport was 'Fit for Five'. Second, communications should be designed for impact so that the clear message is supported by strong visuals. Third, the choice of communications media is important. Face to face meetings should supplement regular e-mail, and newsletter channels. Fourth, employee engagement is important and this can be achieved through workshops. The BA 'Fit for Five' campaign engaged trade union leaders, inviting them to see successful strategies in action overseas and enlisting them as strategy champions.

Different models of communication of strategy may be located on a continuum which includes:

- ◊ Democratic
- ◊ Educative
- ◊ Autocratic.

Democratic

Democratic communication: encouragement of wide participation in strategic formulation.

Democratic communication of strategy occurs where stakeholders of an organisation are encouraged at an early stage to participate in the process of strategic formulation. This represents a bottom-up system of communication. A common method utilised here is to establish a series of task groups or working parties which encompass a wide representation of groups and interests. The objective is to improve the quality of decision making and to ensure the wide ownership of strategy that emerges from such a process. Since a large proportion of stakeholders are involved in strategy formulation, communication will be built into the process rather than being a separate add-on at the end.

Of course, problems arise with such an approach. It may be difficult to reach agreement, information of a highly technical nature may be mishandled by people who are not experts, co-ordination of activities may be laborious and the process may just be too time consuming. It may also be difficult to escape from the existing cultural perspective.

Educative

Educative communication: encourages a two-way flow of communications.

Although essentially a top-down model, the educative process encourages a two-way flow of communications. Thus strategy is likely to originate from the boardroom, but understanding and legitimisation is sought. This will take place by a series of meetings and briefings where the objectives and purposes of a particular strategy are discussed. Strategy may be amended in the light of feedback, encouraging feelings of participation and empowerment among the wider workforce. Legitimisation may be sought through the participation of trade unions.

Hodgkinson *et al.* (2006) presented the results of an exploration of the role of strategy workshops in strategy development through a survey of managerial experience of these events. Their findings showed that strategy workshops play an important part in formal strategic planning processes. Further, the authors noted that the approaches to strategy formation in such workshops rely on discursive rather than analytical techniques. In relation to communication they also found that they typically do not include middle managers a fact that the authors suggest reinforces elitist approaches to strategy development.

Autocratic

Autocratic communication: communication is one-way, top-down and strategy is handed down from the board for implementation.

This may be characterised as 'management by e-mail' where communication is one-way, top-down and the strategy is handed down from the board for implementation. Such a move may be necessary in crisis management where a rapid change in direction is sought, but it may easily alienate those whose job it is to carry out directions. Alienation may arise from resentment at being excluded from decision making, and frustrations arising from an inability to influence matters. Additionally, strategies implemented in such a way are open to misunderstanding and misinterpretation.

Culture

As noted earlier, organisational culture may be an important factor in inhibiting change, since change will represent a threat to established routines, beliefs and values which may be deeply embedded or frozen within the organisation.
The following highlights some cultural problems from the Air France case:

> *I am worried because most of you do not have an economic culture.*
> *(previous chairman M. Blanc, speaking to an audience of managers)*

> *you can't alter attitudes just by redrawing the organisational chart.*
> *(M. Dupuy, SMG Consultancy group)*

> *There are many people who are unwilling or unable to change their attitudes.*
> *(M. Dupuy, SMG Consultancy group)*

These quotations illustrate some general cultural barriers to change. First, the lack of an economic or commercial or service culture may be identified. This really means a lack of focus on profitability or customers. Instead employees may be focused on the specifics of their task and see themselves as information technologists, or accountants rather than as contributors to a corporate goal or mission. Second, cultural patterns are less easily changed than more tangible aspects of the organisation such as the organisational chart.

Higgins and Mcallaster (2004) use the case of the successful turnaround at Continental Airlines to demonstrate the importance of managing cultural artefacts in strategy implementation. They argue that successful strategists create new cultural artefacts or modify the existing ones so that they support the new strategy. They explain that cultural artefacts:

> *include myths and sagas about company successes and the heroes and heroines within the company; language systems and metaphors; rituals, ceremonies, and symbols; certain physical attributes such as the use of space, interior and exterior design, and equipment; and the defining values and norms. (p. 63)*

The authors point out that cultural artefacts, slowly and imperceptibly built up over time, provide support for the existing strategy and can be significant barriers when trying to implement change. Ozdemir (2007) also discusses issues of cultural change management in the tourism industry.

Some of the key factors in promoting cultural change can be summarised as:

◊ Induction programmes for new staff
◊ Change of symbols
◊ Use of language
◊ Training programmes
◊ Appointment of key personnel
◊ Promotion and dismissal policies
◊ Incentive schemes.

Compliance

Compliance: the way to achieve strategic change.

Compliance addresses the question of how strategic change can be achieved, perhaps in the face of opposition. Change may involve deploying political processes, identifying and utilising sources of power (Mintzberg, 1983), and constructing a power base from which to operate. Key issues for achieving compliance include:

◊ Control of resources
◊ Alliances
◊ Rewards and punishments
◊ Charisma
◊ Managing of change skills.

Resources

Acquisition and control of resources is central to the exercise of power and thus a review and reformulation of resource allocation within the organisation can be an important way of implementing change. Resources may be withdrawn from areas within the organisation where resistance is evident and reallocated to areas where the new strategic policy is supported.

Groups, alliances and networks

The forging of groups, alliances and networks can be important in promoting change. The former may be comprised of task groups to achieve particular ends. It may also be important to consider alliances with a wider group of stakeholders other than just employees if, for example, shareholder support is needed for a major policy change. Networking involves a more informal web of contacts and supporters who permeate the organisation more widely.

Rewards and punishments

Part of the process of gaining support may involve improving the status of those who back the new strategic direction whilst sidelining those in opposition. This may involve adjustments to perks, status, salary and ultimately may be underpinned by a radical hiring and firing policy.

Charismatic leadership

Charismatic leader: one who inspires others to follow a particular path.

Writers such as Peters and Waterman (1982) have emphasised the importance of personality and the power of the charismatic leader. In this view of things, the personality traits of managers of change are held to be significant. A charismatic leader is one who inspires others to follow a particular path. Vision, enthusiasm and communications and leadership skills have been identified as key attributes of charismatic leaders. Erkutlu (2008) examined the influence of leader effectiveness at boutique hotels. The findings of this study supported the existing literature on leadership by underlining the importance of transformational leadership qualities in achieving organisational objectives.

Skills and methods for managing change

Theory E: strategic change based on the pursuit of economic value.

Theory O: strategic change based on the development of organisational capability.

Beer and Nohria (2000) distinguish between two distinct approaches to strategic change. They label these 'theory E' and 'theory O'. Theory E, the hard approach, is change based on the pursuit of economic value whilst theory O, a soft approach, is change based on the development of organisational capability. In addition, Beer and Nohria identify six key dimensions of change:

- Goals
- Leadership
- Focus
- Process
- Reward systems
- Use of consultants.

Table 11.2 shows the main differences between theories E and O in terms of these key dimensions. Beer and Nohria do not advocate one theory in preference to the other but rather use the framework to suggest that effective change needs to embrace aspects of both. First, this might involve appropriate sequencing. That is starting with theory E then establishing theory O approaches. Second, it might be appropriate to set goals from the top whilst encouraging participation from below. Third, incentives should embrace a package of financial and intrinsic rewards. Finally, the challenge of integrating theories E and O is to manage the contradictions that may arise.

Table 11.2: Theory E and Theory O

Dimensions of change	Theory E	Theory O
Goals	Economic value	Organisational capability
Leadership	Top down, hierarchical	Bottom up and participative
Focus	Systems and structures	Culture, behaviour and attitudes
Process	Planning and implementation	Experimentation and evolution
Reward systems	Financial	Intrinsic and financial
Use of consultants	Lead change processes	Support and advise

Source: Based on Beer & Nohria (2000)

Buchanan and Boddy's (1992) study of the perceived effectiveness of managers of change included the following as crucial competences:

- ◊ Sensitivity to internal and external environment
- ◊ Clear expression of goals
- ◊ Team building skills
- ◊ Networking skills
- ◊ Ability to cope with uncertainty surrounding change
- ◊ Communication skills
- ◊ Inspirational skills
- ◊ Negotiation skills
- ◊ Political skills
- ◊ Strategic perspective.

Heracleous and Wirtz (2009) examined how Singapore Airlines achieved outstanding performance and sustained its competitive advantage with the airline consistently outperforming its competitors despite a difficult industry environment. They noted that the airline pursues a dual strategy achieving differentiation through innovation and service excellence at the same time as cost leadership. Heracleous and Wirtz also outlined the key success factors of Singapore Airlines' strategy which include:

- ◊ Rigorous service design and development
- ◊ Total innovation
- ◊ 'Profit-consciousness' ingrained in all employees
- ◊ Achieving strategic synergies through related diversification and infrastructure
- ◊ Developing staff holistically.

Control mechanisms

Control mechanism: checks performance and takes corrective action to minimise deviation from strategic objectives.

The strategy process is incomplete without attention to control and evaluation. A control mechanism checks performance and takes corrective action to minimise deviation from strategic objectives. Control mechanisms are necessary to ensure that the strategy which was outlined and broken down into objectives is delivered according to specification. Strategic control is the way in which managers are able to drive the delivery of a given strategy. Merchant and Van der Stede (2007, p. xii) define management control systems as:

> *everything managers do to help ensure that their organization's strategies and plans are carried out.*

Merchant and Van der Stede also stress the importance of identifying the objects of control which they define as results, actions, personnel and culture.

An effective control mechanism is typically composed of four interconnected elements:

- ◊ Performance targets
- ◊ Control systems
- ◊ Measurement of performance
- ◊ Corrective feedback.

Performance targets

Performance target: an outcome that is set for an organization or employee to reach within a specified period of time.

A performance target is an outcome that is set for an organisation or employee to reach within a specified period of time. The concept of management by objectives (MBO) has been discussed earlier in the book but MBO can also be a central part of target setting in management control. This entails the setting of the objectives for a strategy and in turn for those charged with delivery of the objectives. Box 11.2 sets out some high-level performance targets for tourism in Jordan related to its vision and overall goal.

Box 11.2 Performance targets for Jordan's tourism strategy 2010

Vision

Tourism is an essential and vibrant growth sector that will contribute to improving the long-term economic and social well-being of Jordanians.

Goal

Double Jordan's tourism economy by 2010 in real terms.

Results

- Increase tourism receipts from JD570 million in 2003 to 1.3 billion (US$1.84 billion)
- Increase tourism-supported jobs from 40,791 in 2003 to 91,719, thus creating over 51,000 jobs.
- Achieve taxation yield to the government of more than JD455 million (US$637 million)

Source: Jordan National Tourism Strategy 2004–2010

Control systems

Control system: for monitoring progress against strategic objectives.

A control system should establish the process for monitoring progress against strategic objectives. It will typically specify: a schedule for control; who is responsible for the process; key targets for monitoring; what data is to be produced; who the data will be reported to; and how remedial actions will be instigated.

Measurement of performance

Monitoring strategic success includes measurement of the performance targets stated above. These may include:

- ◊ Quality indicators
- ◊ Financial indicators
- ◊ Other indicators.

Quality indicators

Quality assurance: the system by which standards are controlled.

Quality assurance is the name given to the system by which standards are controlled. A common tool of quality assurance is the use of performance indicators. At the level of control, performance indicators in the tourism sector may include items such as:

- ◊ Number of on-time departures
- ◊ Queuing time for attractions
- ◊ Customer satisfaction surveys
- ◊ Number of complaints received
- ◊ Amount of repeat business.

These items will be particularly important for strategies which have a high value-added dimension. Other performance indicators include factors such as occupancy levels. However, there are many aspects of the tourism experience that are difficult to measure, such as atmosphere, excitement, design, and aesthetics.

SERVQUAL: measures satisfaction against customer expectations.

The SERVQUAL questionnaire (Parasuraman *et al.*, 1988) was developed to assess customer satisfaction in the service sector. It measures satisfaction against customer expectations, focusing on:

- ◊ Tangibles, e.g. the appearance of a hotel room, the grooming of resort representatives.
- ◊ Reliability, e.g. do flights depart on time, does the air conditioning work?
- ◊ Responsiveness, e.g. the promptness of service, helpfulness of employees.
- ◊ Assurance, e.g. the knowledge and professionalism of employees.
- ◊ Empathy, e.g. attention to individuals.

SERVQUAL investigations have been carried out in hotels (Saleh and Ryan, 1992), airlines, ski areas (Fick and Ritchie, 1991) and in destinations (Tribe and Snaith, 1998).

Benchmark: a level of acceptable standard.

Benchmarking is a common technique for interpreting performance indicators. A benchmark is a level of acceptable standard. It may be derived from referencing with competitors' services or from an objective analysis of what an appropriate level is deemed to be.

Total quality management: a system that guarantees quality standards.

Total Quality Management (TQM) (Hackman and Wageman, 1995) is an attempt to build systems within organisations which guarantee quality standards. They are built around a procedure which sets and monitors standards, identifies corrective actions arising from monitoring and implements corrective actions – a sort of quality auto-pilot. The concept has also been applied extensively in tourism (Witt and Muhlemann, 1994; Camison, 1996; Kandampully *et al.*, 2001).

Financial indicators

Whilst quality indicators measure the effectiveness of strategy with a mixture of qualitative and quantitative data, financial indicators gauge the efficiency of a strategy using mainly quantitative techniques. Thus for organisations with mainly profit-centred missions, evaluation will be largely quantitative and may utilise data on:

- ◊ Return on capital employed
- ◊ Earnings per share
- ◊ Dividends paid to shareholders
- ◊ Turnover
- ◊ Market share
- ◊ Profit before tax
- ◊ Movement in share prices.

Figures such as these may be interpreted according to specific targets that may have been expressed in the organisations mission e.g. '10 per cent growth in earnings per share', or performance may be related to industry norms. A typical target might be:

> *to achieve above-average growth in normalised earnings per share over the medium term*

Box 11.3 Carnival Cruise Corporation

Carnival Corporation & plc is a global cruise company with headquarters in Miami and London. Its portfolio includes Carnival Cruise Lines and Princess Cruises in North America; P&O Cruises and Cunard Line in the United Kingdom; AIDA in Germany; Costa Cruises in southern Europe; Iberocruceros in Spain; and P&O Cruises in Australia.

Carnival Cruise Lines, was started in 1972 by Ted Arison and in 1987 it launched a public offer of 20 per cent of its shares providing the capital for expansion through acquisition. Targets included Holland America Line, Seabourn Cruise Line, Costa Cruises, and Cunard Line. In 2003 Carnival Corporation merged with P&O Princess Cruises plc, creating the world's largest cruise operator.

Carnival's mission is:

> to deliver exceptional vacation experiences through the world's best-known cruise brands that cater to a variety of different lifestyles and budgets, all at an outstanding value unrivaled on land or at sea.

Headline reporting data for the period 2005–2008 includes the following:

	2008	2007	2006	2005
Revenues ($m)	14,646	13,033	11,839	11,094
Net income ($m)	2,330	2,408	2,279	2,253
Earnings per share ($)	2.90	2.95	2.77	2.70
Passengers carried (000s)	8,183	7,672	7,008	6,848

Source: Annual Report 2008

Carnival Cruise (P&O) "Oriana" docked in Sydney. How well is Carnival delivering its strategic objectives?

Financial information is illustrated in Box 11.3 for the Carnival Cruise Corporation. It can be seen that revenues and passengers carried have increased year on year but net income and earnings per share both declined between 2007 and 2008. However, care needs to be taken in using such data, for two reasons. First, it is sometimes difficult to determine the performance of a specific strategy in the generality of these kinds of global figures. Second, there may be a time lag between a change of strategy and its reflection in changed profitability.

Other indicators

For organisations with non-profit missions, evaluation will utilise different tools. For example, whilst national tourism organisations may use quantitative data such as number of tourist arrivals, organisations such as Tourism Concern will find it difficult to offer precise qualitative or quantitative indicators of their success. They may resort to more discursive reporting such as the use of case studies which can demonstrate the effectiveness of their campaigning.

Corrective feedback

Corrective feedback: identify performance gaps, identify the causes of performance gaps, identify corrective action, instigate corrective action plan.

The system of management control should follow up the cycle of performance measurement with any corrective measures that are to be taken in the case that actual performance does not match up to the performance targets of the strategy. This will involve the following steps:

- ◊ Identify performance gaps
- ◊ Identify causes of performance gaps
- ◊ Identify corrective action
- ◊ Instigate corrective action plan.

Effective implementation

Strategic implementation is putting a strategy into action. Implementation is in many ways more of a challenge than design of strategy. This is because design of strategy is largely an abstract, theoretical exercise involving a sound approach, good data collection and analytical skills and effective evaluation of alternatives. On the other hand, implementation is a practical exercise. It is something that has to be put into place and involves change. As has been previously discussed, effective implementation is pitted against the sometimes deeply embedded traditions of existing culture, structures and people. This section considers three approaches to implementation:

- ◊ Obstacles to effective strategy implementation
- ◊ Critical success factors
- ◊ The 7S Framework.

Obstacles to effective strategy implementation

Hrebiniak (2006) identifies five common obstacles to effective implementation of strategy. These are:

Strategic implementation: putting a strategy into action.

- ◊ **Managers are trained to plan, not execute.** Hrebiniak argues that there is an imbalance in training of managers with insufficient emphasis on implementation.
- ◊ **Managers let the 'grunts' handle execution.** The obstacle here is that top managers are willing to participate in strategic planning but that implementation is a task that can be readily delegated. Implementation therefore does not benefit from best management.
- ◊ **Planning and execution are seen as interdependent.** Whilst Hrebiniak sees a logical distinction between these areas he notes that in practice it is beneficial to encourage mutuality between them. In particular, a feel for the practicalities of implementation means that attention is given to whether strategic goals are actually achievable. Haugen and Davis (2010) also note the gap between strategy formulation and implementation and argue that there is a need to bridge the divide between organisational thinkers and doers.
- ◊ **Implementation is a process that takes longer than formulation.** the longer time frame required for implementation can make it harder for managers to control the process and unforeseen circumstances may disrupt the original plan.
- ◊ **Execution involves more people than strategy formulation.** this makes communication and coordination more difficult.

Additionally, Hrebiniak identified six top obstacles to strategy implementation that resulted from two surveys of 443 managers. The top obstacles were:

- ◊ An inability to manage change
- ◊ Poor or vague strategy

- ◊ Not having guidelines or a model to guide implementation efforts
- ◊ Poor or inadequate information sharing
- ◊ Unclear responsibility and accountability
- ◊ Working against the organisational power structure.

Tan (2007) also investigated barriers to strategy implementation using the case study of Air New Zealand. The research included participants from all levels of the organisation and findings revealed that participants from different levels of the organisation had unique perceptions of the implementation process. The findings also found leadership and power to be two crucial aspects that could impede or enhance implementation. Finally, commitment and loyalty were also seen to be important.

Critical success factors

Pettigrew and Whipp's (1992) study of the management of change concluded that there were five critical success factors common in organisations where change had been successfully implemented. These were:

- ◊ **Sensitivity to the external environment.** Successful organisations avoid strategic drift. They monitor the external environment and adapt to it. They are externally oriented.
- ◊ **Formulation of a strategy for change.** Implementation requires change to be addressed as an important issue. The particular way in which change is managed should be sensitive to the circumstances of each organisation.
- ◊ **Translation of strategic plans to operational outcomes.** This underlines the importance of operationalising strategy. Key elements include resource plans, setting and monitoring objectives and good communications.
- ◊ **Effective human resource management.** This needs to be carefully integrated into the strategy process. This is particularly true for tourism organisations where service quality is often vital for success.
- ◊ **Consistency and coherence of strategic planning**. There are a lot of elements to successful strategic management. It is important that these elements are consistent so that there is no conflict between different parts of the strategy. For example, ambitious expansion plans, funded at high interest rates would be inconsistent with an external environment which was heading for a period of recession. Consistency also demands not only that that strategy, and operations move in the same direction but also that strategy is reinforced by managerial behaviour.

The 7S Framework

Waterman *et al.* (1980) claimed that effective organisational change resulted from a successful relationship between several factors:

- ◊ Structure
- ◊ Strategy

◊ Systems
◊ Style
◊ Skills
◊ Staff and,
◊ Superordinate goals

In other words, successful change needs more than just an appropriate strategy and company structure. Systems – or how an organisation goes about its daily business of routines and procedures – are important. Here the emphasis is on getting the detail right as well as the broad brush of strategy. Style refers to the way the management team projects strategy to the rest of the organisation – do they sell the vision? Socialisation is an important issue in terms of staff. Waterman *et al.* report that successful companies induct and groom new recruits with great care. They also note that it is important for companies to develop distinctive skills focusing on improving on what they do best. Finally superordinate goals are explained as the guiding concept – above all else – of the organisation. They therefore emerge from strategy and objectives and identify the direction of the organisation and give it its drive.

Review of key terms

- Management of change: the process by which strategic change is identified and implemented.
- A frozen organisation: one which has become rigidly routinised.
- Four Cs of change: calculation, communication, culture and compliance.
- Calculation: the identification of the likely impacts of a strategy with a view to discovering where critical blockages may occur.
- Force field analysis: investigates forces that are either driving movement toward an objective (driving forces) or blocking such movement (resisting forces).
- Models of communication of strategy: democratic, educative and autocratic.
- Democratic communication: encouragement of wide participation in strategic formulation.
- Educative communication: encourages a two-way flow of communications.
- Autocratic communication: communication is one-way, top-down and strategy is handed down from the board for implementation.
- Key factors in promoting cultural change: induction programmes for new staff, change of symbols, use of language, training programmes, appointment of key personnel, promotion and dismissal policies, incentive schemes.
- Compliance: the way to achieve strategic change.
- Key factors in promoting compliance: control of resources, alliances, rewards and punishments, charisma, and managing of change skills.
- Charismatic leader: one who inspires others to follow a particular path.

- Theory E: strategic change based on the pursuit of economic value.
- Theory O: strategic change based on the development of organisational capability.
- Control mechanism: checks performance and takes corrective action to minimise deviation from strategic objectives.
- Performance target: an outcome that is set for an organization or employee to reach within a specified period of time.
- Control system: the process for monitoring progress against strategic objectives.
- Performance measures: these include quality, financial and other indicators.
- Quality assurance: the system by which standards are controlled.
- SERVQUAL: measures satisfaction against customer expectations.
- Benchmark: a level of acceptable standard.
- Total quality management (TQM): a system that guarantees quality standards.
- Financial indicators: these include return on capital employed, earnings per share, dividends to shareholders, turnover, market share, profit before tax, movement in share prices
- Corrective feedback: identify performance gaps, identify the causes of performance gaps, identify corrective action, instigate corrective action plan.
- Strategic implementation: putting a strategy into action.

Multiple choice questions

1 Which of the following is not one of the 4Cs of change?
- A Communication
- B Capture
- C Compliance
- D Calculation

2 Which of the following is true?
- A Democratic communication encourages top-down flows
- B Refreezing is important to institutionalise strategic change
- C Autocratic communication is a two-way process
- D Strategy formulation takes longer than implementation

3 Which of the following are not considered cultural artefacts:
- A Myths and sagas
- B Heroes and heroines
- C Ceremonies and symbols
- D Research and development

4 Which of the following is true?
- A Theory E favours economic value
- B Theory O favours owner value
- C Theory E is a soft approach
- D Theory O is a hard approach

5 According to Hrebiniak (2006) which of the following is an obstacle to effective implementation?
   A The use of performance targets
   B Charismatic leadership
   C Lack of training in implementation
   D Superordinate goals

Discussion questions

1. Many airlines are resorting to strategic alliances or horizontal mergers in moves towards more globalisation. Choose an airline and conduct a force field analysis for such a strategy.
2. Explain how success could be encouraged in implementing a tourism destination strategy using Pettigrew and Whipp's (1992) five critical success factors and Hrebiniak's (2006) discussion of obstacles.
3. Using examples from the tourism sector to discuss the importance of control systems in strategy implementation.
4. Discuss the significance of the 4Cs in the management of change in a tourism organisation.
5. Explain what Lewin (1951) meant by the freezing and unfreezing process in achieving strategic change.

References

Beer, M. and Nohria, N. (2000) Cracking the code of change. *Harvard Business Review*, **78**, 133-141.

Brager, G. and Holloway, S. (1992) Assessing prospects for organizational change: the uses of force field analysis. *Administration in Social Work*, **16**, 15-25.

Buchanan, D. and Boddy, D. (1992) *The Expertise of the Change Agent: Public Performance and Backstage Activity*. London: Prentice Hall.

Camison, C. (1996) Total quality management in hospitality: an application of the EFQM model. *Tourism Management*, **17**, 191-201.

Department of Resources Energy and Tourism (2008) *Tourism and Climate Change – A Framework for Action*. Canberra: Department of Resources, Energy and Tourism.

Erkutlu, H. (2008) The impact of transformational leadership on organizational and leadership effectiveness. *Journal of Management Development*, **27**, 708-726.

Fick, G.R. and Ritchie, B. (1991) Measuring service quality in the travel and tourism industry. *Journal of Travel Research*, **30**, 2.

Hackman, J.R. and Wageman, R. (1995) Total quality management: empirical, conceptual, and practical issues. *Administrative Science Quarterly*, **40**, 309-342.

Haugen, L.K. and Davis, A.S. (2010) Bridging the thinking-doing divide: engaged in strategy implementation. *International Journal of Learning and Intellectual Capital*, **7**, 40-54.

Heracleous, L. and Wirtz, J. (2009) Strategy and organization at Singapore Airlines: achieving sustainable advantage through dual strategy. *Journal of Air Transport Management*, **15**, 274-279.

Higgins, J.M. and Mcallaster, C. (2004) If you want strategic change, don't forget to change your cultural artifacts. *Journal of Change Management*, **4**, 63-73.

Hodgkinson, G.P., Whittington, R., Johnson, G., and Schwarz, M. (2006) The role of strategy workshops in strategy development processes: formality, communication, co-ordination and inclusion. *Long Range Planning*, **39**, 479-496.

Hrebiniak, L. (2006) Obstacles to effective strategy implementation. *Organizational Dynamics*, **35**, 12-31.

Kandampully, J., Mok, C. and Sparks, B.A. (2001) *Service Quality Management in Hospitality, Tourism, and Leisure*. London: Routledge.

Lewin, K. (1951) *Field Theory in Social Science*. London: Tavistock.

Merchant, K.A. and Van der Stede, W.A. (2007) *Management Control Systems: Performance Measurement, Evaluation and Incentives*. New York: Prentice Hall.

Mintzberg, H. (1983) *Power In and Around Organizations*. New York: Prentice Hall.

Nutt, P. (1989) Selecting tactics to implement strategic plans. *Strategic Management Journal*, **10**, 145-161.

Ozdemir, G. (2007) Cultural change management and quality in the tourism industry. *Journal of Yasar University*, **2**, 505-523.

Page, S. (2007) *Tourism Management: Managing for Change*. Oxford: Butterworth-Heinemann.

Parasuraman, A., Zeithaml, V. and Berry, L. (1988) SERVQUAL: a multiple-item scale for measuring consumer perceptions of service quality. *Journal of Retailing*, **64**, 12-40.

Paton, R. and McCalman, J. (2008) *Change Management: a Guide to Effective Implementation*. London: Sage.

Peters, T.J. and Waterman, R. h. (1982). *In Search of Excellence*. New York: Harper and Row.

Pettigrew,A. and Whipp,R. (1992) *Managing Change for Competitive Success.* Oxford: Blackwell

Saleh, F. and Ryan, C. (1992) Conviviality - a source of satisfaction for hotel guests? An application of the Servqual model. In P.Johnson and B. Thomas (eds), *Choice and Demand in Tourism*, London: Mansell, pp. 107-122.

Tan, Y.T. (2007) Barriers to strategy implementation: a case study of Air New Zealand. Unpublished dissertation. Auckland University of Technology.

Thatcher, M. (2006) Breathing life into business strategy. *Strategic Communications Management*, **10**, 14-18.

Tribe, J. (1997) *Corporate Strategy for Tourism*. London: International Thomson Business Press.

Tribe, J. and Snaith, T. (1998) From SERVQUAL to HOLSAT: holiday satisfaction in Varadero, Cuba. *Tourism Management*, **19**, 25-34.

Waterman, R.H., Peters, T.J. and Phillips, J.R. (1980) Structure is not organisation. *Business Horizon*, **23**, 14-26.

Witt, C.A. and Muhlemann, A.P. (1994) The implementation of total quality management in tourism: some guidelines. *Tourism Management*, **15**, 416-424.

12 Strategy in Action

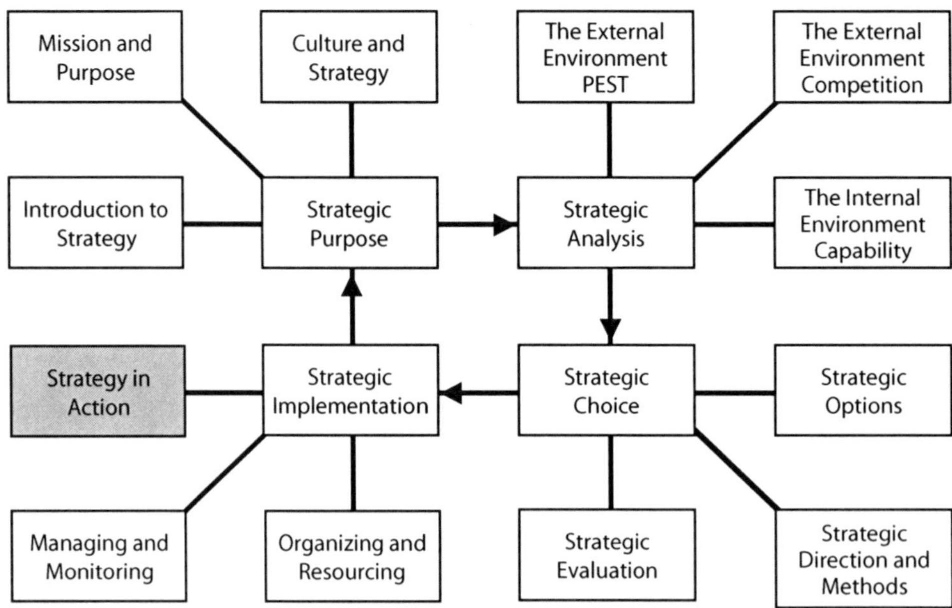

Figure 12.1

Learning outcomes

After studying this chapter and related materials you should be able to understand:

- How to prepare a public strategy document
- Strategists
- Gender and strategy
- Backstage considerations for strategy
- Review of strategy
- Turnaround strategies
- Crisis management strategies
- Concluding issues

and critically evaluate, explain and apply the above concepts.

Introduction

This chapter is about strategy in action. Its starting point offers advice on how to write a strategy document. Here the major headings and contents are set out. Of course not all of the information that has been used to formulate a strategy appears in publicly circulating documents and consideration is given to these backstage issues. Attention is next turned to the fact that a strategy needs to be reviewed to ensure that it continues to make a strong contribution to achieving the organisation's mission and remains appropriate as circumstances change. Next it discusses the roles of the people and agencies responsible for formulating strategy – the strategists. This is followed by a review of issues of gender.

In some cases, review and revision are not adequate since major unforeseen events can quickly render a strategy redundant. Mindful of this problem, the latter part of the chapter looks at the issues surrounding turnaround strategies and crisis management before concluding with some brief remarks.

Case study 12 illustrates a strategy with the particular focus of encouraging pro-poor tourism in Ethiopia. It also shows the role of a key international agency – the World Bank – and other specialist consultants who were recruited to assist in the formulation of the strategy.

Case Study 12: A pro-poor strategy for Ethiopia

Rationale

Ethiopia is one of the world's least developed countries. Approximately 31 million people live in conditions of poverty and of these perhaps 13 million people are at risk of starvation. The country has an over-dependence on the agricultural sector where the terms of trade have deteriorated in the past 40 years. Against this the World Bank report notes that the development potential of tourism is increasingly important in development strategies and that tourism is one of the focal sectors of Ethiopia's five-year development plan. This potential is underlined by data from the UNWTO showing that 35.6 per cent of all international tourists travelled to developing countries in 2003. But the challenge for Ethiopia is to ensure that tourism does not benefit just a few entrepreneurs, or its overseas investors, but that income remains in the country and is widely distributed, hence the focus on Pro Poor Tourism.

Approach

In 2006, The World Bank published a strategy for the government of Ethiopia *Ethiopia in Makeda's Footsteps: Towards a Strategy for Pro-Poor Tourism Development* (World Bank, 2006). The strategy was informed by a working group consisting of both public and private sector representatives and also sought input from independent consultants. For example, data on expenditure and economic impacts was provided by WAAS International (Ethiopia), a value chain analysis was undertaken by Global Development Solutions (USA and Japan) and Acorn International (UK) provided data on market perception. The report identified the following key stages in strategy development:

- Situation analysis
- Set strategic and sector objectives
- Understand the market
- Position product to meet market demand
- Develop action plans.

Situation analysis

The major weaknesses identified in the report included:

- An institutional structure that failed to generate policies, regulate the sector and define strategies.
- A shortage of qualified and skilled labour in the tourism sector.
- Insufficient training institutions in the country.
- Limited hotel stock often of poor quality and with few facilities.
- Weak demand.
- Weak products.
- Limited capacity of Ethiopian tour operators to promote and deliver their services.
- Weak and shallow supply chains with very little value rippling into the wider community.

Other areas that received poor ratings were convenient payment transactions, visitor information, telecommunications, foreign exchange facilities, quality of guides, convenience and access to local transport and access to and interpretation at historical heritage sites.

On the other hand strengths identified included:

- High satisfaction with the tourism experience among specialist consumers who recognise its uniqueness.

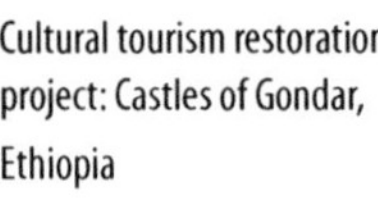

Cultural tourism restoration project: Castles of Gondar, Ethiopia

- Ethiopia's 7 UNESCO World Heritage Sites: Axum's Obelisks; the Monolithic Churches of Lalibela; the Castles of Gondar; the Omo Valley; Hadar (where the skeleton of Lucy was discovered); the carved standing stones of Tia and the Semien National Park.
- Ethiopia's other tourism resources including Lake Tana and the Blue Nile Falls; the Bale Mountains National Park; Awash National Park and Nechisar National Park.

Opportunities included:

- UNWTO estimates for growth in the worldwide cultural tourism market.

Threats included:

- Competition from similar destinations.

Set strategic and sector objectives

The World Bank (2006) reports that:

> The long-term vision of the Government is to make Ethiopia one of the top ten tourist destinations in Africa by the year 2020, with an emphasis on maximizing the poverty-reducing impacts of tourism, and utilizing tourism to transform the image of the country. (p. 11)

It further identifies an emerging Government of Ethiopia vision for tourism which it summarises as:

> Tourism should be sustainably developed and utilized for economic growth, image rehabilitation and poverty reduction whilst preserving and enhancing the social, cultural and environmental assets of Ethiopia. (p.58)

Understand the market

The strategy identifies a specific type of tourist profile associated with Ethiopia's product:

> "This type of tourist is usually in the post family life stage (children have left home) as follows:
>
> - Typical age group 50-60
> - No dependent children
> - Well-travelled
> - Quality conscious, but prepared to 'rough it'
> - Well-educated
> - Sensitive to environmental and social concerns
> - Take holidays in off-peak periods." (pp. 38–39)

It also identifies and a number of countries to target. These are: USA, UK, Germany, Italy, France, Canada, Saudi Arabia, Netherlands, and UAE.

Position product to meet market demand

The report recommends developing the product around two distinct geographical areas each with a different focus. These are:

- A northern circuit based on historic features
- A southern circuit based on ethnological and nature features.

Develop action plans

The World Bank strategy identifies four strategic objectives. These are listed below together with examples of recommendations for action:

- Improving sector management: recommendations here include the creation of a dedicated Tourism Ministry; the establishment of a Tourism Council to provide a public/ platform; the establishment of regional culture and tourism centres and the need to improve the linkages between tourism activities and poverty reduction.
- Enhancing the enabling environment: recommendations include commissioning of a human resources needs assessment study and the collection of key tourism statistics.
- Strengthening the supply chain: recommendations include public/private partnership developments of the Ghion hotel chain and a domestic airline; product development and the completion of destination development plans for the Northern Historic Route, the Southern Cultural Route and for Lalibela.
- Market development: the main recommendation here is to implement a rebranding strategy for Ethiopia.

Preparation of a strategy

Central to the idea of successful planning is the preparation of a detailed strategy. The key to this will be a master document which encompasses the main headings of this book. There will generally be restricted internal, internal and public versions of the strategy since some parts will contain confidential management tactics and information of value to competitors. Of course, all strategy documents vary considerably in their format but a typical strategy will have the following key parts:

◊ Title page
◊ Publication details and contents page
◊ Introduction/endorsement
◊ Executive summary
◊ Strategic analysis
◊ Mission and objectives
◊ Strategy
◊ Strategic implementation
◊ Appendices
◊ (Design features)
◊ (Backstage issues).

A strategy will inform an organisation's activities for the medium term – typically five years but most organisations also have a rolling programme of strategic planning where the strategy is reviewed and amended regularly. A strategy will be the product of detailed research but will generally confine itself to the main findings of that research, avoiding over-complex detail.

Title page

The title page typically includes:

◊ A title – this is generally functional and includes the time period of the strategy, e.g. 'Strategy 2010 – 2016'.
◊ One or two sentences which capture the essence of the strategy.
◊ A picture or graphic.
◊ The name and logo of the entity.

Publication details and contents page

This will include:

◊ Authorship
◊ Printer and publisher
◊ ISBN and copyright details (if applicable)
◊ Date of publication
◊ Table of contents.

Introduction/endorsement

Some strategies have a brief introduction. This might be from the Chief Executive Officer (in the case of a private sector organisation) or the Tourism Minister (in the case of a national tourism strategy) or a high-profile supporter (in the case of an NGO). The purpose of an introduction is often to show high-level support for a strategy and to sell the strategy to a variety of audiences emphasising the benefits that it will achieve.

Executive summary

Executive summary: a precis of the main features of a strategy.

The executive summary should be a precis of the whole document to enable the reader (for example, a busy executive) to understand the main features of the strategy without having to read it all. Key features of an executive summary:

◊ About one page in length
◊ Uses non-technical language
◊ Uses coherent paragraphs, e.g.:
  ♦ Brief statement of the organisation
  ♦ Brief statement of the context/problem
  ♦ Concise situational analysis
  ♦ Key elements of the strategy
  ♦ Key points for delivery of strategy
  ♦ What the strategy will achieve.

Strategic analysis

The aim of this section is to provide the rationale for the strategy and address the twin questions of how the external environment is changing and how well the organisation's capabilities can respond to these changes. It will therefore mirror the contents of Chapters 4, 5, and 6 of this book. A typical format will be:

◊ The external environment
◊ Organisational capabilities
◊ SWOT analysis.

The external environment

This part of the strategy will analyse the following environments in terms of potential opportunities and threats. It is therefore important that these opportunities and threats are not couched at a general level but are specific to the organisation at hand.

◊ **The political environment:** how will the organisation be affected by changes in government policies and legislation?
◊ **The economic environment:** this will include forecasts of main economic data and an analysis of how it will affect the organisation.
◊ **The socio-cultural environment:** how will changes in populations, their characteristics, culture and lifestyles affect the organisation?
◊ **The technological environment:** what opportunities and threats are presented by developments in information communication technology and other technology?
◊ **The competitive environment:** who are the key current and potential competitors and how are their actions likely to affect the organisation?

Organisational capabilities

This part of the strategy will analyse the strengths and weaknesses of the organisation's resources and products or services. Specifically it should address:

◊ The resources and core competences of the organisation
◊ The performance of the organisation
◊ An evaluation of product and services.

SWOT analysis

This part of the strategy often concludes with a summary of the main points of its analysis presented by a SWOT analysis in tabular form. This is illustrated in Table 12.1.

Table 12.1: SWOT table

External environment	Opportunities	Threats
Organisational capability	Strengths	Weaknesses

Mission and objectives

The mission of the organisation will succinctly describe the purpose of the organisation and its overall aim and answer the question 'What does this organisation exist to do?' A mission statement is typically a couple of sentences.

The objectives spell out in further detail how the mission is to be accomplished and answer the question 'what does the organisation have to do to achieve its mission?' The objectives will typically be between 4–8 short separate sentences and should conform to SMART principles. That is they should be:

- ◊ Specific
- ◊ Measurable
- ◊ Agreed with those who must attain them
- ◊ Realistic
- ◊ Time-constrained.

Strategy

This part of the document is likely to cover issues such as:

- ◊ Generic type of strategy
- ◊ Directions
- ◊ Methods.

Generic type of strategy

This is likely to be a statement around one of the generic types of strategy, i.e.:

- ◊ **Price based:** a price leadership strategy will stress the ways in which the organisation will compete in the market in terms of price.
- ◊ **Differentiation based:** a differentiation based strategy will emphasise the points about which the entity wishes to distinguish its goods or services from those offered by competitors, generally by reference to qualities that add value
- ◊ **Hybrid:** a hybrid strategy will demonstrate how an organisation will achieve a combination of low prices and high added value.
- ◊ **Other**: classic generic strategies are not applicable to all organisations. For example, NGOs are likely to have other strategies that enable them to achieve their mission.

Directions

This part of the strategy will explain how an organisation seeks to achieve its strategy by directions such as:

- ◊ **Consolidation**: this would be where an organisation set out its plans to concentrate its efforts on existing products and existing markets.
- ◊ **Market penetration**: here it would explain how it plans to increase market share in exiting markets using existing products or services.

- ◊ **Market development:** this would entail a plan for taking an existing product range into new market areas.
- ◊ **Product development:** here an organisation would outline how it would develop new markets for existing products and completely new products for existing markets.
- ◊ **Diversification:** following this direction an organisation would explain its plans to move into completely new products and markets which are unrelated to its present portfolio.
- ◊ **Withdrawal:** in some cases an appropriate strategic direction would mean planning to remove a product or service or pull out from a market.

Methods

This part of the document will indicate the methods that will be deployed to deliver a strategy. Method to support a strategy may include one or more of:

- ◊ **Internal growth:** an explanation of the case in which an organisation develops markets and products without recourse to mergers with other organisations.
- ◊ **Horizontal integration:** proposals for merging with another organisation operating at the same stage of production in the same industry.
- ◊ **Vertical integration:** proposals for merging with another organisation at different stages of production in the same industry.
- ◊ **Diversification**: proposals for taking over of an organisation in a different line of business.
- ◊ **Franchising**: details of how to use a licensing model to recruit new owners and businesses to replicate an organisation's successful business model.
- ◊ **Joint venture:** plans to join forces with other organisations to cooperate for a specific purpose.
- ◊ **Strategic alliance**: details of any agreement with similar organisations to co-operate on some aspects of mutual interest while remaining independent organisations.
- ◊ **Innovation**: an explanation of how an organisation might bring newness or positive change to products, processes, thinking, or to the whole organisation.

Strategic implementation

This final part of the strategy document will address the two key issues of:

- ◊ Organising and resourcing
- ◊ Monitoring change.

Organising and resourcing

The following three aspects will be covered in this part of the strategy:

- **Resource planning:** this part of the document will discuss how the strategy is to be financed, what adjustments are needed in large-scale physical resources, human resource plans and the deployment of information and technology resources.
- **Formulation of a coordinating plan**: any major logistical considerations should be noted and displayed in a GANT chart.
- **Design of organisational structure**: a change in strategic direction means that thought needs to be given to how the organisational structure will need to change to implement that strategy. This should be illustrated with an organisation chart.

Monitoring change

The final part of the strategy is likely to indicate what control mechanisms will be put into place to monitor progress. These generally include:

- **Performance targets**: here a strategy will list what outcomes are to be delivered to demonstrate that a strategy has been achieved.
- **Control systems**: here information can be given on a schedule for control, who is responsible for the process, what data is to be produced, who the data will be reported to.
- **Measurement of performance**: here attention will be given to how performance targets are to be monitored. This typically involves the measurement of service quality indicators and financial indicators.

Appendices

The main strategy may be accompanied by appendices which include issues such as:

- The process of formulating the strategy
- Details of the strategy team
- Details of stakeholder involvement
- Details of consultation events
- Supporting evidence.

Design features

A strategy should also incorporate the following design features. It should:

- Be professionally designed
- Include graphs to illustrate key trends
- Include illustrative pictures
- Include illustrative 'pull out' quotes.

Backstage issues

Backstage issues: aspects of strategy that are not be available in the public domain.

Some aspects of strategic thinking will not be available in the public domain. First, this may be to restrict access to information that would be advantageous to competitors. Restricted access information may include:

- Specific targets for takeovers
- Sales targets
- Pricing data
- Specific details of product development
- Specific details of plans for market penetration.

Second, some of the issues may be too sensitive to be made publically available. This information will only be made available to senior management, on a confidential basis and can include:

- Force field analysis
- Job losses.
- Plans for achieving compliance (especially tactics for negotiating with trade unions).

Strategists

There are three main groupings of strategists. These are chief executives, strategic planners and external consultants.

Chief executives

Some organisation make a clear distinction between those involved in strategy and those involved in operations management. A key function of the chief executive officer (CEO) is to be the chief strategist. The logic of this separation is that it is easy to get bogged down in the detail, volume and deadlines of operations and this can prevent sufficient attention being given to long-term strategic issues. Also strategies often require tough decisions to be made about parts of an organisation which are not performing well. These decisions may be easier to take by a CEO who is operating at arm's length where a more detached, objective view may be taken.

On the other hand, excessive concentration of strategic power in a CEO and complete divorce between strategy and operations can lead to CEOs becoming out of touch with reality and making decisions that cause deep resentment throughout the organisation. Adler (2005) offers some interesting insights into the roles of CEOs in an article which contains an interview with Joe McKiernan, President and CEO of the American Hotel and Lodging Association.

Strategic planners

Strategic planning departments are increasingly found in large corporations and in the public sector. These do not supplant the role of the CEO as the main strategic leader but provide the resources to enable the CEO to function more effectively as a strategist. Typically strategic planning department perform three roles. First, they are able to provide data, data analysis and also the effective presentation of analysis. Second, they can assume management and co-ordination of the strategy cycle. Third, strategic planners are able to provide support for special strategic projects. These may include takeovers and restructuring.

External consultants

External consultancies that provide services in strategy development include large generalist multinational organisations such as McKinsey as well as smaller firms specialising in the tourism sector. As well as providing complete strategies they also provide related services. First, they may provide a data collection and analysis service. Second, consultancies can provide a range of strategic options and give advice on choosing between options. Third, they can provide training and assistance in change management. Fourth, they can assist in the process of strategic implementation. Box 12.1 shows the activities of The Tourism Company – a specialist consultancy.

Box 12.1 The Tourism Company

The Tourism Company is a small, specialist consultancy which was founded in 1990. Its services range from project development to tourism plans and strategies. Its clients include government departments, national bodies, commercial operators and the voluntary sector as well as the European Commission, UN World Tourism Organization, WWF and UNEP. Examples of their work include the following.

1. **Rural development and sustainable tourism in Kyrgyzstan.** The Tourism Company was responsible for the tourism component of a regional development strategy together with ADAS International. The project was funded by the European Union under its TACIS programme. The Tourism Company developed strategic priorities for tourism in the region, which include improvements in:

   Tourist information and orientation

   The quality of the tourism product

   Access to international markets.

2. **Tourism strategy for Oxford.** Oxford City and Oxfordshire County Councils commissioned The Tourism Company to write a tourism strategy for the city of Oxford. A number of challenges were identified including how to manage the visitor experience, how to manage impacts on the local community, how to respond to competition from other destinations and how to maintain its appeal.

The strategy carried out a detailed review of existing research and policies and engaged in widespread consultation with key stakeholders including tourism enterprises and the University.

The strategy highlighted three objectives:

- Developing more focused marketing and communication
- Making the experience of visiting Oxford special
- Improving the management and co-ordination of tourism

Source: The Tourism Company, www.thetourismcompany.com

The advantages that external consultancies bring include an external, detached view, accumulated sector expertise and a target for deflecting criticism for unpopular decisions. Key disadvantages include their costs, the fact that they often follow standard formulae, that they cannot get a real insight into the business and that they often require unexpected resources, support and management. A further criticism is that in some cases consultants are hired to provide and implement an unpopular solution predetermined by the organisation.

Gender and strategy

Gender issues in strategy: these include the representation of women at strategic levels of management and gender differences in strategic philosophies.

A number of issues arise relating to gender and strategy. The first concerns the representation of women at strategic levels of management and the second relates to any differences in strategic philosophies between the sexes. Smith and Crimes (2007, p. 1) note that:

> *whilst women account for approximately half the UK workforce and one third of managers but they are still conspicuous by their absence in senior management. This situation is mirrored in travel and tourism, despite this sector having a majority of female employees.*

They point to research by Hemmati (1999) that highlights the 'gender pyramid' in the tourism sector where lower level occupations are dominated by women, whilst key management positions are dominated by men. Skalpe (2007) finds a slightly better situation in Norway (at least in the tourism sector) where it is found that more than 20 per cent of the CEOs are women, as opposed to less than 6 per cent in a sample of manufacturing firms. But when the gender pay gap is investigated in Norwegian tourism and manufacturing firms the results find that female CEOs are wage-discriminated against in both sectors.

Olsson (2000) hints at key differences in leadership and strategy styles between men and women. She notes the continuing pervasiveness of what she terms heroic masculiness which she sees as the traditional and hierarchical form of management This she notes, depicts executives as solitary (male) heroes engaged in unending trials of endurance. Olsen continues that official organisational myths and stories perpetuate this archetype type of leadership. These myths and stories function as vehicles of communication management that support male-orientated organisational goals and provide role models for young executives. Kabacoff (2000) investigated gender and leadership in the corporate boardroom. He found that male leaders were more restrained in their emotional expression. On the other hand females exhibited:

> *a greater degree of energy, intensity and emotional expressions and … a greater capacity to keep others enthusiastic and involved. (p. 3)*

Other differences in management styles were also noted but Kabacoff also suggested that many potential differences were minimised initially by selection criteria for promotion and then by some assimilation and imitation of male behaviour characteristics by successful female leaders. This brief discussion alerts us to a continuing gender imbalance in strategy leadership and the impact that this might have on the selection and implementation of strategic goals. Peeters and Ateljevic (2009) progress this argument by investigating the factors that can lead to greater empowerment of women and the consequent community development, social innovation and change.

Strategy review

Strategy review: assessment of the success of the new strategy.

All strategies should be regularly reviewed. Review entails assessment of the success of a new strategy. Review then is the ultimate test of a strategy – has it been successful? Review should be related back to the mission of the organisation and indeed ask whether the mission is still valid. Additionally, all strategies are based on assumptions about how the external environment will change in the future. An important part of review should therefore include assumptions testing, that is a regular review that the assumptions underlying a particular strategy still hold. Review represents the check phase of the Deming (Noguchi, 1995) cycle of plan–do–check–act which is at the heart of strategic planning. The outcome of strategy review will be action to revise the existing strategy in the light of any new circumstances. This will be part of evolutionary change. Many organisations produce an annual report and these often include evaluation of current strategy as well as signalling any changes for the future. Box 12.2 contains extracts from the 2008 annual report of the Canadian Tourism Commission which includes a review of its strategy and also signals some changes for the future year.

Box 12.2 Canadian Tourism Commission

Our goal: Grow tourism export revenues for Canada.

Our vision: Inspire the world to explore Canada.

Key Results

- Total tourism revenue: $74.9 billion UP 5.8% over 2007
- Total international tourism revenue $15.7 billion DOWN 3.1% from 2007
- Total domestic tourism revenue $59.2 billion UP 8.5% over 2007
- Tourism's contribution to Canadian GDP $30.7 billion UP 7.3% over 2007

- Government revenues generated by tourism \$22.2 billion UP 5.7% over 2007
- Total number of Canadians employed in tourism industry 660,000 UP 1.0% over 2007
- CTC core markets with increased performance 5 out of 9 UNCHANGED from 2007
- Average yield per night per traveller from CTC markets \$119.70 DOWN from \$120.90 in 2007 (section 1.2)

Despite the challenges, the Canadian tourism sector outperformed not only the primary industries, but the overall economy. Our strategy to target high-yield consumers was validated as this group has the passion and means for international travel even in difficult economic times.

... In the coming year, we will focus on a domestic advertising campaign and entry into the new, high growth emerging markets of India and Brazil. (p.5)

Source: Annual report 2008

http://www.corporate.canada.travel/docs/about_ctc/CTC_AR08_EN.pdf

Turnaround strategies

Turnaround strategy: the action taken to prevent the occurrence of financial disaster.

Sometimes organisations are faced with a sudden and profound deterioration of their well-being. In these circumstances there is insufficient time to follow the path of strategy revision that is associated with evolutionary change. Such situations include the threat of impending bankruptcy or the possibility of a hostile takeover. In this case, an organisation will need to embark on a turnaround strategy (Slater and Lovett, 1999) and introduce urgent measures to reverse its fortunes. Turnaround is defined as the action taken to prevent the occurrence of financial disaster.

Box 12.3 Japan Airlines turnaround

In 2010 Japan Airlines (JAL) was facing bankruptcy. Its plight was caused by a combination of terrorism, SARS, fuel prices and global recession that had led to steep declines in passenger numbers (particularly business class) and cargo. JAL announced that it had filed for court-led restructuring and that the Enterprise Turnaround Initiative Corporation of Japan (ETICJ) would lead its rescue.

Haruka Nishimatsu, the president of the airline, resigned along with other directors admitting responsibility for causing the situation and the appointment of younger executives is a key priority in creating a new management structure.

To restore financial stability, JAL would petition for a debt-waiver of ¥730 billion, receive an injection of capital from ETICJ with a ¥100 billion cash injection from the Development Bank of Japan and other private institutions. This would be followed by deep cost cutting with a reduction of its workforce by 15,700 staff with better efficiencies at JAL's corporate headquarters and improved productivity on flight operations. A move away from low efficiency large aircraft would also reduce costs. At the same time unprofitable operations would be withdrawn, consolidated and restructured and consideration given to introducing a low-cost model on short-haul flights.

Box 12.3 describes the key features of the turnaround strategy for Japan Airlines and these are some of the generic elements of a turnaround strategy:

- ◊ **Act with speed and precision**: a quick recovery reduces the likelihood of long-term damage.
- ◊ **Clear focus on the cause of the predicament:** it is important not to get sidetracked by peripheral issues.
- ◊ **Communication of the critical nature of problem to key stakeholders**: stakeholders are likely to accept drastic changes if they understand that an organisation is on the brink of extinction.
- ◊ **Ensure financial solvency**: this may involve renegotiating terms with creditors and/or seeking additional capital.
- ◊ **Replacement of CEO**: this may be necessary as the old regime will be identified with the problem and the replacement CEO may need experience in recovery strategies.
- ◊ **Stabilisation of problem**: this will often involve speedy attention to cutting costs and improving revenues. Stabilisation activities include divestment, liquidation, product elimination and reduction in employees.
- ◊ **Re-engineer**: jettison unprofitable activities and create a new core around profitable areas.

Cathoth *et al.* (2006) noted that the hospitality industry has a high rate of business failure but that some organisations are able to successfully navigate a turnaround of their fortunes. They base their study on Pearce and Robbins (1994) article which advocates a retrenchment stage followed by a recovery stage: Cathoth *et al.* conclude their analysis of turnaround strategies in restaurant firms with four propositions:

- *For successful turnaround, restaurant firms will need to initiate retrenchment strategies first before implementing recovery-phase strategies.*
- *Successful turnaround strategies for restaurant firms will not entail simultaneous initiation of retrenchment and recovery-phase strategies.*
- *Retrenchment strategies for restaurant firms will be more operating oriented, focusing on stringent cost cutting tactics on the short term.*
- *Retrenchment measures will be used by restaurant firms for successful turnaround irrespective of the causes of decline, i.e., internal and external factors.*

(p. 619)

Crisis management strategies

Crisis management strategy: strategy to deal with major, extraordinary, sudden and unforeseen events.

From time to time organisations and entities are overcome by major, extraordinary, sudden and unforeseen events that can pose a grave threat to their existence. Crisis management (Glaesser, 2003) is the process by which an organisation deals with such events. Lerbinger (1997) identified the main causes of crises which include:

◊ **Natural disasters:** these include floods, landslides, tidal waves, earthquakes, volcanic eruptions, hurricanes, storms, and droughts.

◊ **Technology**: technology failures can disrupts the supply side and the demand side of organisations and include ICT failures, structural and materials failures and mechanical failures.

◊ **Malevolence**: this includes criminal or political intent that uses extreme tactics such as kidnapping, terrorism and product tampering.

◊ **Confrontation**: this can arise where political interest groups wage successful campaigns against an organisation with whom they have a major disagreement and includes boycotts, blockades, occupations and other form of direct and indirect action.

◊ **Skewed management values**: this occurs where an organisation's management pursues ill-judged values and aims that ultimately cause harm to an organisation.

◊ **Deception**: in these cases organisations deliberately communicate false information to governments and consumers. Deception also includes major employee crime.

Ritchie (2004) suggests that there are strong parallels between disaster management models and classic strategy models. In common with Faulkner (2001) he identifies six main stages in strategic crisis management:

1 Pre-event stage: prevention and contingency measures are put into place.
2 Predromal stage: at this stage the impending crisis is inevitable.
3 Emergency stage: the crisis has arrived and main objective is damage limitation, immediate rescue and clear communications.
4 Short term stage: restoration of basic functions, utilities and essential services to return to normality.
5 Long-term (recovery) stage: continuation of restoration with attention to non-priority actions. Lessons learned incorporated into revised prevention and contingency strategies.
6 Resolution stage: routine strategic management replaces crisis management.

There are many examples of crises that have affected tourism. Natural disasters have included earthquakes, forest fires, disease outbreaks and tsunamis. For example Huang *et al.* (2008) examined crisis management in the light of the devastating earthquake that struck Taiwan in 1999 causing severe damage to the local population and the tourism industry. They generated an integrated crisis management framework which emphasised the role of effective communications in showing secure images for tourists in order to promote tourism recovery in the long-term stage. Hystad and Keller's (2008) research analysed the crisis management of a major forest fire disaster that occurred during the summer of 2003 near Kelowna, British Columbia, Canada. They also noted the importance of marketing and advertising to the recovery of tourism in Kelowna. Additionally they noted how natural disasters cut across many organisations making stakeholder co-ordination an important challenge. Miller and Ritchie (2003) described how an outbreak of foot-and-mouth disease in the UK in 2001 led to restrictions on tourism and vivid worldwide media images showing the burning carcasses of culled animals. Its impact on tourism was estimated as £8.5 billion. Carlsen and Hughes (2008) investigated the recovery rates in ten source markets for the Maldives in the wake of the 2004 Indian Ocean tsunami. They noted that the recovery rates varied significantly between the ten markets and concluded that that a 'one size fits all' marketing strategy is not effective in achieving recovery following a disaster. Box 12.4 outlines the main points in the Tsunami recovery strategy for Sri Lanka.

Box 12.4 Post-tsunami recovery and reconstruction strategy for Sri Lanka

Sri Lanka was one of the countries worst affected by the tsunami tidal waves that swept across the Indian Ocean on 26 December 2004. The tsunami killed over 38,000 people in Sri Lanka and caused extensive damage to infrastructure, property and people's livelihoods. The immediate need was to remove corpses and rescue and care for the injured and this was followed by a relief and rehabilitation phase which provided basic needs such as food, shelter, clothing, and water for around 120,000 displaced families. The Centre for National Operations was formed to oversee and monitor these emergency programmes.

Table 12.2: Investment needs of the post-tsunami reconstruction strategy

Priority area	US$m
Road development	353
Rail transport	313
Telecommunications	18
Water supply and sanitation	205
Electricity	115
Education	170
Health	100
Housing and urban development	400
Fisheries	200
Livelihood and micro financing	157
Tourism	58
Total	2089

The rebuilding operation was led by the Task Force on Rebuilding the Nation. A needs assessment that was undertaken for the reconstruction and rehabilitation phase identified the key investment priorities. One of these was the provision for setting up a tsunami early warning system which was incorporated into the Fisheries plan.

A plan to fund reconstruction identified a total of US$2145 million pledged by various donors including bilateral aid, multilateral agency assistance and NGO support.

In the tourism sector there was considerable damage to hotels and disruption to many micro enterprises. This was exacerbated by adverse impacts on the formal and informal financial sectors. Several bank branches in the coastal areas were destroyed and the micro finance sector suffered. The reduction in the number of tourists meant a net foreign exchange loss of about US$50 million in 2005. The Sri Lanka Tourist Board developed a specific strategy to restore the sector with minimum delay. This included:

- A Marketing Recovery Programme to restore the Sri Lanka tourism brand (US$ 5.3m).
- A Tourism Resort Zoning Plan which identified 15 badly affected tourist towns for rehabilitation and reconstruction.
- A Community Restoration Plan to resettle the displaced communities in the 15 tourist towns
- Incentives to hoteliers and tourism related enterprises which included a waiver on import duties for hotel refurbishment and loans of up to Rs.10 million with no repayment in the first year.

Tourism has also suffered many crises due to terrorism including the 11 September 2001 destruction of the Twin Towers in New York, and the Bali bombings. Sommez *et al.* (1999) argue that tourist destinations that are vulnerable to terrorism should incorporate crisis management planning into their development strategies to protect and rebuild their image of safety/attractiveness:

> *to reassure potential visitors of the safety of the area, to re-establish the area's functionality/attractiveness, and to aid local travel and tourism industry members in their economic recovery.* (p.13)

Blake and Sinclair (2003) constructed a computable general equilibrium model to understand the effects of the September 11-induced tourism crisis and to consider potential and actual policy responses to the crisis in the USA. They recommended sector-specific targeted subsidies and tax reductions as the most efficient means of tourism crisis management. Hitchcock and Putra (2005) note how a combination of bombings, SARS, the Iraq War and bird flu brought about a crisis for tourism in Bali. In particular, the bombings had the potential to escalate into grave domestic political strife. However the authors noted the success of measures designed to avoid conflict. These included Bali's politicians urging restraint, using a range of media and Bali's network of village councils as well as cultural and religious strategies such as inter-religious worship and village security capacity.

Avraham and Ketter (2008) stress the importance of effective media strategies for (re)marketing destinations in crisis. They propose a multi-step model for rescuing place image that has been affected by a crisis. The first step of this is a preliminary analysis which involves understanding the characteristics of the crisis as well as those of the place and the potential the audience affected by the crisis. The next stage relates to goals and timing and focuses on promoting consumption and marketing of the destination. The third stage is about the message. Here the authors stress the importance of influencing the source of the message, choosing the level of acknowledgement of the crisis and ways of influencing the audience. Finally Avraham and Ketter consider appropriate techniques such as PR, direct marketing and advertising as well as channels including broadcast, print and Internet media. The authors point to successful image enhancement strategies following the Madrid bombings (2004) but rather inconsistent strategies to enhance the image of Israel in the face of the Israeli-Palestinian conflict.

Concluding remarks

Figure 12.1, which has provided the analytical structure throughout this book is useful in depicting the strategy process in a logical, organised and coherent way. Thus the first step towards effective strategic management has been taken and a simple overview of the process provided. There is no doubt that an effective strategic understanding is a key element in the successful development of tourism organisations and destinations. However several caveats should be made at this stage.

First, to aid understanding, strategy has been depicted as a logical, linear process where we move neatly from stage to stage. In the real world it is a much more messy business, and the arrows in Figure 12.1 in fact often cut across the diagram. Second, it should be emphasised that the strategy process is a circular one. Note the arrow in Figure 12.1 that links implementation back to strategic purpose showing a continuous process. Strategy should always be under review. Finally it is reiterated that this text has essentially taken a classical view of the strategy process. There is considerable debate surrounding reliance on this method. This would therefore be an appropriate moment to review the Section in Chapter 1 entitled 'The contested nature of strategy'.

Review of key terms

- Executive summary: a precis of the main features of a strategy.
- Backstage issues: aspects of strategy that are not be available in the public domain.
- Strategists: these include chief executives, strategic planners and external consultants.
- Gender issues in strategy: these include the representation of women at strategic levels of management and gender differences in strategic philosophies.

- Strategy review: assessment of the success of the new strategy.
- Turnaround strategy: the action taken to prevent the occurrence of financial disaster.
- Key phases of turnaround strategy: a retrenchment stage followed by a recovery stage.
- Crisis management strategy: strategy to deal with major, extraordinary, sudden and unforeseen events.
- Main causes of crises: natural disasters, technology, malevolence, confrontation, skewed management values, deception.
- Prodromal stage of crisis: The stage when an impending crisis is inevitable.

Multiple choice questions

1 Which of the following is most likely to be restricted access (backstage) information and not included in a publicly available strategy?
   A Specific targets for takeover
   B Mission
   C Performance targets
   D SWOT analysis

2 Which of the following is not true?
   A Turnaround strategies are designed to rescue an organisation from financial disaster
   B An executive summary is a short precis of a strategy
   C External consultants can be used as strategists
   D Strategy review is an example of the Mintzberg cycle

3 Which of the following is one of Pearce and Robbins (1994) four propositions for successful turnaround in restaurants?
   A Retrenchment strategies should be initiated before implementing recovery strategies
   B There should be simultaneous initiation of retrenchment and recovery-phase strategies
   C Recovery strategies should be initiated before implementing retrenchment strategies
   D Neither retrenchment measures nor recovery strategies are effective

4 Which of the following is the correct order of events in a crisis management strategy?
   A Emergency stage, prodromal stage, long-term (recovery) stage, resolution stage
   B Pre-event stage, prodromal stage, short-term stage, resolution stage
   C Emergency stage, pre-event stage, prodromal stage, resolution stage
   D Pre-event stage, emergency stage, prodromal stage, long-term (recovery) stage

5 Which of the following is true?
   A Real world strategy is logical and linear
   B At the prodromal stage a crisis is impending and inevitable
   C It is important to retain the incumbent CEO to bring continuity in a turnaround strategy
   D The first stage of successful destination image recovery is choice of an appropriate communications channel

Discussion questions

1 Discuss which information would be appropriate and which would be inappropriate to include in a strategy document.

2 Distinguish between a turnaround strategy and a crisis management strategy using tourism examples.

3 Discuss the relative merits of using the CEO, a strategy planning department or external consultants as strategists for a tourism organisation.

4 Identify three major recent crises that have affected tourism destinations and discuss common elements for effective crisis management.

5 How does strategy review differ from performance management?

References

Adler, H. (2005) Interview with Joe McInerney, President and CEO, American Hotel and Lodging Association, Fall 2004. *Journal of Human Resources in Hospitality and Tourism*, **4**, 85-93.

Avraham, E. and Ketter, E. (2008) *Media Strategies for Marketing Places in Crisis: Improving the Image of Cities, Countries and Tourist Destinations*. Oxford: Butterworth-Heinemann.

Blake, A. and Sinclair, M.T. (2003) Tourism crisis management: US response to September 11. *Annals of Tourism Research*, **30**, 813-832.

Carlsen, J.C. and Hughes, M. (2008) Tourism market recovery in the Maldives after the 2004 Indian Ocean tsunami. *Journal of Travel and Tourism Marketing*, **23**, 139-149.

Chathoth, P. K., Tse, E. C. Y., & Olsen, M. D. (2006) Turnaround strategy: A study of restaurant firms. *International Journal of Hospitality Management*, **25**, 602-622.

Faulkner, B. (2001) Towards a framework for tourism disaster management. *Tourism Management*, **22**, 135-147.

Glaesser, D. (2003) *Crisis Management in the Tourist Industry*. Oxford: Butterworth- Heinemann.

Hemmati, M. (1999) *Gender and Tourism. Women's Employment and Participation*. London: UNED-UK.

Hitchcock, M. and Putra, I. (2005) The Bali bombings: tourism crisis management and conflict avoidance. *Current Issues in Tourism*, **8**, 62-76.

Huang, Y.C., Tseng, Y.P., and Petrick, J.F. (2008) Crisis management planning to restore tourism after disasters. *Journal of Travel & Tourism Marketing*, **23**, 203-221.

Hystad, P.W. and Keller, P.C. (2008) Towards a destination tourism disaster management framework: long-term lessons from a forest fire disaster. *Tourism Management*, **29**, 151-162.

Kabacoff, R. (2000) *Gender and Leadership in the Corporate Boardroom*. Portland, ME: Management Research Group.

Lerbinger, O. (1997) *The Crisis Manager: Facing Risk and Responsibility*. Mahwah, NJ: Erlbaum.

Miller, G.A. and Ritchie, B.W. (2003) A farming crisis or a tourism disaster? An analysis of the foot and mouth disease in the UK. *Current Issues in Tourism*, **6**, 150-171.

Noguchi, J. (1995) The legacy of W. Edwards Deming. *Quality Progress*, **28**, 35-38.

Olsson, S. (2000) Acknowledging the female archetype: women managers' narratives of gender. *Women in Management Review*, **15**, 296-302.

Pearce, J.A. and Robbins, D.K. (1994) Retrenchment remains the foundation of business turnaround. *Strategic Management Journal*, **15**, 407-417.

Peeters, L.W.J. and Ateljevic, I. (2009) Women empowerment entrepreneurship nexus in tourism: processes of social innovation. In J.Ateljevic and S. Page (eds), *Tourism and Entrepreneurship: International Perspectives*, Oxford: Butterworth-Heinemann, pp. 75-88.

Ritchie, B.W. (2004) Chaos, crises and disasters: a strategic approach to crisis management in the tourism industry. *Tourism Management*, **25**, 669-683.

Skalpe, O. (2007) The CEO gender pay gap in the tourism industry - evidence from Norway. *Tourism Management*, **28**, 845-853.

Slatter, S. and Lovett, D. (1999) *Corporate Turnaround*. London: Penguin.

Smith, P.E. and Crimes, B. (2007) *Women in Management, a Case of a Glass Ceiling? An Investigation into the Relative Under-representation of Women in Senior Management Positions in UK Travel and Tourism*. From: https://uhra.herts.ac.uk/dspace/bitstream/2299/2155/1/901976.pdf.

Sonmez, S.F., Apostolopoulos, Y. and Tarlow, P. (1999) Tourism in crisis: managing the effects of terrorism. *Journal of Travel Research*, **38**, 13-18.

World Bank (2006) *Ethiopia. In Makeda's Footsteps: Towards a Strategy for Pro-poor Tourism Development*. Washington, DC: World Bank.

Index